COMMITMENT TO DIVERSITY

COMMITMENT TO DIVERSITY

CATHOLICS AND EDUCATION IN A CHANGING WORLD

Edited by

MARY EATON, JANE LONGMORE AND ARTHUR NAYLOR

CASSELL

London and New York

Cassell

Wellington House, 125 Strand, London WC2R 0BB

370 Lexington Avenue, New York, NY 10017–6550

First published 2000

British Library Cataloguing-in-Publication Data

A catalogue record for this book is available from the British Library

ISBN 0–304–70541–1 Hardback
ISBN 0–304–70542–X Paperback

Typeset by York House Typographic Ltd
Printed and bound in Great Britain by Bookcraft (Bath) Ltd, Midsomer Norton

CONTENTS

PREFACE

This volume has been written in celebration of the 150th anniversary of St Mary's College. It has not been planned as a history of the College, although a number of articles relate to important periods in the College's development. Its purpose is to explore the interaction during this 150-year period of changes in Church and society, and the effects of government policy on the development of Catholic education, in particular teacher education.

The story of St Mary's during this period is inseparable from the story of the Catholic population it was established to serve. The origins of the College lay in training teachers to meet the educational needs of a rapidly growing Catholic immigrant population. The benefits conferred on the Catholic community by generations of teachers trained at St Mary's are immeasurable.

At the High Mass to celebrate the College's Centenary in 1950, Dr Shannon CM, a former Principal of the College, reminded those present that it is not buildings that matter: 'A college is not merely a solid material construction distinct from its members. Bricks and mortar know no birthdays. A College is built up with living stones.'

The identity of St Mary's has been deeply influenced in its response to educational and academic needs by its Christian vision and inspiration. The Christian vision of the student and scholarly community is founded on the search for truth and justice, and is enlivened by love. In that view of education, individuality and community flourish together, and the development of knowledge is pursued in a spirit of mutual respect. It is this Christian vision of education that has inspired St Mary's for 150 years. It is on this vision that we build our future with confidence.

Dr Arthur Naylor
Principal of St Mary's College

CONTRIBUTORS

Richard Cunningham was educated at Grace Dieu School and Ratcliffe College, Leicestershire and read history at Peterhouse, Cambridge. He served as Assistant Principal and Principal in the Ministry of Education 1953–59 and as Secretary of the Catholic Education Council for England and Wales 1968–91.

Stephen J. Denig, CM is a member of the Eastern United States Province of the Vincentians. After ordination in 1975 he served as a parish priest in Michigan, as a high school teacher in Philadelphia, and as the principal of the Vincentian minor seminary in New Jersey. Father Denig earned a doctorate in educational administration from Rutgers University in New Jersey. Currently he is an assistant professor and an assistant dean at Saint John's University, New York where his research interests are the history of Catholic education and the effects on students of the organizational differences between religious and public schools.

Michele Dowling is the Leverhulme Research Fellow at the Centre for the Study of Social History and the Centre for Educational Appraisal, Development and Research at the University of Warwick. She is working on a project on teacher education in the post-war period, funded by the Leverhulme Trust.

Mary Eaton is Vice Principal of St Mary's College, Strawberry Hill. As a sociologist she has written extensively on women and social control. Her books include *Justice for Women* (Open University Press, 1986) and *Women After Prison* (Open University Press, 1993). Much of her working life has been spent in Catholic education at the Sacred Heart School in Roehampton, Maria Assumpta College in Kensington and St Mary's College, Strawberry Hill.

John Fulton is Professor of Sociology at St Mary's College, Strawberry Hill. He has written *Tragedy of Belief: Division, Politics and Religion in Ireland* (Clarendon, 1991), edited two books on the sociology of religion and co-authored with M. P. Hornsby-Smith and N. Norris *The Politics of Spirituality* (Clarendon, 1995), and written numerous articles on religion and on Ireland. He is presently directing an international study on young Catholic adults in seven different Western countries.

Mary J. Hickman is Reader in European Studies and Director of the Irish Studies Centre at the University of North London. She is the author of *Religion, Class and Identity: The State, the Catholic Church and the Education of the Irish in Britain* (Avebury Press, 1995) and (with Bronwen Walter) *Discrimination and the Irish Community in Britain* (CRE, 1997).

Michael P. Hornsby-Smith is Professor of Sociology at the University of Surrey. For the past 25 years his main research concern has been the social and religious transformations of English Catholicism. He is the author of *Catholic Education* (Sheed and Ward, 1978), *Roman Catholics in England* (CUP, 1987), *The Changing Parish* (Routledge, 1989), *Roman Catholic Beliefs in England* (CUP, 1991), and co-author of *Roman Catholic Opinion* (University of Surrey, 1979) and *The Politics of Spirituality* (OUP, 1995).

Jane Longmore is Head of the School of Humanities at the University of Greenwich. She was formerly Head of Historical, Social and Cultural Studies at St Mary's College, Strawberry Hill, having taught previously at the universities of Reading and Sussex. She has published in the field of urban history and is currently working on a study of the development of Georgian Liverpool. She also acts as an auditor for the Quality Assurance Agency.

Kim Lowden is a feminist historian who is currently researching women's denominational teacher training in the nineteenth century for her doctorate at Liverpool Hope. She has lectured in women's studies at Liverpool John Moores University and in history at Liverpool Hope.

Arthur Naylor is Principal of St Mary's College, Strawberry Hill. He has taught in secondary schools and lectured in higher education.

His research has been in the field of educational administration in Scotland and management development in education. He has served on a range of advisory committees and planning groups for education in Scotland, England and Wales. Currently he is Chair of the Council of Church and Associated Colleges.

Noreen Nicholson is a former administrator, teacher and trainer in higher and professional education with qualifications in history, international relations and the history of education. Her research interests relate mainly to the development of Catholic elementary education in the nineteenth century, including the training of teachers and the inspectorate of Catholic schools.

John Sullivan is an Educational Management Consultant with the External Services Department of St Mary's College, Strawberry Hill and the Course Director for the MA in Catholic School Leadership. He has many years experience as a teacher and headteacher and has written widely on both educational and religious themes.

Philip Walshe, CM is a member of the Vincentian Congregation and was formerly on the staff of St Mary's College, Strawberry Hill teaching in the Department of Theology and Religious Studies and in the Department of Education. He has been on the staffs of St Patrick's College of Education in Dublin and St Patrick's College, Maynooth and has been headmaster of two Vincentian schools. He is now retired.

ACKNOWLEDGEMENTS

Jill Storey, Administrative Assistant to the Vice Principal at St Mary's College, Strawberry Hill co-ordinated this enterprise. She liaised with publishers and contributors, constructed and negotiated schedules. She ensured a consistency of presentation and format. All this she did with patience and perspicacity, tact and good humour. The editors are extremely grateful to her.

INTRODUCTION

Jane Longmore

THIS VOLUME marks the 150th anniversary of the establishment of St Mary's College. It is a celebration of the value and purpose of Catholic higher education. In part, it is a story of survival, transformation and renewal in the face of difficulty, but it is also an acknowledgement of the fundamental strength of an educational philosophy which emphasizes the importance and dignity of each human being. Such a philosophy based on spiritual and moral values sits uneasily with the ruthless materialism and self-centred individualism of the advanced industrial economies in the closing decades of the twentieth century. Yet there are signs of shifting perspectives as the third millennium opens. In Britain today there are striking parallels between New Labour's 'third way' that presents an alternative to both capitalism and communism and Catholic social teaching developed over the past century in response to the forces of industrialization and modernization.[1] On the wider stage, world leaders debate the cost of commercial exploitation of the global environment and seek economic policies with a more ethical dimension. The philosophy of contemporary Catholic education echoes all of these concerns with its emphasis on social justice and community. Thus, the major challenge for Catholic higher education is to emphasize its distinctive identity and the contribution that it is able to make to society in the new millennium.

As Arthur Naylor demonstrates in his chapter dealing with contemporary teacher education in Catholic colleges in England this is a complex and difficult task. His analysis outlines the importance of broadening the remit of the Catholic Church's mission in education in the twenty-first century as part of the current expansion of lifelong learning. This task must be undertaken in the midst of ongoing and profound changes in the nature of the Catholic community in

Britain: in particular, the emergence of a Catholic middle class with wider educational aspirations than their forebears. On the one hand, this provides opportunities for the educational work of the Catholic colleges; on the other, it presents challenges due to the pluralism of belief and practice which is increasingly evident in the modern Catholic community.

In historical terms 'commitment to diversity' refers to the struggle to introduce Catholic education into the hostile environment of nineteenth-century Britain. This period witnessed the foundation and development of St Mary's from a small training college for Catholic teaching brothers in 1850 to a higher education college offering a wide range of degree programmes and numbering approximately 2000 male and female students at the end of the twentieth century. The 150 years of St Mary's College provide a chronological framework and a central focus for the contributors to this volume. However, the chapters do not offer a narrative history of the oldest Catholic college of higher education in England but a combination of perspectives – historical, sociological and educational – on the development of Catholic higher education in the past, present and future.

The impact of social change on Catholic education is a constant theme running through the contributions to this volume. In the nineteenth century one of the most far-reaching social changes was the development of a system of mass education. This development was a consequence of both economic and social concerns. Introducing his Act of 1870 to provide a national system of education in England and Wales W.E. Forster stated:

> Upon the speedy provision of elementary education depends our industrial prosperity. It is of no use trying to give technical teaching to our citizens without elementary education; uneducated labourers – and many of our labourers are utterly uneducated – are, for the most part, unskilled labourers, and if we leave our work-folk any longer unskilled, notwithstanding their strong sinews and determined energy, they will become overmatched in the competition of the world.

Education was also perceived as contributing to the maintenance of social stability which had become a particular issue during the Chartist disturbances and economic turbulence of the 1830s and 1840s. Middle-class observers linked the economic and social benefits of mass education:

The first need of society is order. If order is to be produced in men
and women, what kind of preparation for it is that which leaves the
children as wild as young ostriches in the desert? When for the first
ten or twelve years of life there has been no discipline, either of
mind or body. . . is it to be expected that they will quietly and
industriously settle down in the mills, workshops, warehouses, or at
any trade, or in the orderly routine of any family to work continuously, day by day, from morning till evening, from Monday till
Saturday?[2]

It was such considerations that prompted the provision of government grants from 1833 to contribute to the cost of building schools
incurred by the various voluntary societies. Construction advanced
rapidly and the number of voluntary schools totalled 20,000 by 1870.[3]
Initially this state aid was not extended to Catholic schools in order to
avoid further public hostility of the kind which had accompanied the
passage of the Catholic Emancipation Act of 1829. However, the
demand for places in Catholic schools became urgent, especially
after the famine of 1845–9 produced a massive influx of Irish
immigrants and the creation of concentrations of the Irish poor in
cities such as Liverpool and Manchester. The estimated Catholic
population rose from 700,000 in 1840 to 900,000 in 1851 and
continued to rise steadily thereafter.[4] Mary Hickman describes the
extension of state grant aid to Catholic schools through the Catholic
Poor School Committee, established in 1847. Her chapter also suggests a degree of collusion between the Roman Catholic Hierarchy
(restored to Britain in 1850) and the British state over this arrangement. In return for financial support and autonomy over the
Catholic schools, she argues that the Hierarchy contributed to the
suppression of the cultural identity of Irish pupils by stressing the
Catholic, to the exclusion of the Irish, dimension in their lives. In this
instance, commitment to diversity required a heavy price: the 'incorporation' of Irish working-class children into the culture of the
dominant Protestant community.

The prolonged struggle to obtain adequate state support for
Catholic education has been a crucial part of the effort to maintain
diversity. Richard Cunningham describes the tortuous process
through which Catholic schools gained state aid during the nineteenth and early twentieth centuries, culminating in the 1944
Education Act, 'the greatest gift to the Catholic community'. An
international perspective on this struggle is provided by Stephen
Denig who demonstrates that the process of gaining state aid for

Catholic schools in nineteenth-century America was equally complex and difficult. The parallels are striking in that both systems were developed to cope with the huge influx of immigrants. However, there is also an important difference: Catholic universities were established by the Vincentian community in the USA in the nineteenth century and the Vincentians only moved into the training of teachers for Catholic schools in the early twentieth century. The existence of Catholic universities in Europe, the establishment of University College, London in 1828 without any religious test and the eventual opening of posts at the ancient universities of Oxford and Cambridge to men of all religious persuasions in 1871 offered a number of routes into higher education to more affluent Catholics in nineteenth-century England. Consequently, the establishment of a Catholic university has never had the same urgency in England as in the USA.

Instead, the task of providing teachers for newly-built Catholic schools had clear and unequivocal priority: the number of children in aided Catholic schools more than trebled between 1855 and 1870 from just under 30,000 to over 95,000. In the first half of the nineteenth century many teachers had been unqualified; some were incompetent. As late as the census of 1851 over 700 individuals listed as 'schoolteachers' had to resort to a thumb-print signature on their census return. It is therefore a surprising contrast to encounter the Sisters of Notre Dame and their educational work with Catholic girls and women in late nineteenth-century Liverpool. These female religious were drawn from a higher social class than women in the teacher training colleges run by other religious denominations; they had travelled more widely and were better educated, often abroad. In her chapter, Kim Lowden draws comparisons regarding the curricula of the two types of female training college. The HMI Reports confirm the high standard achieved by their students in a wide range of subjects, including science. From 1861 a new governmental system of 'payment by results' had been introduced to the schools to encourage proficiency in key subjects. The Notre Dame sisters refused to limit their curriculum in order to place all of the emphasis on income generation. With their emphasis on the breadth of the curriculum and on the importance of disregarding gender in encouraging God-given talents, the Sisters of Notre Dame demonstrated a striking commitment to diversity within as well as beyond the Catholic college.

In contrast to the unusually high social status of the Sisters of Notre

Dame, recent research has confirmed that the teaching profession was dominated by lower middle-class women in the nineteenth century.[5] By 1913 three-quarters of elementary schoolteachers were female, a figure which has remained fairly constant up to the present day. During the nineteenth century only one college was training male teachers for Catholic elementary schools: St Mary's, founded with the support of the Catholic Poor School Committee in 1850. The first two decades of the College's existence were extremely difficult with an average annual intake of only 20 to 30 students, approximately one third of its capacity. The role of the Vincentians was critical in ensuring the College's survival during these early years, especially at points of financial crisis. It is therefore entirely appropriate that the contribution of the order to both St Mary's and to the development of Catholic education in nineteenth-century England should be outlined by a Vincentian, Philip Walshe. This contribution was substantial: as Noreen Nicholson points out, by 1886 it was stated that most male teachers in Catholic schools had passed through the College. Her chapter sets the development of St Mary's in the wider context of teacher training in mid-nineteenth-century England and also offers rare insights into the actual experience of trainees at St Mary's in the 1850s and 1860s.

The more contemporary chapters in this volume indicate a significant shift of emphasis in terms of the manner in which Catholic higher education demonstrated its commitment to diversity. Whereas the earlier chapters examine the external struggle to achieve the establishment of training colleges for teachers in Catholic elementary schools in the nineteenth century, in the later chapters 'commitment to diversity' becomes a reference to the internal world of the contemporary Catholic college and the clarification of the value and purpose of Catholic higher education in the late twentieth century and beyond. Michele Dowling quotes the words of a former Principal of St Mary's, Father Kevin Cronin, CM (1948–69): 'we have always had in our College a well-developed tradition of liberty, and in particular of liberty in the expression of different points of view'. The critical and challenging balance between adherence to a particular faith tradition and encouragement of inclusiveness is explored in her analysis of the self-image and ethos of St Mary's between 1944 and 1972. Respondents to her surveys and questionnaires referred repeatedly to the importance of a sense of community in integrating these elements and generating a positive ethos. It is the communication and dissemination of the values of the contemporary Catholic college rather than the implementation and reinforcement of a particular religious perspective that distinguish the challenges of the twentieth century from the historic struggle of the nineteenth century.

Changes in the social structure of the Catholic community have also complicated the task of the Catholic colleges in the late twentieth century. In his chapter Michael Hornsby-Smith outlines the shift from the 'fortress Catholicism' of a religious minority between 1850 and 1960 to a less exclusive and more liberal approach apparent from the 1960s among the growing Catholic middle class, beneficiaries of the 1944 Education Act. He offers a range of complex explanations for this fundamental change, from external socio-economic trends to the impact of two world wars on the structures of authority. The Catholic Church recognized the need to adapt to these changes in the Second Vatican Council (1962–5); thereafter, it began to appear as if the Catholic community had begun a steady process of convergence with the wider community. From the mid-1960s weekly Mass attendance began to decline and the percentage of Catholic marriages and baptisms fell steadily. These demographic and cultural shifts contributed in turn to the contraction of the Catholic teacher training colleges from fifteen in 1975 to five in 1998.

Further pressures for convergence have come from within higher education. At the beginning of the twentieth century central government had adopted a less interventionist approach to the delivery of education. This is epitomized in a series of *Handbooks of Suggestions for Teachers* issued by the Board of Education. The preface of the 1905 handbook, subsequently repeated in 1927, offered the following observation:

> The only uniformity of practice that the Board of Education desire to see in the teaching of Public Elementary Schools is that each teacher shall think for himself and work out for himself, such methods of teaching as may use his powers to the best advantage and be best suited to the particular conditions and needs of the school. Uniformity in details of practice (except in the mere routine of school management) is not desirable even if it were attainable. But freedom implies a corresponding responsibility in its use.[6]

In contrast, centralizing agencies and mechanisms have emerged within the British system of higher education in the 1990s. The 'quality agenda' seems to reinforce the processes of constant change and the elimination of diversity. This is particularly evident in the emphasis on the issue of standards and the discussion of common subject 'benchmarks' and qualification frameworks. A recent critique of these developments included the observation that 'the protection and management of diversity is the big issue which Dearing ducked',[7] referring to the wide-ranging review of higher education chaired by Sir Ron Dearing in 1997. Compliance and conformity pose considerable threats to a system of higher education which serves a range of diverse intellectual needs, reflecting differences in gender, class, age, ethnicity and religion.

A related development has been the growth of a type of educational 'managerialism' which demonstrates a similar lack of awareness of diverse needs. John Sullivan analyses this development and its impact on the delivery of Catholic education in his chapter. He suggests the establishment of a clear distinction between sound management, which is necessary for the effective daily administration of an educational institution, and 'managerialism' based on an industrial model and driven by standardization and quality control. He emphasizes that 'the ambiguity, complexity, particularity, creativity, unpredictability, open-endedness and essentially personal dimensions of educational practice disappear when too strong an emphasis is laid on "managing" education'. The difficulty of reconciling Catholic values and market values (such as the use of school league tables) within a competitive educational environment is recognized as a major challenge. His proposed solution is to articulate the distinctive nature of Catholic education and to establish a framework of moral and humanitarian values which infuse every aspect of the life of the school and its community.

Emphasis on distinctiveness represents a responsible approach to the challenges of the late twentieth century. Distinctiveness need no longer be synonymous with vulnerability as in the nineteenth-century struggle of the Catholic colleges. As John Fulton demonstrates in his preliminary findings from an international research project on the cultural and spiritual values of young adult Catholics, they have identified a contemporary religiosity grounded in peace, divine presence and community. These priorities of modern young adult spirituality align well with the newly-defined value and purpose of modern Catholic higher education as expressed in Mary Eaton's contribution to this volume. She explores the identity, mission and practice of the five remaining Catholic colleges and confirms their re-orientation around a common theme 'which is recognisably

"Catholic" in the way in which needs are addressed and the church is both served and serving'. The sociologist Anthony Giddens has suggested that in the contemporary period of modernity it is increasingly difficult to experience any sense of community, given the fragmentary nature of all human relationships outside those of familial and sexual intimacy.[8] Drawing on their common heritage the Catholic colleges continue to offer 'commitment to diversity' in their genuine sense of community and holistic educational philosophy. The 150th anniversary of St Mary's, Strawberry Hill, becomes a tribute to the past, present and future of Catholic higher education.

NOTES

1   This argument is more fully developed in P. Vallely, 'In the name of the Father and the Holy Vote', *The Independent*, 17 November 1998.

2   Report of the Manchester and Salford Education Aid Society, 1866.

3   Further details of the development of mass education are provided in M. Sturt, *The Education of the People: A History of Primary Education in England and Wales in the Nineteenth Century* (London: Routledge and Kegan Paul, 1967) and D. Wardle, *English Popular Education 1780–1970* (Cambridge: Cambridge University Press, 1970).

4   A.D. Gilbert, *Religion and Society in Industrial England: Church, Chapel and Social Change, 1740–1914* (London: Longman, 1976), p. 46.

5   See for example D. A. Coppock, 'Respectability as a prerequisite of moral character: the social and occupational mobility of pupil teachers in the late nineteenth and early twentieth centuries', *History of Education*, vol. 26, no. 2, June 1997, pp. 165–86.

6   Board of Education, *Handbook of Suggestions for Teachers* (London, 1927), p. 3 quoted in P. Harnett, 'Heroes and heroines: exploring a nation's past. The History curriculum in state primary schools in the twentieth century', *History of Education Society Bulletin*, no. 62, November 1998, pp. 83–95.

7   *Times Higher Educational Supplement*, 17 October 1997.

8   A. Giddens, *Modernity and Self-Identity* (Cambridge: Polity, 1991).

1

TEACHER EDUCATION IN CATHOLIC COLLEGES IN ENGLAND: HISTORICAL CONTEXT, CURRENT PERSPECTIVES AND FUTURE DIRECTIONS

Arthur Naylor

HISTORICAL CONTEXT

ST MARY'S, established at Hammersmith in 1850 and moved to Strawberry Hill in 1925, marked its centenary in 1950 in confident mood. Preaching at Mass in the College chapel in celebration of the centenary on Thursday 1 June 1950 the Archbishop of Liverpool described St Mary's as the 'mainspring of Catholic education'.[1]

The first century of the College's existence had not always been easy but its place in a vision of Catholic education had been firm. Writing in the *Centenary Record* Father G. Shannon CM, Principal of the College between 1941 and 1948, saw

> the struggle for Catholic education, for schools imparting a valid Christian mission, which has engaged the energies of our people since the middle of the last century . . . seen on close inspection to resolve itself into a campaign for education of Catholic children by Catholic teachers. Only believing, practising Catholic teachers can order the various areas of human knowledge into the focus of eternity.'[2]

In affirming the importance of the work of the College, Father Shannon described the training of Catholic teachers as the keystone of the educational arch. The Catholic teacher training colleges, of which St Mary's was the oldest, were in that centenary year an important and valued part of the church's apostolic mission. The commitment to the colleges by bishops, the religious orders which staffed and administered them and the laity which supported them was deep and secure. That sense of security within the church was reflected in the College itself. The College was formed by a small close community of staff and students who shared a faith and a philosophy of education and who were bonded day by day in worship and in fellowship. The particular ethos that was developed and the bonds of friendship that were formed over the two years of training remain clearly visible whenever former students of that era meet now at college reunions. For these reasons the Archbishop of Liverpool, in his message to governors, staff and students in that centenary sermon could describe St Mary's in 1950 as 'truly a garden enclosed'.[3] In the course of that centenary year, 1950, there was much therefore to celebrate. The value of the colleges to the wider Catholic community was clear, their purpose understood, and shared by staff and students. Over the next twenty-five years, however, as a result of changes in society and in the church, that sense of the purpose and value of the Catholic colleges was increasingly obscured.

Yet the first signs of change offered grounds for optimism. Between 1950 and 1960 the total student intakes to training colleges more than doubled in response to the rising birth rate and the higher levels of pupils staying on beyond the statutory leaving age. Historically, the colleges had been seen as separate from the university sector. The report of the Robbins Committee in 1963 was welcomed generally by colleges as it seemed to strengthen their status by recommending closer links between the colleges and universities and the introduction of degree programmes in addition to the teaching certificate courses: 'The Robbins Report was acclaimed by the colleges. It offered them enhanced status, degree courses in a university context, more attention to the quality of entrants to teaching, and steady expansion for at least fifteen years.'[4] In less than ten years, however, the situation had changed.

In 1972 the James Report on Teacher Education and Training followed within a few months by the White Paper *Education: A Framework for Expansion* brought the brief period of expansion to a close. The Robbins' predictions on the scale of intakes to teacher training by 1981 were halved. The White Paper that followed stated simply: 'some colleges now face the possibility that in due course they will have to be converted to new purposes: some may need to close.'[5] For those not facing conversion or closure, the prospect was diversification. 'The substantial broadening of function proposed for the great majority of the colleges of education will involve their much closer assimilation into the rest of the non-university sector of higher and further education.'[6] On these policies the shape and structure of teacher education in England over the last 25 years have been formed.

The main effects have been closure of programmes, conversion or diversification in parallel with pressure for closer links between colleges and universities and can be seen in the present pattern of Catholic teacher education in England. From a position of fifteen Catholic colleges in 1975, representing 10 per cent of the national system, only five colleges remain: three, Newman, Birmingham, Trinity and All Saints, Leeds, and St Mary's, Strawberry Hill, as autonomous institutions linked through validation or accreditation arrangements with secular universities. Two others, Liverpool Hope and the Roehampton Institute have constituent elements which are Roman Catholic. At Liverpool Hope, which is Catholic and Anglican, Christ's and Notre Dame Hall exist to sustain pastorally and academically its Catholic foundation. Within Roehampton, Digby Stuart College provides a Catholic presence within an ecumenical institute. It is not the purpose of this chapter to analyse or explain what has happened over 25 years to reduce and fundamentally reshape the Catholic presence in teacher training. As Michael Hornsby-Smith has observed in his contribution to this volume:

> The story of contraction of the former system for the training of Catholic teachers in the Teacher Training Colleges and hence the Catholic Community involvement in higher and further education is of first importance but remains to be told. What is clear is that it created much hardship and concern about the decision-making procedures.[7]

There is also a view that it is necessary to look beyond government policy to explain the declining role of the Catholic colleges in teacher education. James Arthur has argued that:

> Government action since the 1970s has adversely affected the provision of Catholic teachers from Catholic colleges, but it cannot be claimed that this is the only reason for the dramatic reduction of new entrants to Catholic schools trained at Catholic colleges. There has been criticism of the colleges from within the Catholic community. Some bemoan their secular outlook on education and it has been claimed that their courses merely duplicate those of other institutions.[8]

These kinds of criticisms from within the Catholic community and issues around the identity, character and continuing relevance of the Catholic colleges have been discussed within and across the colleges over the last ten years in a rapidly changing higher education environment. In particular, the thrust of government policy towards expansion in the creation of mass higher education has brought opportunities and threats for the Catholic colleges. While there has been encouragement for growth in numbers, the competition for students has intensified. None of the Catholic colleges was in a position in terms of scale and range of activity to aspire to university status in its own right in 1992 when the former polytechnics were designated universities. Each Catholic college now finds itself within the university sector but unable to aspire in its own right to university status. Constraints on funding, the evidence of merger activities elsewhere in the higher education sector in the United Kingdom and the example of Australia where a Catholic university was established in 1991 largely from former teacher training colleges, led to a collective review of their situation in the early 1990s by the Catholic colleges.

In February 1994 the members of management teams of the Catholic colleges of higher education of the United Kingdom submitted a statement on 'The purpose and value of contemporary Catholic colleges' for the consideration of the Bishops' Conference of England and Wales at the Low Week meeting. The statement recognized openly that the future presented 'further challenges to the Church, including the possibility of the Colleges' elimination from the work of the higher education altogether or the continued dilution of their religious identity. The Colleges are unable to mark time and continue as before.'[9] Changes to the size and shape of the Catholic presence in higher education over the previous 20 years, the statement accepted, had not been made through carefully evolved plans at national level on the part of the Catholic community but rather at a pragmatic level responding to particular situations where there was danger or opportunity. There was no value, it was argued, simply in looking back nor in marking time and continuing as before. In looking forward, key statements were made about the distinctiveness of Catholic colleges and the renewal of Catholic higher education in support of the claim that it was 'right for the Catholic philosophy of education to have its place within the higher education sector, as well as in primary and secondary schooling'.[10]

The central importance of teacher training within the mission of the colleges was recognized: 'colleges have a long tradition in providing professional degrees for teachers and must continue this practice as one of their principal aims, especially the education of those intending to teach in Catholic schools'.[11] At the same time it was recognized that there should be no plea for special treatment and that sound standards were essential. The statement pointed also to the importance of closer co-operation across the colleges in pursuance of their objectives. There 'is a proper mission today for Catholic higher education colleges, embracing the professional training of teachers and the wider provision of undergraduate courses. The mission is best pursued by the colleges in partnership with each other.'[12]

Unfortunately none of this was sufficient to rescue La Sainte Union College (LSU) from closure in 1997 following highly critical reports by the Office for Standards in Education on the quality of its primary teaching courses. The La Sainte Union situation did send out a strong message to the Catholic colleges. More than they realized they were dependent on teacher training and if standards fell, support from the Catholic educational community quickly slipped away. While strenuous efforts had been made to diversify into new academic areas, La Sainte Union was unable to sustain the loss of its accreditation for teacher training and closed within a matter of months of its failed primary inspection. Moreover, the lack of an effective joint response on behalf of the Catholic colleges allowed the LSU training places to be lost to the Catholic sector. A consequence was that the Catholic presence in teacher education within the higher education sector in England is now located in four cities: London, Birmingham, Liverpool and Leeds. The result is that large parts of the country are at some distance from the nearest Catholic college but it is also the case that the colleges that remain are in strategically important locations in terms of the future development of the role of the Catholic colleges in teacher education.

CURRENT PERSPECTIVES

It has to be recognized that following the closure of La Sainte Union the current position of the Catholic colleges in terms of student numbers in teacher education may weaken further in the short term. An analysis of intakes, real and projected, over an eight-year period 1993–2001 indicates that the number of primary undergraduate and postgraduate places in the Catholic colleges will have fallen from around 1300 in 1993 to around 600 by 2001.[13] This results in part from loss of places following the closure of LSU but also from the general reduction in primary intake numbers. The situation in secondary training may appear even less promising. In 1997–8, 6.5 per cent of students on primary Initial Teacher Training (ITT) programmes were in Catholic colleges while the figure for secondary is only 3.3 per cent. In each Catholic college Religious Education is offered as a main secondary subject but the pattern of other subject provision is patchy across the colleges. Moreover, in recent years with the encouragement of the Department for Education and Employment (DfEE) and the Teacher Training Agency (TTA), school-centred courses of initial teacher training have been established. This has led to the development, albeit on a very limited and local basis of postgraduate secondary ITT programmes organized by Catholic schools. There have also been experiments with Catholic pathways on secondary ITT programmes in Anglican colleges in areas where there is no nearby Catholic college.

These issues of falling numbers and competition from new providers are important. There is no special place for Catholic teacher education providers. However, they should not obscure another more fundamental discussion of the extent to which the programmes that are on offer in Catholic colleges are located within a vision of the purposes of Catholic education. The increasing move towards a national curriculum for teacher training has focused the attention of initial teacher trainers very firmly on an agenda of compliance with DfEE requirements, national standards and competencies. Awareness of these issues in forming a current and accurate perspective on initial teacher education within the Catholic colleges is important.

There are, however, other dimensions of the work of the Catholic colleges in teacher education that need to be considered when discussing a comprehensive view of their present position. Against the background of falling numbers in initial training, the scope and potential for the development of in-service training activities have expanded rapidly. Historically, the share of funding allocated to the Catholic colleges in support of in-service provision has, however, always been small. In 1998 for the first time a competitive bidding process was introduced by the Teacher Training Agency. A further sign of weakness is that in the first round of bidding covering 1998–9 to 2000–01 no Catholic college was successful in gaining an allocation of funds.

The position of research in education within the Catholic colleges has also been problematic. In the national Research Assessment Exercises in 1992 and 1996, the Catholic colleges and the broader church college sector of which they are part did not perform well in attracting funds for research in Education. It can be argued that research has not been central to the mission of the Catholic colleges where, historically, learning and teaching have been at the heart of their endeavours. However, there are issues in Catholic education, such as the reasons for the success of Catholic schools and the relationship of mission statements based on gospel values to the realitities of management, that currently would benefit from research, and where at present the main research centres are to be found outside the Catholic colleges.

Before attempting an analysis of the future directions for Catholic colleges in teacher education it is important to begin from the basis of a realistic assessment of the present position of the Catholic colleges in teacher education. First, the Catholic colleges will not, and indeed cannot, return to the position of earlier decades when the majority of Catholic teachers trained there. The nature of recruit-ment to the profession has changed, the colleges are too few in number and attitudes and loyalties to the Catholic colleges have changed. It is understandable that a proportion of those who enter training and whose experience of school education has been in the Catholic sector may wish to undertake a different higher education environment. This does not, however, diminish the case for a strong presence of Catholic colleges in teacher education. For Catholic schools, it is important that there are guaranteed sources of well-qualified teachers whose training has been undertaken within a philosophy and framework of Catholic education and where there is an opportunity to gain the Catholic Certificate in Religious Studies and to undertake placements in Catholic schools. It is through support for the Catholic colleges that there can be assurance that there will be teacher education institutions that can fully share that responsibility with Catholic schools.

Second, there can be no basis for the future development of the Catholic colleges in teacher education that relies on a case for special treatment or historical precedent. The future of Catholic colleges in teacher education must rest on their distinctiveness and on the quality of their work now, their capacity to recruit able entrants to training and the employability of their graduates. For these reasons, the claim to 'historic share' on training places is no longer relevant. Nevertheless, there must be substantial pressure on funding agencies to ensure that they fulfil their obligations in respect of denomina-tional provision. These obligations were restated by the government when the Teacher Training Agency was established. It can be argued that the Teacher Training Agency has not yet grasped these responsibilities.

Third, the Catholic colleges must be prepared to plan together so as to strengthen each other, to share good practice and to present to government and national agencies a common position on matters of mutual interest in teacher education. Individually, the colleges are relatively small and vulnerable to changing patterns of student recruitment, funding arrangements and bidding. Collectively, their voice is greatly strengthened. The commitment to partnership was set out in the statement to the Bishops' Conference in 1994. It suffered a setback in 1997 with the failure of any joint strategy to prevent the closure of La Sainte Union College, Southampton. The challenge for the future is to strengthen the relationships between the colleges.

Fourth, the reduction in numbers of Catholic colleges and training places over 25 years and the most recent loss in 1997 of La Sainte Union have created in parts of the broader Catholic education world a perception of decline in the colleges. In the more geographically isolated areas of the country the Catholic colleges, now only in London, Birmingham, Leeds and Liverpool, can appear irrelevant to the needs of Catholic schools in teacher supply and continuing professional development. Yet, at the same time, the most positive basis for future development is the existence of a Catholic college in four strategic centres. There is the potential through technology to form stronger networks across the country from these centres. There are also the largely unexploited networks of collaboration through links between the Catholic higher education and further education colleges. The scope to work ecumenically with Anglican and Methodist colleges within the Council of Church and Associated Colleges (CCAC) should also be more fully developed.

Fifth, there continues to be a great reservoir of support and goodwill for the colleges within Catholic schools. In recent years this has been tested by the market conditions that were introduced through payments to schools where institutions were encouraged to compete with each other. The continuing presence of the many teachers in Catholic schools trained in the Catholic colleges remains a great strength. More critically, the colleges must again strengthen partnerships with Catholic schools and dioceses in initial teacher education and in continuing professional development in ways that relate closely to needs, particularly where these needs, such as in

Religious Education and leadership training have quite distinctive characteristics in Catholic education.

In summary, the Catholic colleges in seeking to discover their future directions in teacher education must recognize that they will not return to the monopoly of training they all enjoyed but can find a distinctive, indeed, unique contribution to the future development of Catholic education. The colleges must be prepared to work collaboratively with each other and with others who share a Christian vision of education. They must look also to relationships with Catholic further education colleges where there can be mutual interest in extending the geographical presence of Catholic teacher education. Most significantly, they must build a new relationship with Catholic schools. It is the nature of that relationship that will shape the further directions of Catholic teacher education.

FUTURE DIRECTIONS

The challenge of the future for the colleges will be in the part they can play in helping to construct and to support a vision of the Church's mission in education in the twenty-first century which will be wider than its current vision while remaining responsive to the needs of Catholic primary and secondary schools. Schools will continue to be central to vision but cannot (as they have done) carry the weight of expectation they currently bear within the church's overall mission in education.

The future will be different. In the information and knowledge-based revolution in which we are living, described as the learning age, learning is seen as lifelong and no longer restricted by time and place. Learning is considered to be the key to economic prosperity and individual fulfilment. The 1998 Government White Paper on lifelong learning required the power of learning for individuals which 'stimulates enquiring minds and nourishes our souls'.[14] In this vision of a learning age, education and the development of the person are the means by which economies and societies can be transformed. The significance of this shift in the importance that government places on learning and lifelong learning needs to be recognized as the way that the church's mission in education is expressed. The church's mission in education in the twenty-first century must become much broader than solely the provision of Catholic schools. Almost twenty years ago this was recognized in a report to the Bishops' Conference of England and Wales which expressed a vision of education in which

> the total activity of the Church is educative. Its purpose under the guidance of the Holy Spirit is to communicate Christ to mankind and to elucidate the meaning and significance of this communication to each succeeding age. The Church's mission is to all men and women, and all members of the Church share in this mission. Their task is to embody Christ's presence, to continue his work and so to transform the world.[15]

There has been an enormous investment over more than 150 years in Catholic primary and secondary education in England and Wales and it is right that this should continue because of the responsibility that parents and schools share for the religious, moral and spiritual development as well as for the intellectual and social development of young people. Increasingly, however, it will not be enough. The potential of community, adult and family learning has to be harnessed in support of the church's mission in education in its fullest sense. If we can no longer expect individuals to sustain themselves throughout their lives as workers and citizens on what they have acquired through their years of formal education, we cannot expect that their religious, moral and spiritual development can be sustained solely on the basis of the preparation that the primary and secondary school provides. At today's participation rate 60 per cent of school leavers can expect to enter higher education at some time in their lives: 'the 18–25 cohort is not easily approached through traditional parish structures but . . . are very specially accessible in the higher education scene; they are intellectually, emotionally, spiritually very challengable at this time both individually and in peer groups'.[16]

Historically, the principal instrument of the church's mission in higher education in the secular universities is the chaplaincy. While all higher education institutions provide some facilities for chaplaincies, the standard of facilities, support and interest varies significantly across the sector at a time when many students 'regard their faith as marginal to their everyday life within the university'[17] and their commitment to religious values and practice decreases.

Beyond further and higher education and within the broad area of Catholic adult education, training and formation there is a great deal of activity at local level but it can appear fragmented, unstructured and variable in quality. Attention to structure can drive out the spontaneity and creativity of adult and community learning. However, there is clearly a place for strategy at parish and diocesan level in partnership with Catholic schools, further and higher education to provide programmes that can be formative of individuals and groups, for example, in exploring the religious, moral and spiritual dimensions of life at the different stages. In short, a strategy for lifelong learning in support of the church's mission in education, with the church alongside and supporting the vision of a learning society communicating its message of the Gospel.

Therefore, the Catholic colleges can play an important part in constructing and supporting a vision of the church's mission in education in the twenty-first century which embraces more fully adult and community learning and, in so doing, broadens the vision of Catholic education – a vision in which schools will remain foundation stones – within a strategy for lifelong learning.

The role of the Catholic college in relation to schools will be in responding to their needs in the training of teachers and in offering leadership and support in professional development. The key issues will include: sustaining and seeking to improve recruitment to meet the teacher supply needs of Catholic schools; developing partnership in training with Catholic schools; offering relevant continuing professional development opportunities and defining a more significant contribution to research in Catholic education.

The issue of recruitment is among the most important and sensitive. Catholic colleges, particularly where they are offering courses of acknowledged high quality, and in a situation where more students will be looking locally to study, become very attractive to a wide range of potential students who are not Catholic but who feel at home in a college with strong ethical traditions. In secondary education the challenge is to meet the present shortage of qualified applicants of whatever background. However, in primary training, where places are as a rule oversubscribed, the criterion by which applicants are chosen is very significant. Its significance is underlined by the importance that primary school governing bodies place on the recruitment of Catholic staff. There is an obligation on the Catholic colleges to support the schools that they serve by actively seeking to recruit well-qualified and motivated Catholic applicants. The colleges do no service to the Catholic schools by lowering entry standards simply to admit a higher proportion of Catholic students to training. Their goal, always, has to be to fill their training places with the best qualified and motivated candidates that they can attract. However, through targeted recruitment this can at the same time bring into training high proportions of students whose first destination on qualification will be employment in a Catholic school.

In initial teacher training, generally, the future emphasis will remain on partnership between schools and higher education with schools increasingly being asked to take on increased responsibilities. There are distinctive elements of Catholic partnership in training. In broad terms these have been defined as the preparation of newly qualified teachers 'to recognize, support and promote the faith values and ethos particular to the Catholic Christian Mission'. This includes a Catholic understanding of the following:

- the nature and purposes of mission statements; their impact on policy and practice; organization and management;
- curricular policy and provision; provision for those with special education needs/abilities; cross-curricular themes (e.g. health education, PSE, sex education); extra-curricular activities (including retreats, work with parishes/community); multi-cultural education;
- religious education; spiritual and moral development across the curriculum; liturgy, worship;
- pastoral care; personal relationships; counselling; rewards and sanctions; liaison with parents, parishes, the wider community;
- assessment, recording and reporting; academic counselling; careers advice;
- staffing; recruitment policies; deployment; appraisal and professional development; contractual rights and obligations;
- legal status of voluntary aided schools.[18]

The Catholic Certificate in Religious Studies, which is validated through the Bishops' Conference and is offered to students training in each of the Catholic colleges, is also a key part of that distinctive contribution.

Issues will have to be addressed to maintain the balance between preparation of teachers to meet increasingly detailed government requirements and to understand and to be confident and effective in a Catholic school. In the future direction of Catholic initial teacher education there is a critical balance to be struck in order that students can be educated and trained in a way that contributes to their personal, spiritual and moral development as well as to their growing professional competence.

A major shift in balance in the future direction of Catholic teacher education is in the growing involvement of the colleges in the continuing professional development of teachers. John Sullivan in his contribution to this volume describes work (at St Mary's) on the training under way to equip those who aspire to exercise leadership roles and responsibilities in Catholic education. This work is of fundamental importance in view of the present difficulties that Catholic schools, particularly primary schools, are experiencing in attracting suitably qualified candidates for posts of headteacher and deputy headteacher. The involvement of Catholic colleges across the whole range of continuing professional development work can be expected to expand but in two areas in particular it is essential that this happens if the colleges are to offer a distinctive contribution to the future needs of Catholic schools.

The first area, as already identified, is in training and preparation for leadership and management roles in a way which brings together theology, a vision of Catholic education and current leadership management theory and practice. The second is in the development of Religious Education. The national project of catechesis and Religious Education, as its work develops, will require strong in-service and consultancy support from dioceses and colleges. The scale of the task is likely to outweigh the resources, particularly in terms of experienced religious educators who have the time to devote to providing curriculum development and consultancy support. It does provide, however, an excellent opportunity for collaboration between the colleges, dioceses and schools to make the best use of available resources. The close involvement of Catholic colleges in major national projects in Religious Education offers one of the best opportunities for the colleges to play a dynamic part in the future developments of Catholic education.

In seeking a future direction in teacher education, whether in initial teacher training, continuing professional development or research, the challenge is threefold: to be clear about focus; to be distinctive, and to be excellent. In initial teacher training and continuing professional development with sustained and targeted effort all of this can be achieved and the resources are, in most areas, ready to be harnessed. The strengths of Catholic primary and secondary schools can be drawn into effective partnerships in training. For these reasons it is important to pay attention to the continued recruitment of both a strong cadre of staff who can locate their high professional standards within a vision of Catholic education and of able students, a high proportion of whom share a commitment to

Catholic education. Moreover, through in-service and consultancy focused closely on areas such as leadership and Religious Education, the Catholic Colleges can play a major part in continuing professional development which can be distinctive in content and methodology.

Undoubtedly the most challenging area of development will be establishing research bases in education in the Catholic colleges. It may be that this can only be brought about through collaboration with interested and supportive researchers in Catholic education whose bases are in secular universities with strong research track records. With the emphasis now placed on national and international collaboration, this may be more possible to achieve than might have been the case in the past ten years.

After 150 years of Catholic teacher education there is a need to define a new rationale for the next stages. It will not bring the same security that existed for so much of the twentieth century, nor for that matter the sense of drift of which the colleges were accused in more recent years. It can, however, through a clearer focus and new forms of partnerships between Catholic colleges, schools and dioceses support the mission of the church in education which is in quite different ways as urgent and difficult now as it was in 1850 when St Mary's was founded.

NOTES

1   *Centenary Record 1850–1950*, St Mary's College, 1950, p. 129. Report of the Centenary sermon preached by the Most Rev Richard Downey, Archbishop of Liverpool.

2   Ibid., p. 84.

3   Ibid., p. 129.

4   G. P. McGregor, *A Church College for the 21st century?* (York: University College of Ripon and York St John, 1991), p. 179.

5   *Education: A Framework for Expansion* CMND 5174 (London: HMSO, December 1972), pp. 44–5.

6   Ibid., p. 46.

7   M. P. Hornsby-Smith (this volume), 'The changing social and religious context of Catholic schooling in England and Wales'.

8   J. Arthur, *The Ebbing Tide: Policy and Principles of Catholic Education* (Gracewing: Leominster, 1995), pp. 189–90.

9   'The purpose and value of contemporary Catholic Colleges of Higher Education in the United Kingdom', report to the Bishops' Conference of England and Wales on behalf of the Catholic Colleges Partnership (London: Department for Catholic Education and Formation, 1994), pp. 57–63.

10   Ibid.

11   Ibid.
12   Ibid.
13   Statistics drawn from an analysis (unpublished) by the Director of the Catholic Education Service for a meeting of the Principals of Catholic Colleges with the Chairman of the Catholic Education Service, March 1998.
14   Department of Education and Employment, *The Learning Age* (London: The Stationery Office, 1998), p. 15.
15   Bishops' Conference of England and Wales, *Signposts and Homecomings* (Slough: St Paul Publications, 1998), p. 142.
16   Bishops' Conference of England and Wales, Committee for Higher Education, *The Presence of the Church in the University Culture of England and Wales* (London: Department for Catholic Education and Formation, 1997), p. 17.
17   Ibid., p. 15.
18   *Partnership in the Training of Teachers for Catholic Schools* (London: Catholic Education Service, 1995).

2

CHURCH AND STATE IN EDUCATION IN ENGLAND AND WALES 1833–1975

Richard Cunningham

INTRODUCTION

THIS CHAPTER covers the whole period in outline but considers in more detail the 1944 Education Act and surrounding events. The chapter is divided into five sections detailing the history of the relationship between the Church and the state on the topic of education.

1833–1870

The state first intervened in education in 1833 with £20,000 of grants to schools in membership of voluntary societies promoting education. These were benevolently seeking to provide elementary education for the 'labouring classes' at a time when churchmen and many of the better off accepted a duty of voluntary giving in aid of others.

The structure of local government at that time was still essentially Elizabethan. In towns there were boroughs (reorganized in 1835) but in the country, affairs were conducted by the justice of the peace and various *ad hoc* bodies that had been established over the years for particular purposes such as the provision of roads or bridges, the principal bodies being the Poor Law Guardians who provided the social security of the day from the rates they levied. It was not until 1888–94 that administrative counties, county boroughs, urban districts and rural districts came into being as multi-purpose local government units. No rates were levied in aid of education, and the central government grants were the first public expenditures.

Initially the grants were made to schools in membership of the National Society for the Promotion of Religious Education (of the Established Church) founded in 1811 and associated with the Bell method of teaching in its early days, and of the British and Foreign School Society (BFSS) (supported by some members of the Established Church and a wide range of Nonconformists) founded in 1808 and associated with the Lancaster method of teaching. Later, schools associated with the Methodist Church and the Catholic Poor Schools Committee received grants. The grants were given initially only for school building, but their range was later extended under Kay-Shuttleworth's secretaryship of the Committee of the Privy Council on Education which after its foundation in 1839 became responsible for the administration of these grants. In return for the grants the government sought controls, in the form of requirements as to buildings and of inspections by Her Majesty's Inspectors (HMIs). (There were different Inspectors for Anglican, Catholic and Methodist/BFSS schools, with each set of schools having a say in appointments and dismissals.) In 1843 Kay-Shuttleworth wrote to Lord John Russell saying:

> When your Lordship and Lord Lansdown in 1839 appointed me secretary of the Committee of Council on Education, I understood the design of your Government to be to prevent the successful assertion on the part of the Church then put forth, for a purely ecclesiastical system of education . . . I understood your Lordship's government to determine in 1839 to assert the claim of the civil power to the control of the education of the country.[1]

Under the Kay-Shuttleworth system, grants towards current expenditure were introduced in addition to capital grants. In order to assure quality through grants for the employment of certificated teachers and grants for the supervision of pupil teachers. Inevitably the poorest and most needy were left unaided under this system for they had not the funds to pay their share which exceeded the grant. Robert Lowe's controversial Revised Code of 1862 based grants on results rather than factors which might produce good results, and reduced the level of government grant.

But the tide was running strongly in favour of developing elementary education. In 1850 only 1406 elementary schools received an annual grant and annual inspection, although another 4396 schools were liable to inspection, having received other grants for building, books or apparatus. By 1868 the number of annual grant schools had risen to 12,798, and three years later in 1871 it was 20 per cent higher at 15,434. In those three years the number of pupil–teachers rose by 50 per cent, from 10,677 to 16,941, despite Lowe's 1862 Code having withdrawn the grant for the supervision of pupil–teachers.

It is clear that 'local exertion', the contemporary phrase for the voluntary effort of the various religious societies and their members, had produced remarkable results in terms of the number of schools which had risen to a higher level of efficiency, only partly financed by government grants. But there was a deficiency of school provision and a greater deficiency of efficient school provision. For there were more schools than there were efficient schools (in the sense of schools open to annual inspection by Her Majesty's Inspectorate (HMI)).

In 1851 Horace Mann carried out a census of schools along with the national census. He found no less than 29,425 schools classified as private day schools, but with only 695,422 pupils, i.e. nearly 25 on average. Many were dame schools; others fell into the private venture category, a small number counted as young ladies' academies. The public elementary category had 15,411 schools with 1,413,170 pupils, i.e. nearly 100 on average. Many at that stage were not on the annual grant list.

The number on the annual grant list grew over the years, but in 1870 there were still many schools not on the list, because either their staff or their premises were not adequate, the underlying difficulty being lack of funds. An HMI examination of these schools in 1870 and later was undertaken, using on instruction lenient standards, and many were brought within the annual grant list in the expectation that with better funding they would come up to standard. In some areas they were very numerous; for instance, an HMI report on Suffolk before 1870 estimated that two-thirds of the public elementary schools were in this category.

So far as the dame and private venture schools were concerned, the HMI saw little possibility of improvement. A small number of private venture schools were seen as satisfactory but otherwise the verdict was unfavourable with regard to staff and premises. It is hard to disbelieve HMI opinion and one must therefore dismiss the idea that there was a flourishing and satisfactory private enterprise system of schooling which collectivism displaced post-1870. Apart from inspected schools, most of the others were hard-up voluntary schools of the kind seen in Suffolk.

1870–1902

After the return of the Liberal government in 1868, early legislation was anticipated on elementary education. The government Bill accepted the existing voluntary school as the core of the national system, and provided for their supplementation by board schools, provided and run by school boards, to meet deficiencies in public school accommodation. Controversies followed within the Party on the question of the Religious Education in Board schools funded from the rates, and the extent to which denominational schools should be supported from rates. On the first point, the controversy was between the secularists and the undenominationalists in the liberal ranks. The secularists included some who objected to any rate assistance to religious teaching on the ground that it entailed ratepayers contributing to the support of other people's religions. The undenominationalists were more numerous and carried the day with the Cowper–Temple clause: 'No religious catechism or religious formulary of any particular denomination shall be taught in the school.'

Robert Lowe, then Chancellor of the Exchequer, persuaded his colleagues to remove from school boards any duty to support voluntary schools: 'Increase the Privy Council grant by one half and the thing is done and done in the way most agreeable to the recipients.'[2] But school boards, it was considered, had to be treated in the same way and received the bonus of an increase in Privy Council grant. This contributed to the disparity in coming years between Board schools and voluntary schools and, to be complete, between Board schools in areas of higher rateable values and Board schools in areas of lower rateable value.

Two features of the 1870 Act require note: (1) the legal requirement of a conscience clause, i.e. withdrawal from religious instruction and observance at the parents' wish in any school; (2) the ending of the system of inspection by inspectors approved by the denominational authority for its schools.

The Act required only one school board to be brought into existence, that for London. But it led to a further 2470, ranging from those of Birmingham, Liverpool, and Manchester to boards for small rural parishes with just one school. The achievements of the major boards were to be very considerable.

The elementary education system expanded hugely after the 1870 Act. The 1895–6 Report of the Committee of the Privy Council stated under the heading of 'The Provision of School Accommodation':

> The additional amount of accommodation which has been provided since 1870, to the extent of 1,735,762 seats by Voluntary effort, and 2,322,942 in board schools has been supplied in several ways:

(i)   In the 12 years ending on the 31st December 1882 building grants to the amount of £312,000 were paid by the Education Department, on the completion of the erection or enlargement of 1572 schools and 933 teachers' residences affording new or improved accommodation for 280,146 children. These grants were met by local contributors to the amount of £1,348,169, exclusive of the value of the sites given gratuitously.

(ii)   The great majority of the remaining 4626 voluntary schools, with seats for some 1,456,000 children which have come under inspection since 1870 have been erected, enlarged, or improved without Government aid, at a cost to the providers which was estimated to have been at least £7,000,000. Very large sums have been spent upon the erection and improvement of voluntary schools, but we have no returns which would enable us to give any precise figures.

(iii) School boards – up to 1st April 1895 had been given sanction to 11,452 loans, amounting to £31,782,748, to 2079 school boards. Through these, accommodation, when complete, would have been provided for 2,328,037 pupils, at an estimated cost per pupil of £13 12s.

Expansion on this scale would not have been necessary without the growth of population and its movement. Between 1871 and 1891 the population of England and Wales went from 22,12,266 to 29,002,525 with that of the Metropolitan areas (London) going from 3,266,987 to 4,232,118, municipal boroughs as a whole showing the biggest proportional increase from 6,512,611 to 11,938,451 while the remainder of the country showed a smaller increase, from 12,932,668 to 13,831,956.

By 1895 pupil numbers in Board schools had reached 1,879,218, slightly in excess of the numbers in Church of England schools, i.e. 1,850,545 but well below the total in all voluntary schools, i.e. 2,445,812. Many areas of the country showed a strong determination to keep out school boards and the rates which went with them. The resistance to school boards was not solely a matter of objection on religious principle. Boards were thought likely to be free-spending, and HMIs report cases of local people agreeing that they would contribute to avoid a rate, instead of leaving it to the squire and the parson, indeed, there were even cases of proposals for a voluntary rate designed to be less than that which a board would levy. Local industries had an interest. In the North East there were colliery schools, provided by the collieries; in Crewe the railway company established a voluntary school. Agricultural land was not de-rated in this period as it has been fully since 1929, so landowners who would usually have been subscribers to voluntary schools had an incentive to continue.

The years from 1870 to 1902 were marked by friction and rivalry between Board schools and voluntary schools and by differences between the political parties which were aligned according to denomination, the liberals with the Nonconformists, and the Conservatives with the Church of England. Each party, because of Irish issues, had an ally with an attitude different to its own on church schools and religious education. The Liberals had an ally in the Irish Nationalists who had displaced the former Irish Liberal Party but, as Catholics with a watchful Catholic following at home, sought to protect the interests of Catholic education; the Conservatives had an ally in the Liberal Unionists, who had split from the Liberal Party over Home Rule for Ireland but, led by Joseph Chamberlain, carried over Liberal/Nonconformist views on education.

The major issue to arise was the growing disparity between the funds available to Board schools and voluntary schools. By 1895 Board schools on average, rich and poor, were spending over £2 10s per child while voluntary schools on average were spending slightly under £1 19s. Since teachers' salaries then as now were the main item in school costs, the difference between the costs reflected principally a difference in the average salaries paid, which were significantly higher (in London about 65 per cent) in Board schools than in voluntary schools. On the voluntary school side, the dissatisfaction with current arrangements was most clearly felt by schools in Board areas, rather than schools in non-Board areas, and was voiced particularly strongly by Catholics whose schools were mostly in Board areas.

This chapter has described events in more or less chronological order but is interrupted at this stage to consider the Nonconformist opposition which ran throughout nearly all the period under discussion. This has to be put in the wider context of Nonconformist attitudes to the Church of England. Throughout much of the nineteenth century many elements in Nonconformity through the Liberation Society sought the disestablishment of the church. The Church of Ireland was disestablished in 1869, the Church in Wales in 1913. The Church of England had a stronger base and Nonconformist support for disestablishment faded long before Nonconformist opposition to church schools. Two factors may have helped to keep the latter alive longer, the issue of rates, and the belief in real grievances. The root of Nonconformist objection to using rates to support the giving of religious instruction in accordance with some-one else's beliefs appears to lie in objection to the church rate, an obligation since Tudor times on all civil parishioners to pay a rate to maintain the parish church. This was finally abolished by the Liberal government of 1868–74.

The objection to denominational instruction on the rates led to Nonconformist objections in 1870 to the proposal to allow rate aid for voluntary schools. Objections were carried to what seemed absurd lengths when it was discovered that Section 25 of the 1870 Act allowed school boards to pay the fees for sufficiently necessitous children attending voluntary schools. This provoked enormous pro-test and the 1876 Act transferred the duty to assist to the Poor Law Guardians and the poor rate. Later the 1902 Act gave rise to passive resistance and the slogan 'Rome on the rates'.

The views of Free Churchmen would have had less weight, had they not been accompanied by the claim that the denial of Free Church claims imposed disabilities on them and gave them grounds for grievance. The alleged disabilities were of two main kinds: (1) for pupils and parents – the single school area; and (2) for teachers or intending teachers – the high proportion of Anglican schools.

The complaint under (2) applied originally mainly to becoming a student teacher as a preliminary to entrance to a training college. In Anglican schools a student teacher would be expected to be an Anglican and the same would apply in an Anglican training college. Evidence to the Cross Commission in the late 1880s showed a significant Anglican element in colleges of the British and Foreign Schools Society, open to all denominations. The same was found in Edwardian times. Were the BFSS colleges refusing Nonconformists or were there not enough of them? Student teachers numbers declined in the years preceding 1914, and powers to local education authorities to run training colleges ended the Anglican predom-inance in that field. Thereafter the complaint moved to teaching posts, more specifically headships. The Church of England had headships out of proportion to its pupil numbers. National salary scales from 1920 and the advantage of motor transport (to relieve the isolation), not forgetting waterborne sanitation, made rural head-ships more attractive. The single-school area was a civil parish, normally rural, in which there was only one school and normally only enough children for one school. A majority of these areas had only an Anglican school, but in about a third of them the sole school was a County school at the time of a survey by Canon E.F. Brayley in the 1930s (to be found in Archbishop Temple's papers).

Prior to the 1902 Act, Morant commented on the single-school area grievance to Balfour, making two points. The first, relatively minor, point was that some pupils in a single school area could be nearer to, and could attend, a school in an adjacent parish which corresponded better to their parents' wishes. The main point was, however, to question why the free churches placed so much emphasis on the single-school area, when it must be only part of a wider problem, namely that in many areas of the country, parents could not find a school of their persuasion – denominational or Board – close to hand. The beauty of the single-school area as a grievance was that it was one which could be established without proof in individual cases.

The Cross Commission in the late 1880s examined complaints about the working of the conscience clause in the 1870 Act. The Revd James Duncan, Secretary of the National Society, stated: 'In Church schools, out of 2 million children 2200 are withdrawn from the whole, and 5690 from a part of the religious teaching. The partial withdrawals are probably from the catechism.' Religious instruction in Anglican schools was divided into Scripture (usually three periods) and Catechism (usually two periods). About twenty years later, at a time of later controversies, the National Society quoted similar figures. The anti-voluntary minority on the Commission accepted that the conscience clause was being observed but said that it was not enough because of pressures to conform, and called for a Board school in every single-school area.

1902–14

The new local authorities, created in the period 1888–92, were natural candidates to take on responsibilities in education. The Technical Instruction Act of 1889 authorized the newly created county and county borough councils and other local authorities to levy a penny rate in order to 'supply or aid in supplying technical and manual instruction' and in the following year under the recently introduced scheme of assigned revenues, under which central government revenues were assigned to particular purposes, duty on whisky became available to support technical education – the 'whisky money'. Sir John Gorst's unsuccessful Bill of 1896 proposed the creation of a central authority and local authorities for education. It fell by the wayside but three years later the Board of Education Act 1899 brought together under the Board, the Education Department (elementary schools), the Department of Science and Art at South Kensington (which distributed grants in aid of science classes in grammar schools, higher grade elementary schools and evening schools), and certain Charity Commission functions in respect of endowed schools. The report of the Bryce Commission on Secondary Education in 1895 advocated the creation of new local authorities in every county and every county borough to provide secondary education, but side-stepped the burning question whether secondary education should be entrusted to the school boards or to the county councils, county boroughs and lesser local authorities.

The Act of 1902 is known as the Balfour–Morant Act in recognition of its two authors, the one, Arthur James Balfour who became Prime Minister during its passage and personally steered it through the House of Commons, the other, Robert Morant, his chief adviser who became Permanent Secretary of the Board of Education towards the end of 1902. Previously Morant had written: 'The only way to get up steam for passing any Education Bill at all in the teeth of School Board opposition will be to include in it some scheme for aiding denominational schools.' The latter – aid to denominational schools – proved much more controversial than the abolition of school boards, but it also enlisted strong support from Conservative MPs which the former could not. The Bill replaced school boards by general or multi-purpose authorities. These Part III authorities, as they came to be known (municipal boroughs with over 10,000 inhabitants, urban districts with over 20,000 inhabitants), were the authorities for elementary education in these areas. County boroughs were the authorities for both elementary and secondary education in their areas, as were county councils except in the numerous areas where Part III Authorities existed within the county area and left them with responsibility only for secondary education. The Act imposed on authorities the duty to maintain and keep efficient voluntary schools, in popular parlance, to put them on the rates. In the Bill in its original form in deference to the views of Joseph Chamberlain, there was an option available to local authorities to maintain voluntary schools. Conservative backbenchers converted this into a duty.

The proposals in respect of voluntary schools gave rise to immense controversy. Nonconformists had an attachment to school boards and their proposed abolition was a blow. But the Bill proposed in addition to fly in the face of their cherished principle that rates, whatever might happen over taxes, should not be used to any extent in support of sectarian teaching. The Nonconformist opposition gave rise to the passive resistance movement, whose members declined to pay the education rate. Their opposition was on the ground of conscientious objection to paying the rate, part of which went to voluntary denominational schools and a very small part of which financed their own denominational religious instruction. But others objected on the understandable ground that it would add to the rates.

In face of protests about rate increases in June 1902 Balfour promised an increase of £900,000 in government grants and the Chancellor of the Exchequer, Michael Hicks Beach, resigned on this and other grounds. In the end, the 1902 Act provided for extra grants to local authorities of about £1,550,000 a year but distributed according to a formula which gave much more to areas of lower rateable value than to those of higher rateable value and without regard to the numbers of voluntary school pupils.

The controversy over the 1902 Act reunited the Liberals and roused the Nonconformists, the Baptists and Congregationalist elements of which were traditionally heavily pro-Liberal, to great efforts in anticipation of the General Election. The electoral effect of the 1902 Act seems to have been more in galvanizing Nonconformists than in changing voter minds, and other issues such as tariff reform and Chinese labour played a larger part. The Liberals were returned to power in 1906, on a fairly modest majority in the popular vote which translated into a large majority of seats over all parties, including the Irish Nationalists on whom they had had to depend on previous occasions.

From 1906–10 the Liberals had an overall majority; thereafter they depended on the support of the Irish Members for an effective majority. The years after 1906 saw much debate and legislation proposed over religious education and church schools, but apart from some regulations on teacher training colleges and secondary schools at the end there was nothing to show for it. However, the Liberal years left a legacy which associated the question of church schools with tumult and controversy, so that up to 1944 and beyond politicians would hesitate to touch the issue.

The Birrell Bill was the first of four government Bills to be presented and went through full Parliamentary consideration, failing only when the House of Lords and House of Commons did not agree on amendments. In essence, the Bill was a provision that all public elementary schools should come under the full control of the local education authority and give undenominational instruction except where Clause 4 applied. Clause 4 provided for denominational instruction where the local education authority agreed, and 80 per cent of the parents voted for this. It was explicitly designed to cover Catholic schools and Jewish schools, and possibly also some High Church Anglican schools. The Liberal party acknowledged that not all schools could happily and suitably come within their proposals for undenominational instruction, which they thought suitable for Protestants.

The Bill became a source of contention between the House of Lords and the House of Commons. The breaking point between the House of Commons and House of Lords was whether the school staff were to be allowed to give denominational instruction out of hours or whether this was to be allowed only in the case of non-staff. Liberal Ministers who had to look over their shoulders at their Nonconformists MPs refused to agree to the former and the Bill failed. Some Nonconformists wanted it to fail and looked forward to the next Bill, as well as Anglicans who wanted it to pass if only amendments were made. The papers of Archbishop Davidson contain a full account of the events in the Bill's last days in which he was a participant.

The next Bill, from Birrell's successor, McKenna, was a brief one, charging voluntary schools one-fifteenth of their teachers' salaries in respect of denominational religious instruction. Morant told Davidson that opposition from the Passive Resisters for whom this did not go far enough, had caused this Bill to be dropped. McKenna produced a second Bill but did not pursue it while he started discussions which were continued by his successor Runciman, with Archbishop Davidson. Their proposals contained no equivalent of Clause 4 but instead provided for certain schools to contract out and receive government grant but no rate support. In schools which became controlled by local authorities, attention in the discussions was concentrated on the extent of facilities for denominational instruction. Davidson and Runciman came very near to a complete agreement, until at the last minute disagreement arose over the extent of support to contracted out schools. However, the Representative Church Council (of the Anglican Church) voted against the proposals. The front went quiet. In 1910 the Liberals returned to dependence on Irish Nationalist support.

1918–44

Up to 1902 both church and state were involved in only elementary education. From 1902 the board and local authorities assisted secondary, i.e. grammar schools, which continued until 1944 to charge fees. After 1919 when it was felt that the Board should no longer assist schools through two different channels, i.e. directly and via the LEA, schools were invited to choose which they preferred, and some Church of England and Catholic secondary schools took their aid from one quarter, others from the other. The inter-war years saw much attention given to senior education in the elementary sector.

The early 1920s saw economy measures and the 1930s were marked by the Great Depression. But despite this, efforts to achieve educational advance continued. Increases in the numbers of schools and pupils in the years 1903 and 1938 are shown in Table 2.1. However, the Methodist, BFSS and other schools fell in pupil numbers by 1938 to little more than 10 per cent of the 1903 numbers. Many of the schools were transferred to local authorities, if not the schools, at least their pupils. Methodist schools were regarded by many in Methodism as incompatible with Methodist objections to church schools.

The total number of pupils in elementary schools fell by nearly one-sixteenth between 1903 and 1938. Catholic schools increased in number, and enrolment rose by over 10 per cent. The main changes occurred in council and Church of England schools. The pupil enrolment of the latter halved. In the former it increased by almost 25 per cent, despite the drop in the total of pupils.

Figures from the Board of Education's Annual Reports show that the major factor at work was the shift of population in addition to the lower total of pupils, which resulted in the closing of Council and Church of England schools in some areas, with virtually only Council schools plus some Catholic schools opening in areas of growth. Whilst it maintained and improved the buildings of its continuing

Table 2.1 Numbers of schools and pupils in 1903 and 1938

Type of school	Council Schools	Pupils	Church of England Schools	Pupils	Roman Catholic Schools	Pupils	Others Schools	Pupils
1903	6,003	2,870,213	11,687	23,338,602	1,038	337,295	1,494	42,1168
1938	10,363	3,540,512	8,979	1,125,497	1,266	377,073	308	44,853
	+4,360	+670,299	−2,708	−1,213,105	+228	+39,778	−1,186	−376,315

schools, the Church of England was unable to raise many funds for the building of new schools.

1944–75

The 1944 Act dealt with the position of Religious Education in schools without any of the controversy which had attended the position of church schools. The 1870 Act had left the decision about religious instruction in Board schools to the School Board, subject only to the Cowper–Temple clause, and the 1902 Act continued this provision for local education authorities and Council schools. The tide was running in favour of definite Christian teaching of the kind acceptable to Protestant Churches, advancing beyond the Bible reading or simple Bible instruction common in the years after 1870. This reflected a change in the theological climate, including a less literal interpretation of the Bible. In February 1941 the Archbishops of Canterbury (Lang) and York (Temple) published the Archbishops' Five Points, the chief of which were provision for daily religious worship in all schools and compulsory religious instruction, according to an agreed syllabus in Council schools, in each case subject to a conscience clause. The only opposition to the proposals for worship and instruction to be compulsory for schools came from the associations representing grammar school heads and staff whose representatives argued strongly against them. These schools did not have the traditions in this field to be found in public schools and in elementary schools. The General Secretary of the NUT, which had a virtual monopoly of union representation in elementary schools, said that nearly all teachers in council schools were willing to give syllabus instruction.

The normal practice in elementary schools was to have a period of religious instruction each day of up to 40–45 minutes. A requirement of a period of a minimum of 30 minutes was included in early drafts of the Education Bill. On 4 April 1943 Sir Cyril Norwood, who was chairing a government committee considering the Secondary School Curriculum, wrote to Butler, saying that G.G. Williams, the head of the Board's Secondary Branch, had been telling the Committee of the plans for religious education. He expressed concern at the suggestion of a 30-minute period each day as 30 minutes did not fit in as a unit of time in a grammar school curriculum which was based on 45-minute periods. He suggested a daily service and two periods of no less than 45 minutes per week. Officials examined the pros and cons – to adopt this in the case of primary schools would be to require substantially less time for religious instruction than was customary; to adopt Norwood's suggestion only for secondary schools might suggest that the spiritual needs of children decreased from the age of 11. The Permanent Secretary, Sir Maurice Holmes suggested: 'Perhaps the Parliamentary Secretary with his wide experience of educational administration may be able to suggest a solution which has escaped me'. The Parliamentary Secretary, Mr James Chuter Ede, MP, wrote: 'To prescribe the minimum period to be devoted to a particular subject would be an innovation in educational law and practice'. He suggested bringing the adequacy of time for religious instruction within the purview of HM Inspector. On 15 April Holmes informed the Board's legal adviser that references to duration or frequency of religious instruction should be deleted from the Bill.[3]

The Archbishop's Five Points had not specified the frequency or duration of religious instruction, and these did not attract comment during the passage of the Bill. But arguably the deletion of these provisions in the early drafts of the Bill had a major effect on the success of the Act in the field of religious education. The Newsom Report, barely twenty years later, showed that in most secondary schools (replacing the senior departments or classes of elementary schools), religious education received little more than one period a week, an arrangement often justified on the argument that this was all that the staffing could cover. Had the Act contained provisions requiring more time in total, it would then have been incumbent on authorities and schools to take steps to provide the necessary staffing.

On 25 May 1945, Butler talked to Dr Weitzman, appointed to write a history of the 1944 Act, a work never completed. By this time he was Minister of Education, no longer President of the Board:

> The Minister said that the most interesting part of the whole thing to him had always been the religious issue, and the political background of the feelings which were considered by discussions about educational affairs . . . It was the religious question which took time. The Green Book offered the views of the Board's officers on the future treatment of Church schools.[4]

The Green Book covered a number of topics in education and was written as the basis for consultation with interested parties, principally local authorities and teachers. It was printed as a war-time economy measure to save paper and thereby achieved greater status.

The Green Book Scheme met the predilections of the Board's officers, but encountered Catholic opposition primarily because of the issue of senior schools. It also offended Free Church and NUT opinion by proposing to maintain the denominational character of church schools through reserved teachers, and by suggesting that the Cowper–Temple clause should not apply in secondary modern schools.

The Board next issued the White Memorandum on church schools. This was mainly the work of the Parliamentary Secretary Chuter Ede which had been polished by officials. For a junior Minister he was unusually experienced and knowledgeable in his Department's field. He wrote a diary of the years 1941–5 which casts much light on the events of those years (now in the British Museum).

The White Memorandum held out two alternatives for church or non-founded schools. Schools in single-school areas were restricted to Alternative A, under which the schools would be transferred to the control of the LEA who would appoint and dismiss the teachers but meet all the costs of the school including renovation, the schools being limited to agreed syllabus religious instruction. Under Alternative B, schools would retain control of the appointment and dismissal of teachers, continue to provide denominational instruction as before but receive as a grant from the Board 50 per cent of the cost of renovations or rebuildings, finding the rest themselves, without grant for extensions or new schools. Alternative B was essentially aided status as it emerged in the 1944 Act.

In correspondence and discussions between Butler and Temple, controlled status, as it was named, in the 1944 Act evolved. Alternative A was amended to remove the restriction in the case of single-school areas which Butler, for one, did not like. In addition, provision was to be made for the appointment of teachers to give denominational instruction on a sliding scale, one in a school of three to five staff, two in a school of six to ten staff, and so on. (In the event those provisions have been little used.)

Why did Temple accept Alternative A as modified? Temple received advice from certain members of the National Society, including Sir Robert Martin, a prominent member of the Church Assembly and Chairman of the Leicestershire County Council. Butler later described Martin's speeches before the Church Assembly as 'the most complete summary of the policy from the Anglican view undertaken by anyone on that side'. In response to suggestions from

Bishop Bell of Chichester that the Church of England should call for the Scottish system, Martin wrote to Temple, 'The suggestions in the memorandum prepared last week by the Standing Committee of the National Society have as their object the establishment of a scheme which shall be acceptable – as part of a settlement – to the Free Churches and the NUT whilst insuring the continuance of effective Church teaching in the Church schools.'

The desire of the majority of the Standing Committee to make the scheme acceptable to these two bodies was based, it can be argued, on two considerations. The first of these was their earnest hope that by doing this a real advance would be effected towards co-operation between them both and the church in the improvement of religious teaching in all schools and in fostering of the religious life of the nation. The second was that unless such acceptance were substantially secured, they could see any prospect of the government's adopting the scheme or anything like it. Two main factors necessary to secure acceptance were that the method of appointment of teachers should be the same in the provided and non-provided schools and that in non-provided schools there should be security that agreed syllabus instruction should always be available for the children of Free Church parents.

Both these points are secured by the Memorandum with the exception of the provision of some reserved teachers in church schools. The justice of this provision would not, it can be argued, be contested either by the Free Churches or the NUT.

The Scottish scheme, on the other hand, would not meet the conditions of the first point since it provides that in transferred schools all teachers appointed must be approved as regards their religious belief and character by representatives of the Church or canonical body in whose interest the school had been conducted (Education (Scotland) Act 1918 Sec. 18/3).[5]

Underlying these comments is the pessimism felt by prominent Anglicans and others about the proportion of Anglican schools able to adopt Alternative B. *The Times Educational Supplement* suggested one-eighth; many Anglicans did not dispute this, other people in the Board of Education and educational bodies were happy to accept a similar figure partly from wishful thinking.

Any attempt to improve the terms of Alternative B seemed likely to undermine the desired co-operation with the Free Churches and the NUT over religious education in county schools. Subsequent history shows that there was a serious misjudgement here about the advances likely to be achieved in religious education through this co-operation, but Martin's advice, that of others and Temple's actions were based on high motives. Subsequent history also shows a massive underestimate of the number of Church of England schools willing and able to adopt Alternative B.

Although the White Paper of 1943 contained a description of the dual system as 'an embarrassing feature' of the country's educational system, the White Memorandum effectively buried the view which had become standard in official circles and which dominated the Green Book, that schools from the elementary school stable had to be under full public control by LEAs, subject only to denominational instruction and reserved teachers.

Under Alternative B schools were not offered such favourable terms for renovations and rehabilitations as under the Green Book. But Butler was inaccurate in suggesting (in conversation with Dr Weitzman) that the Green Book would have given a more favourable result to Catholics than the final proposals. The final proposals included the revival of special agreements and on the basis of the estimate of costs made by S. L. Laskey of the Board in 1943, the final proposals were less costly to Catholics. In reality, given the long delays in replacements (more favourably treated under the Green Book) and the early implementation of special agreements (initially to meet rising primary school numbers by reorganizing all-age schools) the final proposals proved much more favourable.

The talks between Butler and the Catholic bishops were not productive in proportion to their frequency. Each side was seeking to persuade the other to accept a proposition it was in no position to prove. Butler said in effect that the government did not wish to push Catholic schools into Alternative A and the 50 per cent grant offered would be sufficient to enable them to adopt Alternative B, given that building work would be spread out over the years. The bishops said that the costs were beyond the Catholic pocket, though there was evident among the bishops some disagreement as to how far this would stretch.

Butler summarized the problem in the letter drafted but not sent of 2 October 1943 to Sir John Anderson, the Chancellor of the Exchequer:

> My problem is that I am always brought up against the fact that since the present plan rests on a financial basis it is impossible in the absence of any feasible scheme of limitation of the Roman Catholics' liabilities to a figure within their capacity, to refute their

contention that if, as they anticipate, they cannot raise their share of the money they will be driven to accept Alternative A of paragraph 56 [of the White Paper], an Alternative which the Government admittedly do not regard as appropriate to them and which they themselves would regard with abhorrence.

It was in 1943 that a measure of agreement was reached on the scale of costs facing Catholic schools when the estimate by Laskey of the Board was accepted by Mgr Canon William Wood (appointed by the bishops to examine it), subject to a reservation about the rate it quoted for post-1939 inflation. Butler in his stand on the 50 per cent rate of grant was not influenced to any great extent by the fear that a higher rate would induce more Anglican schools to adopt Alternative B, so persuaded were the Board of the indigence of Anglican schools. Rather, the fear was of upsetting the Free Churches and the NUT who had accepted the 50 per cent grant rate under Alternative B. Moreover, Butler's colleagues in the government were not sympathetic. A number were Liberal Unionists, some veterans of the educational wars of Edwardian times. Churchill himself, who had initially discouraged educational legislation, had been a Liberal Unionist, who as a young Liberal MP on converting from Conservatism had had to eat his criticisms of Nonconformist attitudes to the 1902 Act. The Catholic popular agitation seems to have aroused hackles at the government level, although it had a different effect among MPs. Traditional Anglicans in the government were limited to Lord Cranborne and Lord Wolmer (the Cecil gang in Butler's phrase), whose hands were tied by Temple's agreement with Butler.

On their side, the bishops were faced with new conditions. Building regulations would specify the accommodation required; schools would have to come up to their standards, and it would no longer be the case that managers made improvements at a time of their choice. The new Archbishop of Westminster, Bernard Griffin, told Butler in 1944 that the costs estimated in the Laskey Memorandum were three times the total expenditure on Catholic schools in the previous 25 years when new schools had been opened and others improved.

Negotiations on the Catholic side proved complex for Butler, mainly because of the poor health and death of Cardinal Hinsley and the subsequent interregnum until the installation of Archbishop Griffin in January 1944. In negotiations in late 1943 as the date for the introduction of the Bill approached, Butler found himself still in disagreement with the Catholic bishops and disposed towards concessions he could make without altering the 50 per cent grant rate.

Alternative B provided grants for renovation of buildings and some-times this would entail a move to a new site. The draft legislation provided for transfers of this kind. Chuter Ede had long urged that where a new school was needed because the population had moved, in the case of a voluntary school, this should be grant-aided. He referred to this, no doubt drawing on his experience as a magistrate as the transfer of licences. In his diary entry of 5 October 1943 he says: 'He [Butler] accepted in one, my licensing suggestion made many months ago and then firmly resisted by him and especially by Cleary.'

The result was the provision for substituted schools included in the Bill at the last stage (Section 16 in the Act). In practice this has been mainly a provision useful in reorganizing schemes, e.g. where two schools might become one, one might increase. But it began life as a means of providing a grant for building for pupils displaced from their previous areas. Since they did not move in whole schools, this was followed by another provision for the movement of pupils in smaller groups.

A second version replaced the first, followed by a third when the Bill was in the House of Lords. This though introduced as a drafting amendment without further explanation, seriously altered the mean-ing of the clause. It had always been considered that the provision should not be worked as a coupon system, i.e. grant per pupil, but rather that it should be used in cases where there was substantial group of pupils. The third version maintained the notion of a substantial group but transferred it from a substantial group in the new school to a substantial fall in each school from which pupils came. Given local authority policies and housing allocation by prior-ities, pupils did not come in groups from schools, and the 'drafting amendments' deprived the clause of much of its effect.

This did not last long. Catholic pressure before the 1950 election led to a response by the Labour government which, in the absence through illness of the Minister of Education, George Tomlinson, put negotiations in the hands of Chuter Ede, by then Home Secretary, who offered the clause which became Section 1 of the 1953 Act, giving a grant for displaced pupils without regard to whether there was any reduction in the schools they might have attended. This became Section 1 of the 1953 Act which was to finance most of the Catholic primary school buildings of the 1950s and 1960s.

In the weeks before the publication of the Education Bill in 1943 Butler also considered the possibility of setting a ceiling on the costs schools would have to meet under Alternative B. The idea of a ceiling was first raised by Bishop Marshall of Salford. Butler was ready to consider a ceiling of £25 per place in primary schools and of £45 per place in secondary schools, after which costs would be covered by the government in full.[6] He secured Treasury agreement to this and it was known to his colleagues on the Lord President's Committee that he would be discussing this with the Catholic bishops. Marshall was thought to be conceding too much by way of Catholic ability to raise money, certainly by Bishop McCormack of Hexham and Newcastle, who made a lower estimate of his flock's capacity to contribute. Marshall, perhaps under pressure from his colleagues, explained that the ceiling he had in mind was £15 which would represent nearly a halving of the voluntary contribution. This effectively ended discussion of a ceiling. Had the bishops seen the ceiling not as a means of reducing the 50 per cent contribution but as a protection against unexpected inflation in building costs, it would have appeared in the Bill and greatly reduced voluntary school costs during the post-war inflation of building prices.

One person who was disappointed at the omission of a ceiling from the Bill was Temple. Chuter Ede records in his diary that he expressed this disappointment in a telephone conversation with Butler. Temple had been following the controversy over grants under Alternative B, for he had been under strong pressure from many church quarters to seek better terms for Alternative B schools. In a draft letter to Sir John Anderson (apparently not sent) Butler wrote, ' At the same time the dissident Anglicans to whom Selborne referred are continually prodding Temple to take a stronger stand for denominational religious teaching and so too are some sections of the Church of England press'. On 3 February 1944, with the Bill past the second reading, Butler wrote the following notes:

> For information I have addressed in the House this week a group of some 40–50 Anglican MPs and some 150 Members of the Conservative Private Members' Committee.

> I think as a result of the first meeting it was possible to say that the cells of dissent which were forming round Mr Crowder, Mr Godfrey Nicholson and others have now been temporarily dissipated.

> It was necessary to say quite sharply to these Honourable Members that an attempt to devise a new settlement at this stage would be impossible.

> Captain Cobb and other Members of Parliament (MPs) are now

tending more to take the view of Mr Colegate that the compromise is an acceptable one.

Mr Raikes, another typical Conservative MP, is, however, in favour of some accommodation being given to the Churches in the form of a loan. The extreme Members are in favour of an interest free loan and these Members are under the influence of 'Roman Catholic propaganda'.[7]

The day before Butler had had a talk with the Bishop of London who had said that he was quite convinced that it was essential for him to support a resolution of the Church Assembly in favour of loans since there was a strong resolution down for discussion at the Assembly for raising the grant to 75 per cent. If this were to be carried the whole scheme would be wrecked. He proposed to come along first with his resolution on loans and then to side-track the second resolution.

In a draft sent to the Treasury, of a paper to be presented to the Lord President's Committee asking for approval to loan arrangements, Butler wrote:

I am somewhat loath to take any step in their direction at all. We have secured general acquiescence in the plan, and do not want to get into trouble with other interests at this stage. On the other hand it is my considered judgement that without some rope it will be impossible to carry the settlement through the Committee Stage of the House of Commons, owing to the desire of Members that there should be no risk of the future burdens upon the supporters of the denominational schools being beyond their capacity.[8]

The final version of the paper omitted this paragraph but it remained in Butler's own briefing notes for the meeting of the Lord President's Committee. It is evident that he had some very anxious moments as the Bill went through the Commons. The loan provision enabled him to reassure MPs. It was to prove of major use to Catholic schools for the next three decades. But although in the paper to the Lord President's Committee Butler said that Griffin had asked for this, it seems that this may have been partly at Butler's prompting. As late as 8 March a deputation led by Griffin was asking for loans at cheap rates and earlier there had been little pressure from Catholics for loans, unless at reduced rates. However, the provision of loans constituted the concession to take the Bill out of danger in the Commons.

Section 16 of the 1944 Act provided for the classification of voluntary schools as controlled or aided or special agreement, the schools wishing to be aided or special agreement having to pass a resolution to this effect within six months of the approval of the development plan for their LEA. A resolution for aided status would not be the end of the matter, since the Minister of Education was required under the Act to be satisfied as to the abilities of the managers to meet the financial obligations of aided status. Given the anxieties expressed by the Catholic bishops before the 1944 Act, what was the position in Catholic schools?

Bishop Beck, the new Chairman of the Catholic Education Council, was concerned on behalf of his fellow bishops that they were asked to commit themselves to repay unknown sums on unknown dates. He came away from a meeting with the Minister, George Tomlinson, in early 1950 with the distinct impression that were the Minister in the position of members of the hierarchy, pledges of huge sums would not 'seriously incommode his conscience'. A little later the Ministry informed the bishop that because there was no immediate prospect of an acceleration in the rate of school building, the Ministry would henceforth require denominational bodies to demonstrate only 'a reasonable prospect' of raising an annual sum to service the estimated loan needed for their building costs and repairs. With this, all fell into place and all but two of Catholic schools received aided status, the two having applied out of time.

It was on the Anglican side that the classification of schools produced a result not expected in the years preceding 1944 when estimates of the number of Anglican schools becoming aided had been variously one-eighth of the total, 1000 or even only 500.

The classification of voluntary schools took a long time to complete. By January 1958 (Ministry of Education Report, 1958) the process was 98 per cent complete in Church of England schools and the 1958 return showed 3291 primary and all age schools with 388,481 pupils as aided 43 per cent of the schools with 46 per cent of the pupils. At the secondary level, where the Church of England had less strength, aided and special agreement schools and their pupils were nearly double the controlled schools and their pupils. The aided status of the 1944 Act derived from the non-provided status of the 1902 Act.

Until 1980 the main feature of church–state relations was the revision on four occasions (1953, 1959, 1967 and 1975) of the legislation relating to grant to voluntary schools. The advance from 50 per cent for mainly replacement or improvement to 85 per cent for all kinds of building reflects unexpected demands: (i) the growth of school population at certain periods; (ii) the movement of population on a scale never expected in 1944; (iii) the growth in building costs; (iv) the cost of conversion to comprehensive organization; and (v) high interest rates. Certainly, without these unexpected demands there would not have been the changes in legislation which have occurred. These four Acts entailed little controversy. The announcement of what became the 1959 Act attracted a leading article in *The Times*; the announcement of what became the 1967 Act began on the front page of *The Times* but was then continued on an inside page; the announcement of what became the 1975 Act was to be found in the Parliamentary Report at that time still a feature of *The Times*, in the obscurity of replies to written Parliamentary questions.

One reason for the lack of controversy is that from the early 1960s, following Pope John XXIII's inauguration of the modern ecumenical movement, major matters relating to church schools became the subject of discussions between Catholics, Anglicans and Free Churchmen usually in the forum of the Churches Joint Education Policy Committee and joint approaches have been made to the Education Department. Table 2.2 shows the numbers of pupils between 1950 and 1988 in schools of different status. In the early part of the period the primary total includes senior pupils in all-age schools, later on primary and secondary totals include middle school pupils, according to whether their schools are deemed primary or secondary. Table 2.2 shows numbers of pupils between 1950 and 1988 in schools of different status. The most significant changes are those for Catholic schools, a substantial increase in primary numbers despite the transfer to secondary schools of senior pupils in all-age schools, and a massive increase in Catholic aided secondary schools far in excess of that arising from the transfer of senior pupils. Behind both changes there lies the great increase in Catholic baptisms from the 1950s to the early 1970s, in substantial part attributable to another wave of Irish immigration. In certain areas, the demand for Catholic schools far out-ran supply. At the secondary level the aided sector was increased by the addition of ex-direct-grant schools in the late 1970s and early 1980s and over a longer period by the inclusion of ex-independent schools. The inter-war years and the post-war years saw the establishment and development of many independent schools covering both primary and secondary levels, by a considerable number of religious orders. The growth and spread of the Catholic population gave the opportunity for many to become aided, either as secondary or as primary schools. They joined others already in the aided sector.

Table 2.2 Numbers of pupils between 1950 and 1988 in schools of different status

	1950	1958	1968	1978	1988
Primary					
County	2,702,852	3,202,529	3,344,241	3,341,225	2,786,060
Church of England	878,703	837,902	799,479	748,862	662,039
Catholic	343,515	417,321	478,724	425,761	377,150
Others	30,402	27,663	23,743	23,037	19,370
Secondary					
County	1,462,910	2,044,269	2,460,325	3,223,192	2,512,266
Church of England	65,186	76,765	86,121	145,570	142,984
Catholic	51,142	92,568	224,049	340,220	284,727
Others	117,165	117,461	124,792	142,186	130,175

Note: The Church of England and Others total includes controlled as well as aided and special agreement schools. The text has earlier indicated the proportions in each of the two categories.

This story ends in 1975 with the Education Act of that year raising the grant for capital building to 85 per cent. Since then there has been no change in the legislation on this point, nor any move for a change.

NOTES

1   H. J. Burgess, *Enterprise in Education* (London: SPCK, 1958), p. 70.
2   D.W. Sylvester, *Robert Lowe and Education* (Cambridge: Cambridge University Press, 1974), p. 130.
3   Public Records Office, Education Department (hereafter E.D.), 136/378.
4   Public Records Office, E.D. 138/20.
5   Lambeth Palace Library *Temple Papers*, 19/363.
6   Public Records Office, E.D. 136/412 and 138/19.
7   Public Records Office, E.D. 136/412.
8   Public Records Office, E.D. 136/520.

3

CATHOLICISM AND THE NATION-STATE IN NINETEENTH-CENTURY BRITAIN

Mary J. Hickman

CONSTRUCTING THE NATION IN NINETEENTH-CENTURY BRITAIN

BRITISHNESS IS a national identity which developed as the appropriate identity for a state constructed on the basis of a series of either forced or negotiated unions of different nations. Between 1801 and 1922 the United Kingdom was made up of England, Wales, Scotland and Ireland. The late eighteenth century had seen the amalgamation of the Celtic elites (including the Anglo-Irish Protestant ascendancy) with the English to forge a genuinely British ruling class that lasted until the twentieth century. The Welsh, Scottish and Anglo-Irish individuals who became part of the British establishment in this period did not become Anglicized but British (Colley, 1992).

In the nineteenth century the state in the form of the central government of the day actively intervened to construct political subjects and foster national consciousness. The state sought to reconstruct political rule in society by reconstructing the political subjectivity of the population (Curtis, 1983). Through various means, amongst which education was very important, the state was nationalized through the social construction of Britishness as an over-arching identity. Other identities – English, Welsh, Scottish, Irish – remained as ethnic/national identities which could become conduits to express socio-economic and political dissatisfactions with the union. Only in England has this not occurred.

In the long term the state was unable to incorporate Irish nationalism, hence the establishment of the Irish Free State in 1922. However, Irish Catholics also lived in England, Wales, Scotland and Northern Ireland. In Britain (i.e. England, Wales and Scotland) Irish migrants filled certain niches in the labour market, however they were problematized as Catholics, because of the historical relationship between Britain and Ireland and because they represented a threatening Other in class-divided British cities. The boundaries of the nation socially constructed to bind together different classes of Protestants in Britain did not accommodate Catholics easily even after Catholic emancipation.

Although they were formally citizens of the state, Irish Catholics were not imagined as part of the nation in the nineteenth century. There are clear parallels with the situation encountered by migrants from the Indian subcontinent and the Caribbean one hundred years later. The majority of labour migrants to Britain have always been formal citizens of the state because the British labour market has turned to its former or current colonies for reserve supplies. Yet this has never been sufficient for these migrants to be automatically included as part of the nation once they arrive in Britain.

ANTI-CATHOLICISM IN THE NINETEENTH CENTURY

In the nineteenth century anti-Catholicism was ingrained amongst all social groupings in Britain and was significantly intertwined with anti-Irish hostility. This became manifest at the time of the campaign for Catholic emancipation, which was eventually achieved in 1829. The aim of the campaign, led by Daniel O'Connell, was to gain full political rights for Catholics as citizens of the state, including the right to vote.

There was a mass popular protest in Britain against Catholic emancipation. Colley (1992) records that the main cities where Irish immigrants had settled all petitioned strongly against it: Glasgow, Dundee, Liverpool. Anti-Irish sentiment may also have been one reason why the Welsh who had rarely petitioned on any issue before 1829 did so on this occasion. There were 3000 petitions, from almost every county, some containing as many as 36,000 or 38,000 signatures. Anti-Irish sentiment was not the sole explanation for the size of the protest. For these men and women Protestantism was not just a species of religious belief, it was a vital part of who they were and the frame through which they looked at the past. Part of their national identity was expressed through anti-Catholicism.

It was the poorer, more marginal and less literate people who were most stridently and devotedly anti-Catholic in 1829, for example, Methodist communities of Devon, Cornwall and north and central

Wales, manual workers such as miners, quarrymen, fishermen, farm labourers and an abundance of women. The year 1829 was the first time in British history that large numbers of women signed petitions to Parliament alongside men. The women who petitioned were predominantly working class and overwhelmingly opposed to Catholic emancipation. This may have owed something to the fact that they were often more assiduous in their church-going than men, also less formally educated and more dependent on that traditional, largely oral, culture in which Protestant intolerance was so deeply embedded (Colley, 1992).

Catholics continued, therefore, in the first half of the nineteenth century to be regarded as guilty of superstitious beliefs, idolatrous worship and vile practices. In addition, 'Catholics were imagined to be potential – and sometimes (as in Ireland) even actual subversives of the Protestant constitution' (Norman, 1968:15). The cornerstone of this conception of the Protestant constitution was the religious establishment. Full Catholic emancipation was seen as undermining the indissoluble link between religious and secular concerns. The Church of England's understanding of herself was as an equal partner of the English state, as the 'most national and natural' of institutions (Gilley, 1982: 411). Not only was the Church of England, with its established churches in Ireland and Wales, set against any further changes to the constitutional position of Catholics, but so also were extensive tracts of the Methodist-Evangelical revival of the nineteenth century.

This alliance against Catholic emancipation was significant in that it combined different regions of the nation and different social classes. As Hexter comments:

> When an old-style Anglican tenant farmer in Dorset or a new-style Methodist mill hand in Lancashire inveighed against villainous popery and the dirty Irish they were not expressing sentiments peculiar to any one religious sect or inherent in any single theological doctrine. They were giving vent to 'the radical and rooted antipathies' of the English masses.
>
> (1936: 319)

The decades that followed the passage of Catholic emancipation demonstrated that anti-Catholicism was still a central element in constructing the boundary of who was or who was not included within the nation. The cultural universalism that underpinned Britishness, Protestantism, had been legally broken in 1829. However, in cultural terms anti-Catholicism remained the sentiment which most clearly defined the nation. The constitutional arguments surrounding Catholic emancipation were, in reality, complicated by the fact that the Roman Catholic question was largely an Irish question (Best, 1958). The popular discourse of the Protestant nation intersected with anti-Irish racism and defined where the danger to the nation lay. These fears were made manifest in the shape of Irish immigrants, who were perceived as threatening the union of church and state, which was the embodiment of 'the English people' (Robbins, 1982: 469).

The Conservative party had split in 1829 over Catholic emancipation and did so again in 1845, over the issue of Parliament increasing its grant to a Catholic seminary in Maynooth, Ireland. The split was mainly between the Peelites (those associated with Sir Robert Peel) and the Ultra Tories. The former broadly accepted the industrial revolution and supported a libertarian fiscal policy in order to head off an alliance of the non-aristocratic classes. In this way the Peelites hoped to preserve and strengthen the traditional constitution of church and state and land (Blake 1985). For the Ultra Tories, on the other hand, no compromise was possible. Largely an aristocratic landed interest group, their shibboleth was 'Protection, Protestantism and no popery'. Blake (1985) comments that the advantage of the Ultra policy was that it corresponded to the actual beliefs of a large section of the political nation.

O'Farrell (1975) has pointed out that 'no popery' was available as a strategy because of the realities of British politics at the time. Both liberals and radicals, among whom dissenters figured highly, were always susceptible to the 'Irish question' being presented as a religious one. In this way the racist nationalism propagated by many in the Tory party and others, and articulating both anti-Catholicism and anti-Irish racism, could garner support from across the political spectrum. Examination of political commentaries in the 1830s and 1840s reveals that anti-Irish racism was present in the writings and ruminations of people often on opposite sides of the political divide.

RELIGION, CLASS AND NATIONAL EDUCATION

The main task for the political aristocracy (Whigs and Peelites) between 1832 and 1848 was to forge a society torn by class antagonisms into a nation-state (Richards, 1980). The interests of the bourgeoisie had to be 'nationalized'. Faced with this 'national question', liberal opinion agreed that the stabilization and reproduction of appropriate social relations required the medium of the state as a 'moralizing' or educational agency, and not solely as a agency of repression (Richards 1980: 66). The 1838–42 period was very turbulent after the collapse of the 1833–6 economic boom, with Chartist demonstrations and the massive unrest which accompanied the economic downswing of the early 1840s and the large increase in unemployment this caused. This period witnessed expansion of industrial capitalism (Richards, 1980; Gash, 1965). The railway construction of the mid-1840s was a key aspect of this strategy. There was also agreement that the renewed industrial and urban expansion had to be accompanied by greater 'physical' and 'moral' regulation of the working population.

There was more agreement about the efficacy of education as a remedy to the problem of order the working class presented than any other method (see Donajgrodzki, 1978; Richards, 1980; Corrigan and Corrigan, 1979). The Whig/Peelite forces which occupied and dominated government throughout most of the 1830s and 1840s developed a consensus concerning the education of the working class. This was broadly that it was necessary to bring as many children into schooling as possible and that a significant degree of state regulation was required, to ensure that the requisite standard of education was being purveyed and that public monies were being well spent. Concern therefore centred on the inability of the voluntary effort to provide sufficient school accommodation. There was a growing consensus in some educational circles that the curriculum should include subjects such as 'Political Economy'. In this way the dominant values of the Victorian era, those of bourgeois capitalism (belief in individualism, enterprise *laissez-faire* liberalism), would be transmitted to the working class.

Part of the process of orchestrating the favourable conditions for capitalist social relations involved the construction of state-funded and controlled educational arrangements which encompassed all children. Governments of the day strove for an interdenominational system of national education but were defeated by Anglican resistance, Tory opposition and the failure of educational experiments (based on the 'Irish system' of interdenominational education) in Liverpool in the late 1830s (see Murphy, 1959). The impact of the latter was to strengthen the influence of anti-Catholicism as a feature of the discourse about religion, nation and state (Hickman, 1995).

The anti-popery of the Anglicans in the late 1830s, and again at the time of the restoration of the Catholic Hierarchy in 1850, was a measure of the Church of England's crisis as a national church; while the anti-popery of many Dissenters in the 1840s and after was a measure of their opposition to the privileged position of the Church of England, and also their own inability to do more than restrain part of the Church of England's plans.

As Anthias and Yuval-Davis (1992) argue, the differential access of different collectivities to the state determines the nature of the hegemonic national ethos in a society. This aptly describes the contestations of the fourth and fifth decades of the nineteenth century. In the 1830s and 1840s the essentials of the Establishment – the Anglican monarchy created by the Act of Settlement; the participation of bishops in the House of Lords; and the inalienable claim of the church to its ecclesiastical property – were all still in place. However, the state church could no longer depend on preferential treatment and it was subject to a Parliament no longer solely Anglican (Gash, 1965). Anti-Catholicism allowed the mythical unity of the imagined community of Protestants who comprised the nation to be continually reasserted. Education particularly was the issue through which all these dilemmas were expressed.

Green's (1990) thesis that it was the dominant *laissez-faire* ideology and the liberal conception of the state, rather than the religious controversies through which they were refracted, that underlay middle-class opposition to state schooling, has to be questioned in its emphasis. To suggest that the central concerns of those opposed to state education were refracted through religious controversies is to underestimate the importance of issues of religion and the nation–state in educational debates. Green, in common with most theorists who reify class-based explanations, fails to take account of the extent to which religious issues, which in that period were redolent with conceptions of 'the nation', animated the real concerns of various class groupings in nineteenth-century Britain.

In fact, as Gash (1965) points out, the 'slide into voluntaryism' did not occur until the 1840s amongst organized Dissent, largely a middle-class body of opinion, although the slide was then rapid. The support for voluntaryism and overt anti-Catholicism (see Wolffe, 1991) on the part of Dissent was occasioned by fears of the power of the Established Church. This fear was expressed through anti-Catholic discourses directed at the rise of the influence of the Oxford Movement within the Church of England. Anti-Catholicism was a critical element in the articulation of religious controversies and ideologies of state intervention. For Dissenters also anti-Catholicism served to define the imagined community of the nation:

a Protestant nation but with severely curtailed powers for the Established Church.

The furore over the 1839 educational proposals of Lord John Russell ensured that the privileged position of the Anglican Church in relation to the state had to be acknowledged, and there was never any serious threat of disestablishment. Equally, the state could not favour the Church of England too much, as the uproar caused by the educational clauses of the 1843 factory legislation proved (see Hickman, 1995). The impossibility of achieving an interdenominational system which included Catholics had been demonstrated by the failure of the Corporation Schools experiment in Liverpool and the widespread hostility of Anglicans and the Conservative party to the idea of introducing the 'Irish System' into Britain.

INCLUDING CATHOLICS IN NATIONAL EDUCATION ARRANGEMENTS

Education was concerned with issues of the relationship between religion and the nation–state. In this context, when religious differences served to demarcate class differences, and nationality was the distinctive feature of a particular group of migrant labourers, there was inevitably a 'Roman Catholic problem' in education. On social and political grounds it was expedient, from the perspective of the state, to include Catholics in a national education system. However, anti-Catholicism and anti-Irishness expressed at the level of municipal government hampered this strategy.

The objective of the governing elite in the 1830s and 1840s (various Whig and Peelite administrations) was to forge closer links between the British state and the Roman Catholic Church to resolve the problem of disorder in Ireland (see Wolffe, 1991; Cash, 1965). Funding Catholic schools in Britain became an extension of this policy. This policy could be safely pursued in alliance with the Catholic Church in England, Wales and Scotland because of the national identity and class formation of the Catholic authorities in these parts of the nation–state.

The consequence of the events of the period 1839–43 was that state aid for education would continue to voluntary societies, and the issue became whether to extend this aid to groups not already in receipt of grants. The Wesleyan Methodists, despite their support for voluntarism, decided to accept grant aid in 1846 as long as it did not preclude them from objecting to the education grant being extended to Roman Catholics. This was agreed to at the time by the Committee of Council (the Education Committee of the Privy Council), but only a year later the government, now a Whig administration, suggested in Parliament that state grants be made to Catholic schools on the same basis as other voluntary societies. The Catholic Poor School Committee was set up by the Catholic Vicars Apostolic (prior to the restoration of the Hierarchy these were the most senior Catholic prelates in Britain) in 1847 for the purpose of receiving this grant aid.

The initial application of the Roman Catholic authorities for state aid in 1846 was refused by the Whigs, on the grounds that the regulations of the Committee of Council required the reading of the Authorized Version of the Bible in schools and they had no wish to provoke controversy just before a general election. The immediate background to this decision was the storm of outrage occasioned in 1845 when the then Tory (Peelite) administration had proposed an increase in government funding to Maynooth College, a Catholic seminary near Dublin. There was widespread mobilization against this measure, led by the Protestant Association (see Cash, 1965 and Wolffe, 1991).

The catalyst for the Whig government's decision to advocate extending grant aid to Catholic schools was a massive increase in Irish immigration, a consequence of the famine in Ireland between 1845 and 1847 (Cruickshank, 1963). This movement of population was attracting considerable attention in the press and in Parliament. Hundreds of thousands of Irish migrants arrived, principally at the port of Liverpool, between 1846 and 1849. As in Ireland the Whigs were ready to extend state funding to the Catholic Church in order to educate Irish Catholics.

Sir James Kay-Shuttleworth had long held the view that educational arrangements for the Irish working class were desirable. He had earlier favoured national interdenominational schools but opposition to the 1839 proposals had convinced him that the education of the poor must remain denominational. Kay-Shuttleworth's brother, Joseph Kay, expressed the view that only Catholicism could influence the most destitute parts of the population:

> What I mean is, that none but the lowest forms of Protestantism will ever affect an ignorant multitude; but that Catholicism is particularly designed for such a multitude; and what I do wish is, that if we may not have an educational system, whereby to fit our people for the reception of Protestantism, that we might again have Roman

Catholicism for the people; believing as I do, that it is infinitely better that the people should be superstitiously religious, than that they should be, as at present, ignorant, sensual, and revolutionary infidels.

(Quoted in the First Report of the Catholic Poor School
Committee, 1848: 55)

Here the notions of ignorance, sensuality and rebelliousness are juxtaposed as representations of the Irish poor whose alien 'nature' was potently symbolized in their resistance to Protestantism. In this context many were reconciled to the public funding of Catholic enterprises as a necessary step in order 'to deal' with Irish migrants. In the context of rising immigration from Ireland, continuing activity against the Union in Ireland and of renewed Chartist agitation in Britain, the Catholic Church seemed the only agency able to restrain and incorporate the Irish Catholic section of the working class.

There was considerable opposition to the extension of grant aid to Roman Catholic schools in 1847, often from evangelicals who saw Catholicism as the root cause of 'the Irish Problem'. In support of the proposal, 'reasons of state' were advanced by the Whig government and supported by the Peelites from the opposition. Peel argued, in a speech in Parliament, that to leave children of Roman Catholic poor 'immersed in ignorance' would harm 'the Protestant community' (*Hansard*, XCL: 1231). Peel, who strongly believed in the Protestant basis of the state, found that this was in constant contradiction to what he viewed as the best policy on Ireland: alliance with the Catholic Church (Wolffe, 1991).

Thus, in 1847 Roman Catholics became the last religious denomination to be in receipt of grant aid for the provision of elementary schools for the children of the Irish Catholic working class in Britain. This was the first time in 300 years that Catholics were permitted to share in the distribution of a public grant in England, Wales and Scotland and it represented a fundamental departure in Catholic relations with the nation-state.

THE EXPANSION OF THE CATHOLIC ELEMENTARY SCHOOL SYSTEM

In the second half of the nineteenth century the Catholic Church oversaw the development of a parish-based, diocesan-organized system of elementary schools. The whole was overseen by the Catholic Poor Schools Committee (CPSC), set up by the bishops to receive and administer government grant aid. The activities of the CPSC were crucial for the long-term influence and control of the Hierarchy over Catholic education. Especially in the early years of its existence the journal of the CPSC, the *Catholic School*, was a means of continuous exhortation by the committee to all involved in Catholic elementary education to increase the provision of Catholic schools. In the pages of the *Catholic School*, school managers were urged to apply for government grants and accept the benefits of inspection. The *Catholic School* was sent free to every school and parish and there is no reason to doubt that it was widely read by the clergy, lay managers and teachers; it was also regularly reviewed in many contemporary publications (Holland, 1987).

The persuasive powers of the CPSC were critical because there was considerable opposition in Catholic circles to the acceptance of government aid. There was a division of opinion amongst the bishops on the subject. Some believed that state inspection, the condition of the grants, was potentially hazardous to the independence of the schools. As Norman (1985: 160) comments, in the circumstances of England's national Protestant culture these fears were entirely reasonable. Bishop Ullathorne of Birmingham, from an old Catholic family, was the main opponent of first Cardinal Wiseman and then Cardinal Manning on this issue.

In 1857 Ullathorne wrote 'Notes on the Education Question', in which he was critical of the terms upon which Catholic schools accepted maintenance grants from the state. The chief danger that he saw was of government interference. Inspection of schools he could accept because it led to improvements, but not control. Ullathorne's motives were compounded of suspicion of the government because of the traditional anti-Catholic prejudices of the English government and suspicion of the rise of the power of the state as such (Norman, 1985: 166). Reluctance to apply for government aid was expressed in certain quarters of the Catholic press, for example, *The Tablet*, and by some of the Irish priests in Britain (Holland, 1987).

The views of Cardinal Wiseman were quite different. A firmly ultramontane prelate, his concern was the provision of adequate Catholic school places. Government aid was essential for a church, the majority of whose congregation were impoverished Irish migrants. Wiseman had not been against schemes of interdenominational elementary education as long as they included adequate safeguards for denominational instruction. Wiseman's education policy appears to have been a pragmatic one, in which the closeness of the aims of the government and the church were apparent. The CPSC articulated these views in the pages of the *Catholic School.*

One of the main messages of the Hierarchy, transmitted by the CPSC, concerned the closeness of the aims of the government and the Catholic authorities about education. A letter from the CPSC to the Committee of Council reproduced in the *Catholic School* states:

> The cause of the Government and Ours is identical, though the object be not the same. Whatever advances the education of Catholics will develop the wisdom of the Government scheme; and, on the other hand, wherever the blessings of the Government provision are widely and wisely diffused, there also Catholicity must reap the more abundant harvest.
>
> (*Catholic School X1*, 1849: 170)

The same theme was still being propounded a quarter of a century later after the introduction of board schools by the 1870 Education Act. Cardinal Manning and the then secretary of the CPSC, Thomas Allies, both urged participation in the new school boards being set up. Allies put the case for government aid in the following terms: 'The prime and chief value of the grants lay in the improvement of education, of which they were the instrument. It lies in the hearty co-operation in a good work of two powers, which had been enemies for centuries' (quoted in Bland, 1976: 44). The relationship with the government was the basis of the existence of the CPSC. There were a number of dissenting voices about this course of action.

In the manner described above, bishops gradually exerted control over the system of elementary schools. The role of the parish priest was to raise money, to manage the school once built and to oversee efforts to increase the number of parents who sent their children to school. The long-term strategy to transform the children of Irish migrants had no chance of success until the children were presented for education. The Irish were part of that section of the population with ostensibly the least incentive to send their children to school. Because of the predominance of Irish men and women in casual labouring jobs, the families often depended for survival on the small sums children earned, for example, as street sellers. However, substantial numbers of Irish Catholics became involved in the funding, building and use of the schools. This became a significant aspect of their incorporation. Catholic schools were 'their schools' and, in the process of creating and defending the schools, the Catholic identity of the Irish in Britain was strengthened.

As the number of Catholic elementary schools increased, what developed was a hierarchically organized system which united the Catholic body in England, Wales and Scotland as no other enterprise did. The clergy and many of the English Catholic laity were convinced of the charitable necessity of educating the Catholic poor. The clergy were able to elicit the participation of Irish Catholics in the parish on the issue of the education of their children, if not any other issue. The whole enterprise was overseen by the bishops through the agency of the CPSC.

In line with their contemporaries, the Catholic Church put great faith in the powers of education to transform its Irish working-class congregation, especially the children of Irish migrants. In its first report the CPSC asserted:

> It is now commonly allowed, even by persons whose opinions force them to explain away the fact, that the Catholic religion alone is qualified to influence the masses. What these masses now are, it is beside the purpose to describe. Suffice it to say, that the education of the Catholic Church, and not one or all of the many devices which have been tried, or may be tried, can, and, as far as that education is diffused, will convert these masses into useful citizens, loyal subjects, and good men.
>
> (CPSC Report, 1848: 13)

Useful citizens must be disciplined and hard-working; loyal subjects must not involve themselves in Irish politics; goodness before God was signified by obedience and attendance at Mass on Sundays. The long-term transformation that Catholic schools were trying to bring about was described a year later in the *Catholic School*: 'A working man with a cottage and garden, his own freehold property, and Catholic county voters are charming pictures; and it would rejoice us to think that nothing worse ever became of our School Boys' (*Catholic School XI*, 1849: 166).

The production of respectable working-class Catholics out of the Irish masses was the long-term aim of the church. Loyalty and hard work would bring its own reward in modest participation in the fruits of British society. These aspirations were, in part, inspired by the motive of placing the Catholic poor on an equal footing with their Protestant neighbours (Ullathorne, 1857; Murphy, 1991); the amelioration of the poverty of Irish Catholics would be a step towards the greater respectability of Catholicism.

THE CURRICULUM AND NATIONAL IDENTITY

The strengthening of Catholic identity became the principal strata-
gem of Catholic elementary schools. This was a strategy designed not
only to arrest lapsation but also to weaken Irish national identity. In
the mid-nineteenth century, in addition to denominational instruction, schools were expected to provide some secular education.
Under the arrangements agreed by the government with the various
churches in the 1840s, each denomination was given sole control of
religious instruction, but the secular curriculum was subject to government inspection and direction. In Catholic elementary schools
the greatest priority was placed on religious instruction and this
dominated the curriculum. This set a pattern that was to continue
throughout much of the next century.

Lyn Hollen Lees (1979) points out that we do not know exactly
what effects Catholic education had upon Irish workers' children, but
she thinks it may be surmised that those who passed through the
schools had their Catholic loyalties reinforced and grew in familiarity
with the norms and messages of the church. Considerable effort was
expended on the development of religious education. Cardinal Wiseman had specifically advocated Italian-style missions for the Irish in
London as providing a flamboyant ritual more likely to attract the
Irish working class than the restrained practices of English Catholicism. Much later in the century Dr O'Reilly, the Bishop of Liverpool,
expressed his wish that Catholic schools avoid 'colourless religious
teaching in which there is nothing distinctive and dogmatic' (quoted
in Pritchard, 1983: 116). In mid-century the competition with prose-
lytizing Protestant charitable schools, and later the competition of
Board schools, were in part responsible for the concentration of the
Catholic Church on religious education and the efforts expended to
ensure that religion was a spectacular experience.

This emphasis on the religious education of the children of Irish
migrants should not obscure the significance of the secular instruction they received. If overshadowed at first by religion, the teaching
of other subjects was to take on greater importance, as it did in other
elementary schools. The demand for Catholic pupil-teachers made it
imperative even in the mid-nineteenth century that serious attention
be given to the secular curriculum.

In their secular curriculum Catholic schools differed very little
from other elementary schools for the working class. In the mid-
nineteenth century Catholic pupils would have been given only an

introduction to basic literacy. Lessons centred on reading, writing, arithmetic and religion. Pupils who stayed long enough to reach higher grades might in addition learn geometry or algebra, history, geography and English grammar. There is little comment on the secular curriculum in the early reports of the CPSC. However, school books are discussed and an examination of the recommendations of the CPSC gives an indication of what the CPSC considered was appropriate content for the education of Irish working-class children.

In the second issue of the *Catholic School* in 1848 the CPSC signalled that the long-term plan of the committee was to produce a series of schoolbooks 'adapted in all respects to the requirements of English Catholic Schools'. In the meantime the CPSC stated ... 'a general opinion prevails, that the publications of the Commissioners of National Education in Ireland form the best educational course procurable in the English language' (*Catholic School 11*, 1848: 27). These were the books prepared for the 'Irish System'.

The Irish lesson books came to be widely used in Britain because they were on the Committee of Council's list and therefore grant aid towards their purchase was available. They are an example of direct state influence on the content of schoolbooks. The Irish Commissioners had been instructed to:

> Exercise the most entire control over all books to be used in the schools, whether in the combined moral and literary, or separate religious instruction; none to be employed in the first, except under the sanction of the Board, nor in the latter, but with the approbation of those members of the board who are of the same religious persuasion with those for whose use they are intended.
> (Report of the Irish Education Commissioners, 1841: 172)

In Britain, using the grant system as an incentive, the Committee of Council intended to have a similar influence over secular instruction as existed in the 'Irish System'.

By 1850 the Irish Commissioners had produced 41 titles. On this lengthy list were all the books schools required except for a history text. History was a subject too controversial for the Commissioners to be able to publish an agreed volume. Each volume published had to have the approval of both the Anglican and Roman Catholic Archbishops of Dublin. The fact that the Irish Commissioners' books had been approved by a Catholic authority undoubtedly explains why the CPSC favoured these books rather than others on the Committee of Council's list.

An examination of these books gives some indication of the content of education in Catholic schools in Britain. For example, references to Ireland had proved offensive to some non-Catholics involved in preparing the books in Ireland and so Irish geography, history and folklore all but vanished in later editions of the readers. It was this exclusion of references to Ireland that made the readers suitable for schools in England. The object of the Irish Commissioners' books was to diffuse the major tensions in Irish life:

> These pious conservative textbooks were designed, among other things, to cool down two major tension areas in Irish national life: the tension between the Protestants and the Catholics and the tension between the British rulers and their Irish subjects. The books attempted to diffuse these conflicts by stressing Bible knowledge, Christian virtues and a common Anglo-Saxon heritage. They were, in fact, so successful in ignoring the specifics of the situation that they could be used in any school in British-ruled territory.
>
> (Repo, 1974:121)

Most significantly, while the attitude to other nationalities in the textbooks is not hostile, their inhabitants tend to be stereotyped and emerge in none too favourable a light. But, as Goldstrom (1972) notes, by implication the English are 'normal', so normal that their characteristics need no comment. The ideas in the books stem from England and many of the positive examples of a good and advantageous life are based on stories set in England. These books had an obvious propaganda value in Ireland in the mid-nineteenth century. But because of these national characteristics, intertwined with the appropriate lessons in political economy, the books were considered suitable for use in England. The CPSC, concerned as they were with the possibilities of any Protestant bias, would have found nothing to remark upon in the absence of Ireland from the Irish lesson books.

From the beginning of the Catholic elementary system the content of the secular education of Irish working-class children in Britain contained little reference to Ireland. What mention was made of Ireland in the new Catholic readers, which replaced the Irish lesson books later in the nineteenth century, primarily praised the Catholicity of the Irish as their outstanding feature and otherwise contained lessons on the political economy of Ireland. These characteristics of Catholic schools curriculum were little changed over a century later. The identity of Irish working-class children as Catholics was implanted and constantly reinforced in the schools by the priority placed on religious instruction, in the effort which went into religious instruction, and in the manner in which the religious pervaded all the rituals of school life. This was a strategy of incorporation. There was a corresponding silence in the curriculum content of Catholic schools about Ireland. This was a strategy of denationalization.

CONCLUSION

A separate Catholic elementary schools system did not develop, primarily because of the sectarian tendencies and ghetto mentality of the Catholic Church and Irish Catholics in Britain. Despite internal differences on the issue, the Catholic authorities, including Cardinal Wiseman, in the first half of the nineteenth century would have accepted interdenominational schools as long as the church retained full control of the religious instruction of Catholic children. All through the period under discussion, 1833–47, the Catholic Church did insist on the use of the Douay version of the Bible and on no common prayer, except for infants. However, they were happy to accept the composite Scripture extracts prepared as part of the 'Irish System' as a basis for common instruction as had been demonstrated in their support for the Corporation Schools experiment in Liverpool.

The objections to the children of Irish Catholic migrants being schooled with other working-class children came from the other denominations, especially the Church of England, and from certain political forces, in particular the Conservative party. Their objections centred on the fear of 'contamination' from the Irish Catholic working class. These fears were articulated by the Protestant Association and by the local and national press through the discourse of anti-Catholicism.

In the changed political circumstances of the 1830s and 1840s the state, in the form of various Whig and Peelite administrations, wanted a national system of education to include all working-class children, in order to produce the appropriate workforce and political subjects of the future. Education was the means by which the long-term regulation and transformation of the working class was to be achieved. By the mid-1840s the state had to accept that publicly financed denominational education was the only means of achieving this at the time. In the end, the state successfully introduced grant aid for Catholic schools in 1847, against still significant opposition, by extending a policy objective in Ireland to its consideration of the problem of educating the Irish Catholic working class in Britain. Supporters of the policy stressed the dire educational need, and the consequences if neglected, of the poorest and most alien section of the population.

Education was the crucial national arena in which the issue of the relationship between the nation-state and religion was aired. What emerged by the middle of the nineteenth century, as a result of sustained opposition to the idea of interdenominational education as the basis of a national system, was an education system which segregated and differentiated sections of the working class by religious denomination and thus by ethnicity.

Both the significance of large numbers of Irish working-class Catholics in many large cities and the 'Roman Catholic' problem in education they gave rise to, and the importance of the role of anti-Catholicism in determining the development of the education system, have been underestimated in many previous histories. The resulting compromise was one which, while segregating Irish Catholics from the rest of the working class, also provided the conditions for the incorporation of the children of Irish migrants.

By establishing the Committee of Council for education, the government commenced the process whereby the schooling all working-class children received, other than religious instruction, began to follow identical principles. From the state's point of view, religious instruction could be safely omitted from the jurisdiction of the Committee of Council's inspectors, because all religious authorities in Britain could be relied upon to relay similar messages of respect for authority and private property and acceptance of the rigours of industrial life. This included the Catholic Church which, despite the furore at the time of the restoration of the Hierarchy in 1850, was increasingly seen to be the only agency whose authority was recognized by the Irish working class.

The legendary disregard of the Irish for British authority structures contrasted strikingly with their willingness, in many circumstances, to follow the instructions of the church when the issue concerned the education of their children. Thus, to the English and Scottish Catholic churches fell the prime task of the incorporation of the children of their Irish congregation. The aim of the National Education System in Ireland was to produce support for the Union. In Britain the aim in educating Irish working-class children was incorporation and denationalization.

REFERENCES

Anthias, F. and Yuval-Davis, N. *Racialised Boundaries: Race, Nation, Gender, Colour and Class and the Anti-Racist Struggle* (London: Routledge, 1992).

Best, G.F.A. 'The Protestant Constitution and its supporters, 1800–1829', *Transactions of the Royal Historical Society*, vol. 13, 1958.

Blake, R. *The Conservative Party from Peel to Thatcher.* (London: Collins, 1985).

Colley, L. *Britons: Forging the Nation 1707–1837* (London: Yale University Press, 1992).

Corrigan, P. and Corrigan, V. 'State formation and social policy before 1871', in N. Parry *et al.* (eds), *Social Work, Welfare and the State* (London: Arnold, 1979).

Cruickshank, M. *Church and State in English Education: 1870 to the Present Day* (London: Macmillan, 1963).

Curtis, B. 'Preconditions of the Canadian state: educational reform and the construction of a public in Upper Canada, 1837–1846', *Studies in Political Economy*, no. 10, 1983.

Donajrodski, A.P. *Social Control in Nineteenth Century Britain* (Beckenham: Croom Helm, 1978).

Gash, N. *Reaction and Reconstruction in English Politics 1832–52* (Oxford: Oxford University Press, 1965).

Gilley, S. 'Nationality and liberty, Protestant and Catholic: Robert Southey's Book of the Church', in S. Mews (ed.) *Religion and National Identity*, Studies in Church History, vol. 18 (Oxford: Basil Blackwell, 1982).

Goldstrom, J.M. *The Social Content of Education 1808-1870 (A Study of the Working Class School Reader in England and Ireland)* (Shannon: Irish University Press, 1972).

Green, A. *Education and State Formation: The Rise of Education Systems in England, France and the USA* (London: Macmillan, 1990).

Hexter, J. H. 'The Protestant revival and the Catholic question in England, 1778–1829', *Journal of Modern History*, vol. 8, no. 3, 1936.

Hickman, M. J. *Religion, Class and Identity: The State, the Catholic Church and the Education of the Irish in Britain* (Guildford: Avebury, 1995).

Holland, M.G. *The British Catholic Press and Educational Controversy, 1847–1865* (New York: Garland Publishing, 1987).

Murphy, J. *The Religious Problem in English Education: The Crucial Experiment* (Liverpool: Liverpool University Press, 1959).

Murphy, M. *Catholic Poor Schools in Tower Hamlets 1765–1865. Part One: Wapping and Commercial Road* (Middlesex: Roehampton Institute of Higher Education, 1991).

Norman, E.R. *Anti-Catholicism in Victorian England* (London: George, Allen and Unwin, 1968).

Norman, E.X. *The English Catholic Church in the Nineteenth Century* (Oxford: Clarendon Press, 1985).

O'Farrell, P. *England and Ireland Since 1800* (Oxford: Oxford University Press, 1975).

Repo, S. 'From Pilgrim's Progress to Sesame Street: 125 Years of Colonial Readers', in G. Martell, (ed.) *The Politics of the Canadian School* (Toronto: James Lewis and Samuel, 1974).

Richards, P. 'State formation and class struggle, 1832–48', in P. Corrigan (ed.) *Capitalism, State Formation and Class Struggle 1832–48* (London: Quartet, 1980).

Robbins, K. 'Religion and identity in modern British history', in S. Mews (ed.) *Religion and National Identity*, (Studies in Church History, vol. 18) (Oxford: Basil Blackwell, 1982).

Ullathorne, Right Revd Bishop *Notes on the Education Question* (London: Richardson and Son, 1857).

Wolffe, J. *The Protestant Crusade in Great Britain, 1829–1860* (Oxford: Clarendon Press, 1991).

4

WOMEN RELIGIOUS AND TEACHER EDUCATION: A CASE STUDY OF THE SISTERS OF NOTRE DAME IN THE NINETEENTH CENTURY

Kim Lowden

PRIOR TO the 1830s there had been no serious attempt to develop a national system of elementary education and teacher training in England. Educational provision for the masses was dependent on voluntary effort in the form of philanthropy through the religious denominations.[1] The need for training teachers had not been widely recognized and on the whole was generally considered unnecessary. Consequently, teaching carried very little social standing in society. Before 1840 only the religious denominations made a limited effort to train both men and women as teachers for their voluntary schools, adopting the monitorial method of instruction.[2] However, their primary motive was to ensure that the teacher's knowledge of religion was sufficiently developed to inculcate the desired doctrines and morals into the working-class children under their care. The training was minimal, usually only lasting three months and did little to improve on the intending teachers' previous education or their ability to teach secular subjects.

The general lack of professional teaching qualifications in the first half of the century, meant that the only teaching posts which carried social status or offered attractive salaries were those occupied by clerics. University dons and masters of respected private schools, a select minority, derived their status from their position in the church and generally undertook teaching only as a secondary vocation.[3] Women were prevented from joining these professional elites because they were excluded from the Church Hierarchy and a university education. In mainstream society, teaching was usually undertaken by men and women who opened schools because they had no other way of making a living. Therefore, it was often regarded as the last career resort for men and the only non-manual option open to women, who undertook it, in most cases, out of financial necessity.[4]

However, by the end of the nineteenth century this unsatisfactory state of affairs had largely been transformed. Universal education was almost a reality and the chances of women from all sections of society receiving an education had greatly improved. Female education of every class existed; elementary schools for the poor, middle-class secondary schools for girls and university education for women. Teaching had become a recognized profession, albeit a minor one, and school teaching had been transformed from a last resort into a positive career choice, for women at least. Although in terms of status, elementary school teaching remained the lowliest branch of the profession, it nevertheless provided countless women with a non-manual career choice and allowed them to live relatively independently. Women from the lower-middle and working classes came to dominate elementary teaching as men left the profession for more lucrative work.[5]

This growth was made possible through the network of church teacher training colleges, which developed after 1839 to train elementary school teachers. The financing of these colleges was made possible by the first government grants towards building costs, awarded to the National Society (Anglican) and British and Foreign Society (Dissenters), from 1839 onwards.[6] As a result, the denominations competed with each other to provide colleges to train teachers for their voluntary schools. The Anglicans got off to a head start and by 1846, they ran twenty-six colleges; sixteen for men, eight for women (including Warrington, which opened in 1844) and two mixed-sex. By the same date, the dissenting denominations ran six colleges; three mixed-sex, one for women and two for men. Most of these colleges were very modest affairs in the early years of their existence, catering for only a few students.

The Roman Catholics did not become eligible for government grants until 1848. From that date they could apply for state aid towards building costs on the same terms as the other denominations, through the Catholic Poor School Committee, set up in 1847.[7] The criteria for obtaining a grant stated that the government would provide half the cost of building a college if voluntary contributions provided the other half. The Catholic Poor School Committee exhausted all its funds providing the men's college of St Mary's at Hammersmith, which was also financed in part by state funds, leaving no money to provide a similar establishment for women.[8]

After several failed attempts by religious orders, Mother Cornelia Connelly of the Sisters of the Holy Child Jesus opened a training college for women at St Leonards-on-Sea in 1856. Some 117 students were trained there before it was forced to close in 1863 due to the financial pressures wrought by the Revised Code of 1862.[9] In 1855, Mr Scott Nasmythe Stokes, HMI for Catholic schools, approached the Sisters of Notre Dame, a Belgian teaching order, well established in Liverpool, to provide a training college for Catholic women. Liverpool was the obvious choice for such a venture due to the influx of nearly 300,000 poor Catholic immigrants in 1847 alone who had paid the sixpence passage to the city to escape the potato famine in Ireland.[10]

The Sisters of Notre Dame accepted the request to open a college. Neither the government nor the Catholic Poor School Committee contributed any money to the establishment of the college due to the generous financial help of one of the sisters, Sister Mary of St Francis. She had been the Hon. Mrs Petre, daughter of Lord Stafford. She joined the Sisters of Notre Dame in 1848 after her husband's death and was able to use her considerable fortune to further the cause of Catholic education in England.[11] It is estimated that she donated at least £10,000 to the foundation of the college at Mount Pleasant, Liverpool, where the sisters already had a convent. Our Lady's Training College, for many years the only training college for women teachers in England, opened in February 1856 with 21 students.[12]

The residential denominational church teacher training colleges developed their own religious tradition, and professional training came to be considered an essential part of the curriculum. By the end of the century teachers could legitimately claim to form a trained and qualified body.[13] The gains made in education generally in the nineteenth century, and by women in particular, were considerable. However, historians have largely neglected the contribution made by the women's denominational teacher training colleges to the development of elementary education and teaching training. The absence of gender and religion, as analytical tools, from most historical studies of education and teacher training has marginalized the work of the female church colleges. Thus, the important role played by women, particularly women religious, as educators, in developing elementary education has not been fully highlighted. The aim of this chapter is to explore the class, gendered and religious nature of Our Lady's Catholic Training College. Comparisons will be drawn between the women religious approach to teacher training and recruitment of staff in the nineteenth century and the Anglican approach, focusing in particular on the Anglican training college for women teachers at Warrington.[14]

The successful development of the teacher training colleges in the nineteenth century depended to a large extent on the quality of the teacher training they could provide. This in turn was dependent on their ability to attract able teachers who had not only received a solid education themselves but who also knew how to impart information and inspire learning in others. The evidence suggests that the consistent influence of the convents, as female support networks, which had maintained the tradition of women's learning, facilitated the rapid expansion of Catholic education in the nineteenth century.[15] From the start, Catholic middle-class girls' education and teacher training in England developed with a clear idea of its aims and objectives and the confidence that considerable experience had given it.[16] On the other hand, without a similar organizational network, Anglican and dissenting women were disadvantaged and, consequently, mainstream middle-class girls' education took longer to develop and lagged behind its Catholic counterpart in aim, quality, and organization.[17]

Anglican and dissenting elementary education and teacher training for the poor was well established by the time the Catholics entered the field in any organized form through the Catholic Poor Schools Committee. However, it was not long before the Catholic schools equalled and often excelled their rivals in the breadth and quality of the education they delivered.[18] It is tempting to conclude, therefore, that the loss of the convent tradition in England and the failure of Protestant women to develop an alternative educational network of their own, had a detrimental impact on mainstream middle-class female education and elementary education of the poor as both developed in the nineteenth century.[19]

The existence of the convent system in itself was not the only reason why Catholic educational reform in England progressed relatively smoothly. It was further advanced by the ability of the convents to attract educated middle- and even upper-class women to the teaching profession. Within the Catholic religious tradition, teaching was afforded the highest possible status as it provided the surest way of deepening the faith of the next generation. Middle-class Catholic women, therefore, who developed a vocation and joined a religious order, viewed education as saving souls for God and could not aspire to a higher calling within their congregation, than to become a teaching sister and dedicate their life to teaching the poor.[20]

The number of Catholic teaching orders made up of educated upper- and middle-class women shows this. The Institute of the Blessed Virgin Mary, at York[21] for example, and the Canonesses of the Holy Sepulchre, who began at New Hall, Chelmsford in 1800, both attracted aristocratic women.[22] These were followed after Catholic emancipation in 1829 by religious teaching orders from the Continent and native congregations, predominantly founded by converts, also made up of women from the higher classes who taught both rich and poor in their convent schools.[23] It was because teaching was considered a vocation rather than a profession, and valued for its social and religious usefulness, that Catholic teaching orders attracted a significant number of educated and cultured women to train as teachers.[24] This is certainly true of the Sisters of Notre Dame who conducted Our Lady's Training College and the Sisters of the Society of the Holy Child Jesus who ran the training college at St Leonards. George Bartley, an examiner at the government's Science and Art department wrote a book on the history of schools in 1871 in which he commented that the female Catholic training colleges did not suffer from staff problems to the same extent as the other colleges because

> Ladies of a more superior rank are more readily found, particularly
> in the Roman Catholic Church, to devote their energies to the
> poor; and the obvious necessity of a supply of Mistresses induced a
> number to enter on the work of teaching, frequently as a labour of
> love, and as a religious duty.[25]

Through the medium of these dedicated and cultured religious teachers, a solid education imbued with a French tradition of quality, *le goût*[26] and high moral standards was passed on not only to wealthy Catholic girls but their poorer sisters as well. As role models to the next generation, the nuns were exemplars of the highest ideal of Catholic womanhood. It is perhaps not surprising, therefore, at a time when there were so few choices outside marriage for single women that the convents, through the example of the nuns, provided a positive alternative for middle-class Catholic women to emulate. Furthermore, in the eyes of the Catholic community at least, devoting one's life to God's work through education by becoming a teaching sister was seen as an acceptable alternative to spinsterhood. If not always regarded as highly as marriage and motherhood, the most appropriate choice for women, it never-theless did not involve loss of status.

Conversely, in mainstream society, the poor status of school teach-ing and the stigma attached to paid work meant that the majority of intellectual upper middle-class women, perhaps most qualified by their superior private education to aid in the reform of education, did not as a rule enter the teaching profession. There were, of course, individual exceptions, predominantly single women who were moti-vated by a variety of reasons to involve themselves in education.[27] However, they remained a minority, the majority of middle-class women, particularly married women, continued to adhere to the cultural norm and did not work for money outside the home.

As already outlined, Catholic education had a considerable advan-tage over mainstream education because it was able to mobilize scholarly women from the upper classes to aid in the work of educating Catholic England. One such woman, Frances Mary Lescher, Sister Mary of St Philip in religion, and first Principal of Our Lady's Training College, is a prime example of this kind. Until her mother's death from consumption when Frances was eleven, she was educated at home with her brothers and sisters, receiving regular lessons with their governess, but the father kept in his own hands their instruction in catechism and Scripture, devoting himself to the task every Sunday.[28] After her mother's death, Caroline, William Lescher's unmarried sister, came to look after the household and the older children were sent to school: William to Stonyhurst in Lanca-shire and Frances and Annie to New Hall, a convent school run by religious.[29] Frances was an exceptionally bright child, rising to the head of the school after only two years of formal education and receiving a gold medal, the highest distinction awarded. The Canon-esses of New Hall evidently took her intellectual ability seriously as they recognized the limitations of what they could provide and advised her family that it was useless to leave her in school any longer. Frances returned home to continue her education under the direc-tion of her father. Annie was sent to Bruges to be further educated at the English Convent.[30]

For the next few years, until self-education took over, William Lescher undertook the more serious side of his daughter's studies. At a time when it was rare for girls to learn Latin, Frances read Virgil with her father. She also studied the English classics, Scott, Dickens, Wordsworth and Shakespeare as well as reading Italian and French works in the original. In a letter to her cousin in 1843, Frances records, 'in our house it is a terrible, dull thing not to be addicted to reading'.[31] Her mastery of French became fluent and grammatical with the help of a young French teacher who lived near by and with whom she corresponded all her life. Twice a week she went to London to study music at the Royal Academy where she learnt to play the harp.[32]

Religious instruction was common to the education of all classes at this time. However, for the Leschers and for many other middle-class families, religion was not confined to the arid repetition of the catechism or even to moral inculcation (these were the forms it usually adopted in the church's attempts to educate the poor). Instead, for these men and women religion was a way of life. The committed study of, and deep interest in, religion pervaded all their actions and afforded women the opportunity to expand their scholarship to Latin, history and other subjects. In the case of Frances, after reading Pugin's *First Principles of Pointed Church Architecture* at the age of sixteen, she developed a lifelong interest and expert knowledge of building styles.[33] This self-education was evidently put to good use when she sat her teacher's certificate in 1855 as the examiner praised her essay on 'Medieaval [*sic*] Architecture' as 'more fit for the Quarterly Review than for an examination paper'.[34]

At a time when Catholic emancipation and the Irish question were acutely part of the political agenda, interest in the progress and setbacks of their religion led many Catholic women to actively keep abreast of the religious politics of the day. The Leschers were avid supporters of the Irish 'Liberator', Daniel O'Connell, and Frances accompanied her father to hear him speak in Covent Garden.[35] Thorny theological questions and issues, as well as the opinions of eminent church leaders, gleaned through their religious writings and tracts, became the subjects of serious study, discussion and contemplation for middle-class women. The stirrings of the Oxford Movement, the consequent wave of converts and the move towards the restoration of the Roman Catholic Hierarchy provided ample scope for intellectual, theological and philosophical discussion.[36] Religion also provided the opportunity to put hard-earned talents to the service of the church and offered women a legitimate reason to be actively involved in public affairs. Frances and her sisters played the harmonium in the chapel, organized Sunday Schools for the children of the poor and embroidered vestments for the church.[37]

Foreign travel and pilgrimages to the Continent during which Frances kept a detailed diary relating and extending her knowledge of the art, geography and history of the places she visited, supplemented these already broad intellectual and creative pursuits. Again, an interest in religion informed her decision to seek out churches, cathedrals, museums, art treasures and architectural styles she had read about. Her creative talents were put to use in the brass rubbings and pencil sketches she made of things that caught her eye.[38]

The Leschers, like most women of their class, also enjoyed an active social life with its round of balls, dinners and soirées and they included among their friends prominent churchmen, politicians, writers and artists. From her letters it is evident that Frances Lescher and the majority of her female acquaintances had access to the informed opinion of their intellectual and influential male acquaintances.[39] They themselves were serious, studious, erudite women who wanted more out of life than the feminine ideal of marriage and motherhood promised. In spite of the very privileged upbringing which Frances enjoyed, and an offer of marriage, her deep and all-consuming love of religion, shared by many women of her class, led her to want to become a Roman Catholic nun. She was not drawn to a contemplative order, as throughout her life her faith had been an active one. In a letter to her friend and confidante, Fanny Grehan, written in 1846 when aged twenty-one, Frances declared:

> I want to reform the whole Catholic world – Catholic society and
> Catholic young ladies especially. A grand idea, isn't it? the best of
> which is its *extreme practicability!* Upon my word, though you may
> laugh, I declare I try my hand sometimes on the young lady part,
> but have not as yet been very successful . . . the young ladies, you
> see, are not worked upon by any of these outward movements, and
> it provokes me to see how little interest they take in Catholic affairs,
> and how they shrink from anything *active* in the cause of religion.[40]

It would appear that not all middle-class women had the strength of character to place active religious duty in the public world above the dominant ideologies of appropriate feminine behaviour, which stressed a subordinate and complementary role for women in the private world of the family. This fact annoyed Frances and led her to want to educate women into the benefits of an active religion, one in which it was the duty of women to develop their intellectual and creative potential so that they might work for the church in practical and useful ways. It is hardly surprising that Frances should be drawn to the Sisters of Notre Dame whose avowed mission was to educate girls and women.[41] It is perhaps less surprisingly still, given her intellectual pedigree, that on completion of her noviciate in 1855 as Sister Mary of St Philip, she was chosen to become Principal of the Catholic training college in Liverpool.

The accomplishments of Frances Mary Lescher were exceptional but the other women who joined her on the staff of Our Lady's College were also well educated and cultured in their own right. Among them were her own sister Annie, now Sister Mary of St Michael and her childhood friend Lucy Wallis, Sister Theresa of St Joseph, both of whom had enjoyed a similar intellectual upbringing to Frances, imbued with the same religious, educational and social tradition. Some of the staff were Belgian or French nuns who had received the benefit of a continental convent education. HMI Mr Stokes, in his first report on the college, dated January 1857, noted the wide range of teaching ability and experience of the sisters. He stated that the community consisted of, 'not only English ladies of great accomplishments, but also foreigners not less accomplished, and, moreover, experimentally acquainted with the approved methods of the best primary schools in Belgium, Holland, and Prussia'.[42] The English nuns were fortunate to have received their initial training as teachers under the direction of the sisters at Namur and were therefore familiar with the Francophone tradition as well as the latest European methods so favoured by educational reformers in England at the time. Indeed, James Kay-Shuttleworth, first secretary of the Privy Council for Education, had followed the example he found in The Netherlands when he introduced the pupil–teacher system to England, a system that was already in use in the nuns' schools on the continent.[43]

Inevitably, not all the women who staffed the first training colleges were as highly educated as the Catholic sisters at Our Lady's, nor was their motivation purely to do God's work in a separate female community. Unlike the nuns, many Victorian gentlewomen of lesser means were driven to find respectable employment in order to maintain themselves. Even if deeply pious, as many of them undoubtedly were, not all were attracted to a religious life. In any case, women of the Anglican denominations did not found convents until after 1845 and, even so, to become a nun was generally viewed with suspicion.[44] Therefore financial security, together with the offer of a home within a secular family-like community and the respectable social position attached to it, were often motivating factors for seeking a college post. The absence of formal qualifications, which of course were impossible for women to obtain, made the task of selecting suitable candidates for the position of governess or Lady

Superintendent a difficult one for Anglican training colleges in the early years of their existence. It appears, therefore, that the chief requisite for such employment was an impeccable character and once appointed, women had to prove their academic worth to maintain their position.[45] The Anglican Hierarchy had no ready supply of trained female teachers to whom they could turn for help to staff their colleges.

This situation differed from Our Lady's Training College, where all the staff were Catholic sisters and could, if necessary, be constantly renewed and maintained by fresh recruits of culturally diverse, religious and academically trained middle-class teachers from the mother house in Namur. The sisters had little choice in their teaching destination, rather, they accepted in obedience the work that was allocated to them by the Mother Superior in Belgium. According to the meritocratic ethos of the Notre Dame order, however, this meant their talents were often utilized according to need and the most educated sisters would be sent where they could do the most useful work. This enabled Sister Mary of St Philip to obtain some of the best teachers the order had to offer for the work at Our Lady's, a work which was regarded as being of great importance, to provide the female teachers to educate Catholic England. Her biographer, an anonymous Sister of Notre Dame writes of Sister Mary of St Philip, 'She showed great insight in selecting the *personnel* of her Staff' suggesting that she had some influence in choosing her fellow teaching sisters.[46]

At Warrington and the other Anglican training colleges, there was no such network of well-qualified female teachers on which to draw. The Clerical Principal, who was by definition a man and usually a graduate, was normally the principal teacher in the Anglican colleges. The women staff worked entirely under his direction, having little autonomy or power to make decisions themselves other than in the domestic arrangements of the college of which they took charge. In any case, with no formal academic or teacher training, it is doubtful whether many of them would have had either the confidence or the ability to direct the educational work of the colleges. On the other hand, they were well qualified by their upbringing to deliver the domestic, religious and social training, which the colleges required of their future teachers.[47] These women, therefore, often relied on their respectable middle-class credentials to obtain a teaching position. They were usually motivated by personal circumstance, as single women this often meant having to earn a living while trying to maintain their position in society.[48]

Consequently, the placing of women staff was often made by recommendation or through an informal social network whereby women who moved in the same circles as the men who had the power to employ them would put themselves forward for consideration. Unlike the sisters whose previous informal schooling had been consolidated by religious and teacher training within their congregation, there was no way of assessing the academic qualifications of secular women because of their previous *ad hoc* education. Therefore, they were frequently judged on the strength of their moral and domestic qualities and their respectable pedigrees.[49]

The personality and leadership qualities of the individual Clerical Principals who ruled over each college may have given each one its own peculiar ethos but in many respects they developed along similar lines.[50] During the 1850s the work of the training colleges had gradually became standardized and this was due to the dictates of government grants upon which they increasingly depended for their survival. In 1854 Revd H. Moseley, HMI for training colleges, introduced a syllabus for all the colleges to follow which allowed students across the country to sit the same examinations in all subjects.[51] College staffs were also required to sit examinations to obtain 'Certificates of Merit'. By the mid-1850s the pupil–teacher system had come to fruition and the colleges were guaranteed a continuous supply of Queen's Scholars.[52] The accompanying government grants ensured their financial stability. Grants also became available for the teaching of certain subjects which the government considered 'proper to elementary education', such as history, geography, English, physical science and mathematics.[53] In 1857, the greatest weight was given in examinations to those subjects considered 'compulsory': religious knowledge, arithmetic, English language and grammar and school management.[54] Thus, by the time Our Lady's Catholic Training College opened in February 1856, the foundation of an integrated teacher training system (with a limited curriculum geared towards elementary schooling) had been laid down by the government and in many respects the colleges became very similar.

All the colleges were residential for staff (except in some cases the Clerical Principal) and students. Nearly all were built in the same Gothic style of architecture.[55] They all had a male Clerical Principal, (with the exception of Our Lady's) and each had a Lady Superintendent to oversee the domestic arrangements. All the colleges, including Our Lady's, had Practising Schools attached to them where the students carried out their teaching practice and all placed the emphasis on a religious education. The students also became a more uniform group. Most came from lower middle-class backgrounds and the average age was 18–20 on entry to the college.[56] Nearly all had been pupil–teachers (although a small number were private students who paid for their college education), therefore, they had a more uniform body of knowledge, even if ability varied.

As a result of the government initiatives, Warrington and other church training colleges could afford to employ more staff. It became usual for the colleges to employ a Master or Mistress of Method whose job it was to instruct students in the art of teaching. As a general rule, however, from the mid-1850s onwards the full-time live-in staff was made up of unmarried women, usually recruited from the most promising students in the college. Many of these women completed lifelong careers in the church colleges.[57]

As a result, by the 1870s, the majority of women on the Anglican training college staff, originated from lower middle-class or even working-class backgrounds and had worked their way up through the pupil–teacher apprenticeship system to supplant the 'respectable middle-class lady' governess of earlier days. These women had originally been destined to work in the poor schools. Having been recognized as diligent and bright girls from respectable and god-fearing, if often humble and financially strained homes, they were selected by their school managers to train as pupil–teachers. At the age of thirteen they had begun five years of teaching in an elementary school while at the same time continuing to improve their own education outside school hours. During this time they had sat yearly examinations, taught in front of inspectors, learnt about school management and had worked extremely long hours for little reward. Clergymen, teachers, school managers and inspectors had ensured that the strict moral and religious code deemed necessary for all single women, but particularly for those who would be charged with educating young children, had been upheld.[58] At eighteen, after successfully passing their Queen's scholarship examination they had opted for a free place at one of the church training colleges, which carried a maintenance grant. Here they had completed another two years of teaching practice, narrow academic studies, compulsory church attendance, examinations and long hours of physical and mental work under the strict supervision of the Lady Superintendent and the Clerical Principal. They had emerged at the end of all this with a Teacher's Certificate.[59]

The majority of these women, along with Catholic pupil–teachers of the same class, went straight to work in church elementary schools with little prospect of promotion or prestige. The life of a school-mistress was hard, according to HMI Mr Cook, 'It separated her very much from the class to which she originally belonged, while it did not bring her socially into contact with a different class, and therefore she was very much isolated.'[60] However, for the brightest girls of impeccable character, there existed within the emerging Anglican tradition the opportunity of enhancing their status by obtaining a college post or finding work in a reputable middle-class private girls' school. Therefore, for a few women of lowly origins it was possible to rise to the post of Lady Principal which carried a certain amount of prestige and definite middle-class status[61] (an opportunity not available to Catholic secular teachers as only religious worked at Our Lady's).[62] It seems likely that this social recognition was an important motivating factor for single women and it helped to compensate for the poor remuneration they received.

The average wages for assistant female college staff ranged between £35 to £60 per annum in the early years, with the Lady Principal receiving around £80.[63] All female staff were expected to live in the college and received their board and lodging free of charge. Towards the end of the century, average junior college staff wages had risen to £60–£80 per annum while the Lady Super-intendent could expect to receive £100–£120. When compared to male staff salaries, these amounts seem disproportionately low. Male Principal salaries started at £150 to £300 per annum rising to £300–£500 per annum towards the end of the century.[64] However, the female staff were probably grateful to be employed in academic work and must have considered themselves fortunate to have escaped the usual female domestic employment, particularly in light of the fact that the cook at Warrington earned £15 a year in 1873 and the scullery maids had to make ends meet on £9 per annum.[65]

Personal financial considerations did not trouble the Sisters of Notre Dame or any of the religious congregations. As religious they had taken vows of poverty and were thus prohibited from owning personal property. All their daily needs were met by the community and although they received a nominal salary for their teaching, this amount went directly into communal funds.[66] The sisters received a total of £125 (later increased to £150) per annum from the Catholic Poor School Committee to cover all staff salaries at Our Lady's.[67] Clearly, this amount alone would not have been sufficient for their needs. They supplemented this income with government grants, fees from their High Schools and the sisters' dowries. It must be remembered that before entering the convent, most of these women had been financially secure, in some cases they had been very wealthy and all had brought with them a sizeable dowry which aided the work of their congregation.[68] The dowries, as well as any money which the sisters were able to earn on a daily basis through teaching, were all invested into the good works which the community undertook – enlarging and furnishing buildings, providing resources and investing in people. Thus, although the community as a whole may have suffered financial hardship from time to time, each sister knew that her own personal welfare and old age would be provided for by the congregation leaving her free to devote her energies to less vulgar considerations than earning a living.[69]

Apart from the difficulty and worry of having to provide for personal financial security and old age, which preoccupied the single Anglican female college governess and was of little concern to the Catholic sisters, there was another difference between the staff of the two colleges. This was their culture and life experience, which in turn was tied to social class and wealth. In contrast to the Catholic sisters, none of the Anglican women came from gentry or aristocratic stock – the ruling classes that were used to wielding authority. In fact, most of them originated from a class which was used to their 'betters' prescribing what was good for them and directing their lives. They had been restricted to the field of the elementary school system and therefore they had had few opportunities to widen their horizons.[70] The women who rose through the ranks of the pupil–teacher system to become elementary school teachers and who eventually joined the college staff had learnt to accept discipline, strict supervision and all the constraints demanded of femininity. Every minute of every day, from morning bell to evening lights out, was minutely accounted for and filled with constant work, petty rules and regulations. The power of the management committee to enforce college rules was unquestioned and the least breach of any regulation or lapse in etiquette by female staff or students could lead to dismissal, particularly if the morals of the women were at stake.[71] Under such a limiting regime, only those students who accepted and acquiesced to the system by their adherence to regulations, implicit (such as proper ladylike behaviour, and respectability in dress, manners and habits) and explicit (such as outward piety, domestic diligence and obedience to superiors) could hope to join the college staff. Given these circumstances, it is not surprising that when they became college governesses they maintained and perpetuated the same strict code of conduct and limited field of knowledge to which they themselves, had been subject. They had been socialized to accept subservience, not to be self-reliant or exercise authority. In such a conservative atmosphere of stifled creativity and inhibited personal freedom (to be flamboyant or extrovert was not the role of a female college tutor), the work of the Anglican colleges remained narrow and focused on the job in hand. Mr Robinson, in his evidence to the Newcastle Commission in 1861, noted the effects of the training given in most of the Anglican colleges, 'The present course tends to impart information rather than to develop the faculties and to discipline the mind. The principle in short . . . is cram.'[72]

Such mechanical and narrowly trained minds inevitably affected the ethos and results of the colleges and accounts for the mediocre academic attainments of the students who were taught only what they needed to know to impart to the children under their care.[73] This is not to suggest that there were no intelligent and innovative women among the staff at Warrington and the other church colleges in the later years of the century. Undoubtedly, some intelligent women of natural ability educated themselves beyond the requirements of their job and overcame their social disadvantages to become committed teachers who devoted their lives to their work. Rather, it is merely to point out that most of them had not been given the opportunity to expand their culture or widen their field of experience beyond the limited curricula set by government examinations, the dogmatic principles of the church authorities, or the boundary walls of the college. Considering the disadvantages they faced in terms of their class and cultural position at the onset of their career as teachers, these women succeeded in finding a niche for themselves against all the odds.

This situation contrasts sharply with the well-read and creative minds which characterized the Sisters of Notre Dame who, because of their privileged class position, had travelled widely and had access to different countries and cultures.[74] They too were inflexible in their principles and equally clear that their *raison d'être* was to bring the children of the poor to God. However, it could be argued that they achieved their aims in a more conducive and stimulating learning environment. The difference between the broad culture of the staff at Our Lady's and the narrow culture of the staff at Warrington manifested itself in the contrasting educational ethos of the two institutions. At Our Lady's the students were encouraged to read widely, if selectively, and the library was continually improved[75] whereas the library at Warrington was poorly stocked.[76] The curriculum at Our Lady's was much broader (Sister Mary of St Philip refusing to limit her students to the demands of government inspectors or grant-earning activities),[77] whereas at Warrington the work revolved around cramming for those examinations which carried the most financial weight.[78] The staff at Our Lady's displayed an enthusiasm for education that was infectious; individual talent and potential were motivated and rewarded[79] whereas at Warrington the emphasis was on domestic and religious duty and learning only what they needed to know to do the job.[80] At Our Lady's all second-year students had their own rooms to encourage private study and self-education,[81] whereas at Warrington they shared a partitioned dormitory and had little time to themselves.[82] These differences help to account for the more positive learning environment at Our Lady's which was reflected in the examination results and the reputation which the college gained. It is the unique success of Our Lady's which he attributes to the culture of the sisters that struck the Anglican writer, the Revd Fredrick Fuller, in his doctoral thesis surveying all the church training colleges.

The whole set-up of the training establishment at Mount Pleasant was very successful. This produced a very low rate of failure. As early as 1858 the Mount Pleasant results were unparalleled in the history of training colleges. In 1863 the college had the highest percentage of first class passes. HMIs frequently commented upon the superiority of the students there, pointing out that this was because of the constant contact with cultured women, very different from the usual college governesses.[83]

It is also possible to detect (though difficult to define) a different spiritual ethos between the two colleges which contributed to the advanced female intellectual development at Our Lady's. Although both Warrington and Our Lady's fostered Christian ideals and placed the emphasis on religious training, it appears that a distinctive feminine Catholic 'spirit' was at work at Mount Pleasant. All aspects of college life were imbued with the religious tenets of charity, obedience and poverty, as indeed they were at Warrington. However, at Our Lady's, there co-existed a further belief that all work should be edifying. Human beings (including women) should be encouraged to develop their physical, mental and spiritual capacities to the full. In this way, they could better serve God. Talent and individual gifts were considered to be God-given, not gendered, and should therefore be developed and perfected for His benefit, even if these gifts fell outside society's accepted realm of women's work. The belief that all work could have an edifying dimension if undertaken in God's name, transcended worldly, gendered notions of appropriate spheres of feminine activity. In so doing, a wide range of female industry was justified and made possible, which in other circumstances would not have been considered appropriate or 'ladylike'. For example, Our Lady's actively encouraged those sisters who showed a flair for 'manly' Science to develop their scientific studies and the college was among the first to offer science on the curriculum in 1869, dismissing claims that women were unsuited for such activities.[84] A year later, George Bentley, a Science inspector could write regarding the teaching of the subject, 'In the results which it has obtained this College has not been surpassed by any under the inspection of the Privy Council.'[85] Mount Pleasant training college was among first to encourage its staff and students to take degrees as external candidates at London University and later at Liverpool University after restrictions, imposed by the Catholic Hierarchy, barring Catholic women had been lifted.[86] These activities suggest that the Catholic 'spirit' valued knowledge and learning in women for its own sake as a means of glorifying God. Whether intentional or not, by using their religion as justification for their actions, the sisters successfully extended the boundaries of women's appropriate sphere.

It is not possible to detect an equivalent 'spirit' at Warrington or the other church colleges under the direction of a man. Of course, they too offered a religious education intended to foster Christian ideals. However, these ideals appear to have had a confining, gendered dimension. These colleges do not appear to have tempered Christian duty with a liberating spirit of self-fulfilment and self-development, rather, they offered a restricted ideal of Christian womanhood. While the women were taught to respect others, they were not taught to believe in themselves. If they were talented, their talents were wasted if they were at variance with ideological notions of acceptable feminine spheres of activity or were not needed in their work. They were encouraged to work hard and do their job efficiently but there appears to have been little encouragement to go beyond that and be creative. It is worth considering whether the development of such a liberating, non-confining ethos or 'spirit', such as appears to have been at work at Mount Pleasant, was also dependent on an all-female environment where societal prohibitions on female development held considerably less sway.

Leaving the difficult issue of spiritual difference aside, there are two uncontested, mutually dependent reasons for the difference between the kind of teaching at Our Lady's and the other training colleges, including Warrington. First, Our Lady's was established and run independently by a Catholic teaching congregation of international character. This meant that the Notre Dame order was able to attract women of a high social class and academic attainment from across Catholic Europe to its noviciate (and therefore to its advanced, in comparison to the Anglican tradition, teacher training system). Second, and as a result of this, the college, through the community, was able to draw on some of the best-educated, cultured and trained female minds that the congregation, perhaps even Europe, had to offer. Therefore, Notre Dame and the other Roman Catholic teaching congregations, had access to a different *type* of teacher not available to the employers of the other colleges.[87]

Most had grown up in the kind of comfortable, pious and cultured home epitomized by that of Frances Mary Lescher. This remained the case throughout the nineteenth century. Unlike Warrington, the staff at Our Lady's was not drawn from the ranks of lower middle-class or working-class former students who had been pupil–teachers. This is understandable as the majority of these women, on completion of their college training at Our Lady's, did not become nuns but remained in the world as Catholic teachers working in Catholic poor schools. As already noted, during the nineteenth century only women religious taught on the college staff. However, the influence of the nuns inevitably led some former students from the lower classes who had been educated in their schools as pupil–teachers, to develop a vocation and to join a religious order, most, though not all, becoming Sisters of Notre Dame. Even so, the women who joined the staff at Mount Pleasant later in the century were not generally taken from among these lower middle-class women religious elementary school teachers. They were drawn from a higher social class and had received a broader education.

From the beginning, the sisters had opened superior fee-paying day and boarding schools to cater for the daughters of middle-class Catholics which helped to pay for their work among the poor. In so doing they were fulfilling a mutual need; prominent Catholic families, lacking good middle-class educational provision for their daughters, had no qualms about entrusting their education to ladies of such a high class and reputation so the schools were a success from the beginning. Apart from its middle-class ethos, what made the

High School at Mount Pleasant and similar schools the sisters founded around the country, different from all their other educational ventures, was the fact that they were completely free of all external control. The High School, as a privately funded 'independent' school was unhampered by the restrictive requirements of government grants, inspections and examinations.[88] Therefore, it was here that the sisters were free to pursue their educational ideal of 'godliness and good learning' devoid of outside interference.[89] Moreover, they had the full backing of the parents in their efforts to achieve this aim as the ideal so closely mirrored that of their own. The nuns firmly believed in the distinctiveness of what they were doing as Josephine Murray, a Sister of Notre Dame, demonstrates in her history of the Mount Pleasant High School:

> Wonderful understanding support came wholeheartedly from the parents; the children came, almost without exception, from model Catholic homes . . . There was nothing but the best in personnel; nothing but the best for those they taught . . . Each one was studied individually; each was promoted when she was ready, and habits of independence and self-restraint were inculcated from the start.[90]

This model produced the kind of 'godliness' which many middle-class Catholic families dreamed of for their daughters; it was considered an honour if they developed a vocation and became a nun. For example, the wealthy Mr Neale Lomax educated all his daughters at the sisters' High School, five became Sisters of Notre Dame including Elizabeth Lomax, Sister Theresa of the Passion. She had been one of the sisters' first students when, a week after their arrival in Liverpool, the sisters opened the Select Day School charging six guineas per annum; Elizabeth, then aged ten, started this school on the opening day.[91] From the High School, as it was later called, she continued her education at the sisters' boarding school at Namur and entered the noviciate in 1859. In 1863 she returned to Liverpool to join the college staff as a science teacher and remained at Mount Pleasant for the next 26 years. In 1887, Sister Theresa became First Mistress of the college[92] until she was recalled to work at Namur where she remained until her unexpected death after a short illness in 1891.[93]

The model was no less effective in developing the 'good learning' part of the ideal. The students were subject to the usual middle-class 'accomplishments' such as needlework, ornate handwriting, letter writing and accounts[94] but they also received a broad-based education. Unlike the limited curriculum which was standard fare for their working-class counterparts, the pupil–teachers, their curriculum included French, Music, English Language and Literature, Geography, Botany, Geology, Physiography and History as well as the ubiquitous three Rs and Religious Knowledge.[95] The girls were also directed and encouraged to develop an active apostolic life and were 'taught to think of, and to help to the best of their ability, their fellow Catholics, who in those days were to be found among the very poor'.[96] This was achieved by sewing garments for children in the poor schools and the requirement to give up their free time to help in church work such as teaching the catechism or using their musical talents to provide social evenings for their less fortunate Catholic brothers and sisters.[97] Consequently, from an early age, the girls were made aware of their privileged social position but were also made aware that such a position carried duties and responsibilities as well as privileges. They were, therefore, taught to have empathy towards and if possible help the poor, one of the fundamental doctrines of the Sisters of Notre Dame.

Perhaps not surprisingly, given their exposure to Roman Catholic religious ideals, both at home and through the extensive opportunity they had of observing so many women of their own class as religious role models in the convent school, a high proportion of these middle-class girls developed a vocation, joined the institute and became teaching sisters. In contrast to the governesses at Warrington, their education and socialization, through their constant contact with female religious who demonstrated and commanded authority, led them to expect that they too, through religion, could aspire to responsible positions in society. Their upper middle-class status, their superior education and the exceptional role models whom they sought to emulate, all confirmed to these girls that if they devoted their lives to God, they too would earn respect for their efforts. They too, could be rewarded with an interesting career, which offered opportunities to travel and hold positions of authority. It is perhaps understandable why for some, it proved more tempting than marriage. When they left the High School, the young women were sent to Belgium to continue their education and training both as teachers and novices in the mother house at Namur. It is from this pool of highly educated middle-class women that some of the staff at Our Lady's was drawn in the later years of the nineteenth century.

What is striking about these women is the fact that so many of them were prepared to forgo a privileged and leisured lifestyle as middle-class wives and mistresses of substantial homes, with servants and children of their own, in order to devote themselves to an idealistic life of self-sacrifice among the poor in an all-female environment. Perhaps some of them were merely being pragmatic. Alongside the obvious advantages which they gained by becoming nuns: the opportunity to develop their intellects; increased spiritual status; the lifelong support of a female community; the possibility of reaching a position of authority and the satisfaction of doing useful work, there was the added benefit of avoiding endless pregnancies which claimed the lives of so many married women.[98] Personal wealth and the existence of the convents as a suitable alternative to marriage gave middle-class Catholic women a choice not open to other women. In contrast, the women at Warrington and elsewhere were motivated to become teachers, at least partially, by financial necessity. They needed to work in order to support themselves and teaching was virtually the only occupation open to them. They were compelled to seek respectability to maintain their middle-class status in a society which marginalized and discriminated against single women for not living up to the domestic ideal of good wife and mother. Without independent wealth, their choices were severely limited. Even with wealth, entering a convent was not necessarily a positive option for Protestant women and they could therefore not afford the luxury of idealism.[99]

Throughout the nineteenth century, Our Lady's was fortunate to be able to draw on a pool of widely experienced, cultured, highly educated and well-qualified women – women who would not have entered the teaching profession had it not been for their religious status. These women religious, because of their privileged upper- or middle-class origins, had not been subject to the usual economic and educational restrictions or limited self-autonomy and freedom of movement, which characterized the lives of most women in the period. Active encouragement from their families and religious advisers had allowed them to develop their talents and explore their potential and a spirit of philanthropy. Catholic zeal had enabled them, through religion, to use their considerable attainments for the educational benefit of the poor and girls of their own class. The all-female environment of the convent and college had facilitated the development of their educational ideals and spiritual ethos unhindered by male hierarchical systems of government or negative ideologies, which usually inhibited the capabilities of women and acted as a barrier to their self-development in the nineteenth century.

NOTES

1 For an account of the voluntary schools prior to the nineteenth-century reforms, see M. G. Jones, *The Charity School Movement: A Study of Eighteenth Century Puritanism* (London: Cambridge University Press, 1964).

2 This method, claimed to have been invented simultaneously by Dr Andrew Bell, an Anglican, and Joseph Lancaster, a Quaker, was used in both Anglican National Schools and the Dissenters' British Schools. The teacher would train the older children as monitors and they in turn would pass the information on to the younger children. Thereby, one teacher could, in theory, teach a large number of children, which had the advantage of being cheap. For discussion of this method of training teachers see R. W. Rich, *The Training of Teachers in England and Wales during the Nineteenth Century* (London: Cambridge University Press, 1933), particularly Chapter 1.

3 British Parliamentary Papers (hereafter BPP), Education General, vol. 24, Schools Inquiry, 1867–1968, Mr Bryce's Report, p. 682.

4 Ibid., p. 683.

5 F. Widdowson, *Going Up into the Next Class; Women and Elementary Teacher Training 1840–1914* (London: Hutchinson and Co., 1980), p. 7.

6 Rich, *The Training of Teachers*, p. 52.

7 Revd. F.W.T. Fuller, 'The churches train teachers: a history of teacher training in England and Wales Until 1890', unpublished University of Exeter PhD thesis, 1973, p. 381.

8 M.P. Linscott, 'The educational work of the Sisters of Notre Dame in Lancashire since 1850', University of Liverpool, MA thesis, 1962, p. 191.

9 The Revised Code, instigated by Robert Lowe in 1862, altered the way the training colleges could qualify for government grants and ushered in a period of 'payment by results'. As a result, many of the smaller colleges were forced to close and most of the larger ones had to charge an entrance fee in order to survive. For a detailed discussion of the effects of the Revised Code, see Rich, *The Training of Teachers*, pp. 181–210.

10 T. Burke, *Catholic History of Liverpool* (Liverpool: C. Tinling and Co. Ltd, 1910), p. 93.

11 Fuller, *The Churches Train Teachers*, p. 198.

12 Linscott, *The Educational Work*, p. 197.

13 The expansion of middle-class secondary education for women began with the opening of Bedford and Queen's Colleges in London in the 1840s. These colleges afforded opportunities for middle-class women to become teachers in secondary schools and women's colleges. For an account of the growth of middle-class women's education in the nineteenth century, see J. Purvis, *A History of Women's Education in England* (Milton Keynes: Open University Press, 1991), particularly Chapters 4 and 5.

14 Warrington was founded by the Chester Diocesan Board of Education in 1844 to train female teachers for the diocese of Lancashire and Cheshire on the site of the Clergy Daughters' School, Warrington. After a fire destroyed the building in 1924, a site was purchased in Liverpool and a new college built which opened in 1929 as St. Katharine's College. Today, the Anglican college

of St. Katharine's, together with the Catholic colleges of Our Lady's and Christ's form Liverpool Hope University College.

15   See for example, M. O'Leary, *Education With A Tradition; An Account of the Educational Work of the Society of the Sacred Heart* (London: University of London Press, 1936); C. Bremner, *Education of Girls and Women in Great Britain* (London, 1897).

16   After only three years in existence, Mr Sandiford, Chief Secretary of the Education Department was so impressed with Our Lady's results that he wrote a personal letter of congratulation to Sister Mary of St Philip. He later said of her 'Miss Lescher is a woman who might fearlessly place her hand on the helm of the State'. *Sister Mary of St Philip (Francis Mary Lescher) 1825–1904*, written anonymously by A Sister of Notre Dame (London, 1922), p. 110.

17   See H. C. Barnard, *A History of English Education from 1760* (London: University of London Press, 1969), pp. 156–66 for a description of the inadequacies of mainstream middle-class girls' education.

18   Within four years of its foundation, for example, the poor school of the Society of the Sacred Heart at St Leonards-on-Sea was described by HMI Mr. Marshall, in 1853, as 'one of the most perfect institutions of its class in Europe'. Quoted in A Religious of the Society, *The Life of Cornelia Connelly, 1809-1879, Foundress of the Society of the Holy Child Jesus* (London, 1922), p. 167.

19   See Bridget Hill, 'A refuge from men: the idea of a Protestant nunnery', *Past and Present,* 117 (1987), pp. 107–30.

20   Ibid. p. 56.

21   See Susan O'Brien, 'Terra Incognita: the nun in nineteenth century England', *Past and Present,* 121 (1989), p. 110. For a history of the Institute, see H. J. Coleridge (ed.), *St Mary's Convent: Micklegate Bar, York, 1686–1887* (London, 1887). O'Brien notes that the Institute of the Blessed Virgin Mary or English Ladies' was founded in 1686 when convents were illegal. They lived and worked covertly at the Bar Convent in York and gained a reputation for providing a good quality education, mainly for middle-class girls.

22   O'Leary, *Education With A Tradition,* p. 233.

23   See for example, A Religious of the Society of the Holy Child Jesus, *A Daughter of Coventry Patmore, Sister Mary Christina, S.H.C.J.* (London: Longman, Green and Co., 1924). Also, O'Brien, 'Terra Incognita'. It is important to note that the older congregations were enclosed and undertook the education of girls within the confines of the cloister; devoid of contact with the outside world and increasingly out of touch with the requirements of the rapidly changing times. In contrast, the native and imported English religious orders established in the wake of Catholic emancipation were modelled on the post-Revolutionary Continental congregations, and as such were 'active rather than contemplative, and public rather than cloistered', (ibid., p. 112). See same for a discussion of how this change was achieved.

24   O'Brien, 'Terra Incognita', p. 135. O'Brien notes that this was particularly so of the Continental orders that maintained a distinction between choir and lay sisters. Upper-middle-class women were attracted by the status given to teaching and the leadership opportunities available in these congregations.

25   George C.T. Bartley, *The Schools for the People* (London, 1871), p. 472.

26   The expression *le goût*, literally 'good taste' is widely used by French educators

to mean the training and development of every human faculty in harmony. In 1765, Rollin, writing on education described it thus, 'Good taste, that delicate sensitiveness to what is truly noble, is the most precious fruit of our studies . . . Thus the citizen whose mind has been cultivated by arts so worthy of man's nature, shows in all his actions a grace which betrays him, . . . and proclaims unconsciously the education he has received.' M. Rollin, *La Manière d'enseigner et d'étudier les Belles Lettres par rapport à l'esprit et au cœur*. Quoted in O'Leary, *Education With A Tradition*, p. 19.

27 For information on some of the individual personalities who pioneered mainstream middle-class education, see J. Senders Petersen, *The Reform of Girls' Secondary and Higher Education in Victorian England* (London: Garland, 1987); P. Hirsch, *Barbara Leigh Smith Bodichon: Feminist, Artist and Rebel* (London: Chatto and Windus, 1998); M. P. Gallant, 'Against the odds: Anne Jemima Clough and women's education in England', *History of Education*, 26: 2 (1997), pp. 145–64; M. Forster, *Significant Sisters: The Grassroots of Active Feminism 1839–1939* (London: Penguin, 1984), particularly Chapter 5, 'Education: Emily Davies 1830–1921', pp. 133–65.

28 A Sister of Notre Dame (hereafter SND), *Sister Mary of St Philip*, p.7.

29 See note 20.

30 SND, *Sister Mary of St Philip*, p.11.

31 Ibid., p. 19.

32 Ibid.

33 Ibid., p. 21.

34 Ibid., p. 105.

35 Ibid., p. 20.

36 The Oxford Movement or the Tractarians is the label given to pioneers who contributed to the series of pamphlets, edited by John Henry Newman, entitled *Tracts for the Times*, published between 1833 and 1841. The leading writers were Newman, J. Keble, E.B. Pusey, R.H. Froude, C. Marriott and I. Williams. Their purpose was to stress the apostolic character of the doctrine of the Church of England. They also sought to rouse their fellow clergymen to a higher conception of their sacerdotal office by encouraging them to resist secular encroachments on ecclesiastical power and by repudiating the 'Protestant' elements in Anglicanism. See R.W. Church, *The Oxford Movement: Twelve Years 1833–1845* (London, 1891, republished London: Macmillan & Co., 1970) and E. Norman, *The English Catholic Church in the Nineteenth Century* (Oxford: Clarendon Press, 1984).

37 SND, *Sister Mary of St Philip*, p. 54.

38 Ibid., pp. 26–39.

39 Sisters of Notre Dame Provincial Archives (hereafter SNDPA), Mount Pleasant Training College (hereafter MPTC), Letters of Sister Mary of St Philip.

40 SND, *Sister Mary of St Philip*, pp. 50–1 (original emphasis).

41 In choosing an active apostolate, Frances was also following a trend within the Roman Catholic Church which had gathered pace since the French Revolution. As O'Brien notes, although pioneered with difficulty the nineteenth century is unique in the history of Christian religious life in the number of new, active foundations made by women. An active apostolate matched the needs of the contemporary church, particularly in Protestant countries, as it allowed

women to fulfil social welfare functions. See O'Brien, 'Terra Incognita', pp. 111–12.

42 BPP, Education, Inspector's Reports, HMI Mr Stoke's Report on The Roman Catholic College for Schoolmistresses at Liverpool, 1857, p. 485.

43 It should be noted, however, to avoid confusion, that Kay-Shuttleworth did not adopt the French Catholic system when he started his experimental college at Battersea. He favoured the Swiss model, particularly De Fellenberg's and Vehrli's work at Kreuzlingen. See Rich, *The Training of Teachers*, Chapter 2 for an overview of the various European developments in teacher training.

44 See S. Mumm, 'Lady guerrillas of philanthropy: Anglican sisterhoods in Victorian England', unpublished University of Sussex, PhD thesis, October 1992, particularly Chapter 6 for public opinion of sisterhoods.

45 Warrington Training College Archives, private collection held in the Sheppard Worlock Library (hereafter WTCA, SWL), *The Warrington Training College Magazine*, September 1902, 'Reminiscences of early days' by a former student, p. 139.

46 SND, *Sister Mary of St. Philip*, p. 162.

47 Cheshire Record Office (hereafter CRO), DGR/B/23, Clergy Daughter's School Minute book, December 1844.

48 See for example, M.J. Peterson, 'The Victorian governess: status incongruence in society', in M. Vicinus (ed.) *Suffer and Be Still, Women in the Victorian Age* (London: University of Chicago Press, 1985); K. Hughes, *The Victorian Governess* (London: Hambledon Press, 1993).

49 WTCA, SWL, *The Warrington Training College Magazine*, September 1902, 'Reminiscences of early days' by a former student, p. 140.

50 See Fuller, *The Churches Train Teachers*, for a description of some of the personalities involved.

51 J. Hurt, *Education in Evolution: Church, State, Society and Popular Education 1800–1870* (London: Rupert Hart-Davis, 1971), p. 100.

52 Kay-Shuttleworth introduced the pupil–teacher system in 1846, which allowed government apprenticeship grants to children of thirteen who stayed on at an elementary school for five years to train as teachers. At the end of the apprenticeship they could take the Queen's Scholarship examination and if successful, they were awarded a maintenance grant to attend one of the church training colleges for two years. The colleges were also awarded grants in return for accepting pupil–teachers. For a detailed description of the system see Rich, *The Training of Teachers*, pp. 80–115.

53 Fuller, *The Churches Train Teachers*, p. 105.

54 Ibid., p. 106.

55 Ibid., p. 92.

56 Ibid., p. 95. See also, Widdowson, *Going up into the Next Class*, p. 24.

57 See for example, J.E. Hollingshead (ed.), Liverpool Institute of Higher Education, *In Thy Light: St. Katharine's College 1844–1994* (Liverpool: Stanley Printing Ltd, 1994), p. 14.

58 For a fuller discussion of the character and training of pupil teachers see M. Sturt, *The Education of the People* (London: Routledge and Kegan Paul, 1967), particularly Chapter 10; P. Horn, *Education in Rural England 1800–1914* (Dublin: Gill and Macmillan, 1978), Chapter 3.

59 For descriptions of training college life see, G. P. McGregor, *Bishop Otter College* (London: Pembridge Press, 1981); F. Montgomery, *Edge Hill University College: A History 1885–1997* (Chichester: Phillimore and Co. Ltd., 1997); J. L. Bradbury, *Chester College and the Training of Teachers* (Chester: Chester College, 1975); M. Dobson, *1851–1951: The First Hundred Years of the Diocesan Training College, Derby* (London: Kenrick and Jefferson Ltd, 1951).

60 BPP, Newcastle Report, 1861, vol. XXI, Mr Cook's evidence, p. 163.

61 Hollingshead (ed.), *In Thy Light*, pp. 13–14.

62 SNDPA, The Convent, Woolton, Mount Pleasant Training College, MPTC, ms document by J. Murray, SND, *History of Our Lady's* (1972).

63 WTCA, SWL, *Warrington Training College Minute Book, 1854–1880*, p. 155.

64 Ibid.

65 Ibid.

66 See Linscott, *The Educational Work*, p. 195.

67 SNDPA, MPTC, ms document by J. Murray, SND, *History of Our Lady's*, p. 17.

68 See A.M. Clarke, *Life of the Hon. Mrs Edward Petre* (London, 1899) for an example of the wealthy lady who joined the SND.

69 See S. O'Brien, 'Lay sisters and good mothers: working class women in English convents 1840–1910', pp. 453–469, in W. Sheils and D. Wood, (eds), *Women in the Church*, Studies in Church History vol. 27 (Oxford: Blackwell, 1990) for a discussion of the importance of dowries to religious congregations. O'Brien estimates that choir sisters outnumbered lay sisters by two to one in most communities and that this was necessary because of financial considerations. Unusually, the SND did not make a distinction between choir and lay sisters, though my own research suggests that the ratio of 'ladies' to working-class sisters was similar. It is also evident that although, in theory, everyone was equal within the SND order and exceptional working-class women would not be prevented from exercising positions of authority if they proved themselves worthy. In practice, the difference in culture and upbringing disadvantaged such women from fulfilling all but the manual work of the convent. However, this in itself does not imply a lack of respect for working-class women; all convent work was equally valued in the eyes of God, therefore, 'ladies' were expected to do their share of the domestic work. This, and the heightened emphasis on fulfilling potential and nurturing talent within the SND order, could lead to working-class women of exceptional talent being given positions of authority and responsibility, though the odds, of course, were against it.

70 Fuller, *The Training of Teachers*, p. 103.

71 For example, Warrington Training College dismissed a student from the college in April 1875 for having been detected 'using language of an immoral character'. WTCA, SWL, *Warrington Training College Minute Book, 1854–1880*, p. 182.

72 Revd. H.G. Robinson, Principal of York Training College, statement to the Newcastle Commission quoted in Hurt, *Education in Evolution*, p. 140.

73 WTCA, SWL, *The Warrington Training College Magazine*, September 1902, 'Reminiscences of early days' by a former student, p. 140.

74 SNDPA, MPTC, ms document by J. Murray, SND, *History of Our Lady's*, pp. 62–74.

75 SND, *Sister Mary of St Philip*, p. 185.

76 BPP, Education, Inspector's Reports, HMI Mr Fitch's Report, 1857, p. 492.

77 SND, *Sister Mary of St Philip*, p. 171.

78 BPP, Education, Inspector's Reports, HMI Mr Brookfield's Report, pp. 727–36.

79 SND, *Sister Mary of St Philip*, p. 162.

80 WTCA, SWL, File, student reminiscences, uncatalogued, Memories of Isabel Williams.

81 M. Cullen, 'The growth of the Roman Catholic training colleges for women in England during the nineteenth and twentieth centuries', unpublished University of Durham M. Ed. thesis, 1964, p. 40.

82 WTCA, SWL, File, student reminiscences, uncatalogued. Memories of Isabel Williams.

83 Fuller, *The Churches Train Teachers*, p. 390.

84 SNDPA, MPTC, Murray, *A History of Our Lady's*, p. 34; Linstott, *The Educational Work*, p. 232.

85 Bentley, *Schools for the People*, p. 471.

86 Linstott, *The Educational Work*, p. 246, In 1903, two sisters and one student obtained a Bachelor of Arts degree from London University.

87 This was true of the other Roman Catholic teaching congregations such as the Society of the Sacred Heart. See O'Leary, *Education With a Tradition* and the Society of the Holy Child Jesus; see A Religious of the Society, *The Life of Cornelia Connelly*. For the Irish experience see C. Clear, *Nuns in Nineteenth Century Ireland* (Dublin: Gill and Macmillan, 1987).

88 SNDPA, MPTC, Murray, *History of Our Lady's College*, p. 75.

89 D. Newsome, *Godliness and Good Learning*, (London: Cassell, 1961), p. 17.

90 SNDPA, MPTC, Murray, *History of Our Lady's College*, p. 75.

91 SNDPA, MPTC, A Sister of Notre Dame, *The Foundations of the Sisters of Notre Dame in England and Scotland from 1845 to 1895* (Liverpool, 1895), p. 48.

92 SND, *Sister Mary of St Philip*, p. 223. In 1887, Sister Mary of St Philip became Superior of the Mount Pleasant convent, which meant she had to take charge of the religious as well as the academic side of convent and college life. Sister Theresa of the Passion became acting Principal of the college until 1889 when Sister Mary of St Joseph was appointed.

93 Ibid., pp. 239–40.

94 SNDPA, MPTC, Murray, *History of Our Lady's College*, pp. 77–8.

95 Ibid., p. 85.

96 SNDPA, MPTC, Reminiscence of former High School student quoted in Murray, *History of Our Lady's College*, p. 86.

97 Ibid.

98 In 1870, 3875 women in England and Wales died either of childbirth or puerperal fever. This figure rose to 4,400 in 1899. See Barbara Harrison, 'Women and health', in J. Purvis (ed.), *Women's History: Britain, 1850–1945, An Introduction* (London: UCL Press Ltd., 1997), p. 171.

99 See S. Mumm, 'Lady guerrillas of philanthropy', Chapter 6.

5

THE VINCENTIAN CONTRIBUTION TO ST MARY'S AND TEACHER EDUCATION IN ENGLAND

Philip Walshe, CM

THE PORTRAIT of Canon Thomas Graham in the senior common room at St Mary's College is a reminder of the first 50 years of the college's existence, years summed up in the career of this man as student, member of staff and Principal for 30 years. The Vincentian Fathers in St Mary's College in Hammersmith and later in Strawberry Hill built on the foundations of those 50 years. Canon Graham belonged to the small Brook Green Brotherhood of the early 1850s which had evolved into a college for lay teachers by the time he joined the staff. Under his direction the college quietly prospered. Up to two years before his death the buildings were being expanded. Numbers, nevertheless, were small, at best about 60 students over any two year period. His ill health in the final two years and consequent problems of discipline and administration led the Catholic Poor Schools Committee, the owners of the College, to seek a religious order to provide the continuity and ethos which they desired.[1]

The decision to ask, indeed to pursue, the Vincentians was one of several possible lines of action open to the Committee. The tradition that the college should be administered by priests was taken for granted. That they canvassed privately the religious orders in England traditionally engaged in teaching may be presumed. If so, they soon found that there was little interest in a small, underfunded college for primary teachers serving what was still an impoverished Catholic primary school system. Nor did the Irish province of the Vincentians, with no educational involvement in England at the time, see St Mary's College as anything but an added complication and a burden to their already stretched resources.

On 3 July 1899, clearly aware that a request was likely to be made for staffing for the Hammersmith College, the minutes of the provincial council of the Vincentians record: 'In the event of the

Hammersmith Training College being offered by the Cardinal, except some extraordinary reason be brought forward for accepting it, it be declined without calling a special council.' As late as 1 August the minutes read: 'Ruled that Hammersmith Training College be not taken up for many reasons.'[2]

Cardinal Vaughan wrote on 20 July 1899 to Father Morrissey, the Provincial of the Vincentians: 'I shall be very glad to receive you into the diocese in charge of the Training College.'[3] The Duke of Norfolk, Chairman of the Catholic Schools Committee, wrote tactfully:

> I believe you have expressed a kind willingness to at least consider the proposition as to your Congregation taking charge of St Mary's Training College for Schoolmasters. At a meeting of the Training College Committee here today it was unanimously resolved that your Congregation should be invited to undertake this work . . . I am hoping you may be able to depute one of your Fathers with power to act to come over and arrange matters with us.[4]

On 10 August, writing from Derwent Hall, Sheffield, the Duke of Norfolk sounded less assured:

> I am still entertaining the hope that you may see your way to take the Training College if I meet your difficulty half way as to men. If you would send one man, for instance Fr Byrne of Drumcondra, to take charge, I would furnish him with an assistant priest – a young man, clever and docile, knowing the ways of the place.[5]

Suddenly the picture changed. Cardinal Vaughan wrote, with obvious relief, from his family home at Courtfield, Hay-on-Wye on 25 August: 'I am pleased to find that you can find a second Father to act as Vice-Principal . . . God bless you for having undertaken this work.'[6] Just what finally influenced Father Morrissey and his Council to accept responsibility for St Mary's College does not emerge from the available archival resources. They were severely stretched for personnel with a quickly expanding mission in Australia. They already possessed experience in the administration of a teacher training college in Ireland but cannot have been enamoured of a Committee which was seeking their involvement with only weeks to go before the college was due to reopen for the next academic year.

The agreement, finally signed in January 1900, which entrusted the college to the Congregation of the Mission (Vincentians), gave the appointment of Principal and Directors of the College to the Superior of the Congregation with the proviso that the appointment of the Principal should be as far as possible permanent. Principal and Directors were to be entitled to suitable board, fuel, light, medicine and medical care attendance. The Principal would receive a salary of £120 and the Directors salaries of £80 per annum. The Principal would have full control over the professional staff. The Principal would also have the administration of the finances. The agreement was terminable by either party on six months notice.[7] Thus began for the Vincentians almost a century of involvement with St Mary's and 93 years of direct administration.

It was as administrators that the Vincentians came to St Mary's, responsible for overseeing the work of the professional staff, for the discipline and well-being of the students and for catering and maintenance.[8] This pattern they understood and brought over from previous experience in St Patrick's Teacher Training College in Dublin. In both colleges they had immediate responsibility for religious instruction. In contrast to the Dublin college, at St Mary's the Vincentians fairly quickly began to accept secular teaching appointments, thus increasing the numbers of the resident community and ensuring a greater influence on the students.

The contribution of the Vincentians to St Mary's is first and foremost a matter of continuity of able Principals. Apart from the second decade of the century, these Principals held office for substantial periods of time, and had generally been on the staff of the college for some years before appointment as Principal. Their success as individuals and their contribution reflect in some measure the circumstances of the time in which they held office. It is not easy to make direct comparisons between the small college up to the end of the First World War, the years of educational development and college expansion that continued to the end of the 1960s, and the final third of the century when denominational colleges fought for survival in an educational atmosphere which proclaimed that optimum size was large.

Father William Byrne, Principal 1899–1909, expanded the numbers in the College from 52 when he took office to 116 in his final year. There was an energy evidenced in his administration which caught the attention of the Board of Education Inspectors after he was a year in Office.

> This College now has the prospect of becoming thoroughly efficient. The Principal is energetic and takes a real interest in the welfare of his students. He is ably seconded by his staff . . . The premises have been greatly improved in the past year.[9]

In his 1906 report Father Byrne breezily listed his improvements: 'It only remains for me to chronicle that with our increased numbers the general improvement of the College goes on apace. We have erected a new Manual Training Room, we built a second Fives Court, we have added considerably to the Lavatories, Heating Apparatus, Chapel accommodation etc.'[10] In the previous year the College received approval from the Board of Education to increase its numbers from 70 to 116. Even more important, good administration was enabling the College to fund itself, even with larger numbers, without asking for an increase of grants from the Catholic School Committee. Both the increase in the number of Catholic male teachers coming from the College and the decrease in demand for grants did much to endear Father Byrne to the Committee.

It had not been easy at the start. At the beginning of the decade Father Byrne had to note the

> backwardness of the majority of our candidates both in secular and religious knowledge . . . whilst in religious knowledge only six, that is about 20 per cent of those who entered, passed the Diocesan Examinations . . . Starting with such material we are placed at a decided disadvantage as compared with other Male Training Colleges.[11]

At the same time, as a new broom, anxious to strengthen the discipline of the College, there were complaints against him lodged with the Catholic School Committee, and his dismissal of two members of staff who were deemed unsatisfactory had to be upheld before the Committee. There is evidence too that the Vincentians at this stage were not fully committed to St Mary's, Hammersmith. On 4 June 1905, the Provincial Council in Dublin ruled: 'That Hammersmith be kept on but that the Committee be expected to support the confrères there, and that the Superior and Dean be exempted from teaching.'[12] In his final report in 1909 Father Byrne was able to say:

> The rule was enforced last year of admitting to College only those who had passed the Diocesan Examinations. Candidates who had achieved certain distinction in the Preliminary Certificate List were deliberately passed over, and the preference given to those who had passed the Diocesan Examinations . . . it is much to be hoped that the College shall not be required to make a similar sacrifice again.[13]

The Catholic Education Council summed up their appreciation of

Father Byrne, after his ten years in office, in their resolution at their meeting in June 1909:

> That this Council wishes to express its deep sense of gratitude for the admirable work done by Father Byrne . . . at a time of special difficulty, and for the energy and devotion with which he grappled with a critical situation and also brought about a steady and continuous improvement in the financial condition of the College.[14]

A conventional enough valediction but a good beginning for the Vincentian administration.

His successor, Father Andrew Moynihan (1909–12), dogged by ill health, played a lesser role in the development of the College. Records show that his promotion to the office of Principal was a matter of obedience rather than choice.[15] After the drive of Fr Byrne's years there was space for a Principal whose primary concern was the welfare and happiness of the students. Typically the only building development of his time was a gymnasium. Typically also he did much to foster the annual reunion of Pastmen of the College and the formation of the London, Liverpool, and Manchester and Salford Simmarian Clubs,[16] a tradition of encouragement and support continued by the later Vincentians.

When the question of his successor arose, the rising academic standards of the period brought into question the suitability of Father Edward Sheehy (1912–17) on the grounds that he did not possess an honours degree. The Board of Education and the Catholic Education Council considered that an honours degree was *sine qua non*. Explaining this to his Provincial, Father Moynihan wrote:

> On the occasion of my appointment I represented to the Board that the fact that I was without a University degree should not be a bar on account of the altogether exception (sic) position of Catholics in this matter. I mentioned that it was quite the exception for the Principal of a Catholic Training College or Secondary School to possess a degree and if the regulation was insisted on the area of choice would be seriously limited.[17]

Anderton, Secretary of the Catholic Education Council wrote a revealing letter to the Secretary, Board of Education:

> In reply to your letter of the 20th, 'I would submit that there are certain exceptional circumstances attaching to the above College within the meaning of the regulations. Most of the students are Irishmen and, for disciplinary reasons, it may be desirable that the

Principal should be of the same nationality. Unfortunately, at present, the number of graduates in Honours who are available for the post is somewhat limited, owing to the fact that until recently Irish Catholics [for reasons] which appeared good were not in the habit of frequenting the Universities.[18]

In the end Father Sheehy was appointed for three years only, though this was extended due to the outbreak of war.

Anderton's comment about the desirability of the Principal being an Irishman for disciplinary reasons was illustrated in the problems facing Fr Sheehy in wartime, always a challenge to the administration of an institution. In 1915 the College opened with 112 students. 'One left in October to join the army, and eighteen in December. In February exemption from military service until July was granted to all students.'[19] Disruption of courses would be the pattern for the next five years. Staff also volunteered for service and both staff members and students were soon listed among those who had died on active service. Students on weekend leave regularly stayed in the college. Cutting across this pattern was the agitation connected with Home Rule in Ireland, culminating in the Rebellion of Easter 1916. Father Sheehy had to walk a tightrope between the students, on the one hand, and the Catholic Education Council, on the other, who would regard it as evidence of a failure in discipline if sympathy with the Irish movement were expressed by any of the students.[20]

By 1917 numbers in the College were down to 42 students. Father Sheehy left to become an army chaplain and Father John Campbell (1917–20) was appointed Principal, provisionally due to alleged inadequacy of his degrees. The final year of the war and the re-absorption of demobbed soldiers placed a strain on the College which was not experienced to the same degree by the other Catholic colleges, all of which were women's colleges.

Father Campbell was unfortunate in that the Board of Education chose this time to pressurize the denominational colleges to improve their standards. In his first Report he complained that, 'The work done during the year was hampered considerably by our fluctuating numbers, and the absence of three of the professors in France.'[21] In the following year the College had to provide special courses for 82 students who were ex-servicemen. The Principal's Report recorded that it was 'still a disturbed year with groups leaving at different times'. Under attack, some members of the Catholic Education Council thought that lay staffing of Hammersmith might be a solution. In October 1919 Anderton wrote: 'The Board's officials expressed a strong opinion that the Congregation of the Mission had not been successful in maintaining the efficiency of the College.' A Report of the Joint Meeting of the Training Colleges Sub-Committee declared:

> Some orders have not got the right people wherewith to staff a Training College. At Hammersmith the Vincentians have utterly failed. The Board will not go on with Hammersmith as it is. Hull and Southampton are in danger of losing recognition.[22]

They recommended that the Provincial of the Vincentians be asked whether the community desired to continue managing St Mary's College, Hammersmith.

An examination of the staffing of the College in 1918 suggests that several different agendas were in operation.[23] The staff as listed was a strong one. In the end, the Vincentian Provincial, having sustained Father Campbell in his position as long as possible,[24] appointed two new priests to the staff and appointed Father James Doyle as Principal in the summer 1921.

With the appointment of Father Doyle as Principal the Vincentian administrative contribution to St Mary's College entered a new phase. With an MA and a triple doctorate in divinity no one was likely to query his academic credentials. The uncertainties of the war decade were over. Degree qualification for all teachers was now in the air and this he was well equipped to handle. Yet, to keep things in proportion, we have to note the small scale of the College when the Principal's annual report includes: 'The social life of the College was improved by the addition of a full-sized billiard table.'[25]

There is a vigour about his report for 1921–2, as he expresses pleasure in the approval of degree courses for his students, and regrets that so few take it up due to the desire for immediate employment at the end of the second year. It was a theme of his principalship. Reporting on the first year in Strawberry Hill in 1925–6 he says:

> I must state that it is a matter of much disappointment to the College authorities that few Students are prepared to take a Third-year's Course with a view to obtaining a University Degree. Courses leading to a Degree are taken up by a large number of Students, but unfortunately most Students stop short at a Third-year which would crown their efforts. Excuses for this are invariably based on financial difficulties, but until some means are devised to meet these difficulties, St Mary's College must continue to compare unfav-

ourably with other high-class Training Colleges in the number of Graduates it sends forth from its walls[26]

Deliberately he insisted on taking standards from a larger world than the Catholic community.

His concern with the integration of the training colleges with the universities was recognized in 1925 when the Catholic Education Council appointed him together with its own Chairman to a Board of Education Conference on this subject. By the following year St Mary's College, together with St Charles' College, North Kensington, was included in the draft scheme for the examination of the students in training colleges in and around London in general subjects by the University of London.

He had the energy and imagination to recognize that sentiment should not tie the college to the site in Brook Green, already far too small, despite the building of the past twenty and more years. A satisfactory sale, involving enough money for the purchase of a property at Strawberry Hill and for the building of a college for 150 students was eagerly grasped in 1923 and in two years the college was given a new lease of life in new and unhampered premises. And at no cost to the Catholic Education Council. The Report for 1926 declares with satisfaction:

> St Mary's Training College is now undoubtedly the best building of its kind in the country. The entire cost of the new property and the extensions to the buildings have been met from the proceeds of the sale of the old property at Brook Green, Hammersmith

The Board of Governors of the College also played its part. So too did a sub-committee of the Catholic Education Council set up in 1923 to liaise with the Governors. But Doyle was the Principal on the spot, the active agent in negotiation and in the search for a new site. The day-to-day relationship with architect and builders was his. Moreover, the educational work of the college had to be maintained at a satisfactory level throughout this period of transition.

There were those who sniped at him. As an Irishman with an Irish community he was vulnerable to comment that the facilities of the new College with its 150 places for English students was been taken up unfairly by students from Northern Ireland and from the Orders of Teaching Brothers.

> The acceptance of Students from Northern Ireland, from Malta, and from the Brothers of the De La Salle Community has, I fear, led some people to the belief that outsiders filled vacancies which really

should have been given to Students from England. I take this opportunity of correcting this false impression. The Board of Education limited the number of English Students to 150 at a time when there was no question of accepting Students from Northern Ireland, from Malta, or from the Community of the De La Salle Brothers. These latter Students are supernumerary; they are paid for by their respective Governments, and if their connection with the College ceased, I should have no right to accept a larger number of students from this country. As a matter of fact, the Students from Northern Ireland and the De La Salle Brothers live in separate hostels specially provided for them, and they do not encroach on the accommodation provided for Home Students. Incidentally, I may remark that the admission of these private Students has contributed largely to a better financial condition of the College, as the economic problem of running a College is eased in proportion as the number increases.[27]

The Catholic Education Council had not been imaginative in restricting the new buildings in Strawberry Hill to 150 students. The coming decade would call for a considerable extension. Nevertheless, the pattern until the end of the Second World War was set by the administration of Father Doyle. Numbers of students would remain under 300. The number in the Vincentian Community was sufficient to provide a major contribution to the teaching staff as well as controlling the administration through Principal, Bursar and Dean. As late as 1950 in a staff photograph of 23 members, 9 belonged to the resident clerical community.[28]

In the final years of his principalship Dr Doyle was still complaining: 'I am quite helpless in the matter since the number of vacancies for grant earning students is absolutely limited by the Board of Education.' Gently he prodded the Council: 'Perhaps the time is ripe for approaching the Board with regard to the matter.' As a result, in 1929 we find the Secretary reporting to the Catholic Education Council that 'the Governing Body of St Mary's Training College, Strawberry Hill, has made application to the Board of Education for an increase of the number of recognised places by fifty'.[29] The Board too had approved plans for a further enlargement of the College at the cost of £12,000. Ever conscious of the financial weakness of the Catholic Education Council, Dr Doyle reported that playing fields had been laid out at a cost of £1000 but 'the expense . . . was borne by the College, and there was no appeal for special help from the Council'.[30]

In the same years another ambition of Dr Doyle was achieved when the Training College Delegacy of the University of London was founded, with four male residential colleges in London forming a distinct group under University College, Gower Street. From 1928 onwards the college was to follow a syllabus jointly formulated by University College and the Training Colleges and leading to university certificates. Dr Doyle had been elected by the colleges as their representative on Delegacy and representatives of University College London had been nominated to the Governing Body of St Mary's. Another recognition came in 1929 when the Catholic Education Council appointed him its representative on the Central Advisory Committee for the Certification of Teachers.[31]

Perhaps it was a more gracious age, but certainly his sheer achievement had a lot to do with the sort of recognition he received as he left St Mary's in 1930.

> The Executive Council also invited Dr Doyle to be present at their meeting on Thursday, 30th October 1930, at Caxton Hall, in order that the Chairman of the Council might convey to him personally in the presence of the members an appropriate expression of thanks for his valuable work for the College.[32]

The Report for that year continued: 'The Governing Body of the College have appointed the Revd Vincent MacCarthy, B.A. (Principal 1930–42), the former Vice Principal, as successor to Dr Doyle'.[33] They deliberately underlined his academic and administrative qualification for the position by adding:

> [He] obtained first class honours in mental and moral science in the BA examination of the Royal University of Ireland. He was also for many years Headmaster of Castleknock, and had served on the professional staff of the Irish College in Paris.

The 1930s was for most of its run a period of quiet. It had to be. The Catholic population, like most of the working people of England, was suffering from the financial depression and high unemployment of the early 1930s. The one great social occasion of the period at St Mary's was the hosting in September 1930 of the official Catholic Garden Party in connection with the Catholic Emancipation Centenary Celebration.

In this year too the University Delegacy made an Inspection and reported: 'We understand that the aim of the College is to produce men with an educated and cultural outlook rather than to push as many as possible through the Degree examination'.[34] Was it a snub?

Certainly, it seems to represent a withdrawal from the stance of Dr Doyle who had exerted himself so much to give St Mary's a footing in the university world. Vincent MacCarthy would have rejected neither the report nor the policy of his predecessor. The values recognized by the Delegacy Inspection would have been embraced by all the Vincentian Principals.

In this period pride in the responsibility of administering Strawberry Hill, the eighteenth-century creation of Horace Walpole, led one member of the Vincentian Community, Father John Leonard, to make friends with W.S. Lewis, the American scholar, collector of Walpoliana and editor of the collected works of Horace Walpole. Lewis acknowledged his debts to the Vincentians. Later, during Father Cronin's principalship, a major restoration of the building would be undertaken. Later again, the sheer cost of maintaining the building in an acceptable condition would be one of the financial problems which would weigh heavily on the last Vincentian Principal, Father Beirne.

Through the 1930s there was a certain stagnation in the world of teacher training, even retrogression. In 1933 the Board of Education has been pressing for a reduction of 8 per cent of entrants to training.[35] Towards the end of the decade it seemed that expansion was again possible. In the year before the war there were proposals for a swimming pool and a gymnasium. And Father Vincent MacCarthy, recognized for his persevering work in St Mary's, was reappointed to the Training College Delegacy. But his final years as Principal were to be dominated by the problems of administration in wartime and in preparation for war. There were shelters to be dug, for the Board of Education declared that 'in consequence of the situation of the College in a neutral area, the work of training of teachers should continue in the event of a national emergency'.[36]

Soon the well-organized pattern of college finance was in shreds. Numbers tumbled quickly to about 150. As a result the College was soon in debt, towards which the Vincentian Congregation offered a low interest loan. Uncertainty prevailed as courses were cancelled and then restarted. In November 1940 the college was severely damaged by bombing , greatly reducing its residential capacity and teaching areas. Father MacCarthy had struggled against all these difficulties and early in 1942 his health gave way and he had to retire.

The next six years continued under the cloud of war and its aftermath. The new Principal, Dr Gerald Shannon (1942–8), the only Scot among nine Irish Vincentian Principals, had been on the staff of the College since 1929 and had greatly supported Father MacCarthy in the early war years. To the end of the war the new Principal, still with a greatly reduced number of students, maintained the limited wartime existence of the college. The summer of 1944 brought further bomb damage, laconically reported as: 'luckily most of this was of a superficial nature, although the stained glass window of the Chapel was badly shattered'.[37]

With the war over, this low-key pattern of college life stopped abruptly. Numbers in the college rapidly returned to their pre-war level. There were 232 students in the college in the academic year 1945–6, but courses were out of kilter due to the presence of many ex-servicemen completing their courses or following shortened courses to return them quickly to civilian life and employment. These were older and more experienced men, who found the pattern of training college life and discipline excessively paternalistic. Dr Shannon found these problems of social integration difficult to handle and after six years of service gave way in 1948 to Father Kevin Cronin who in his nineteen years as Principal, 1948–69, would reshape the college both academically and socially.

From 1946 onwards the Secretariat of the Catholic Education Council was in constant touch with the Ministry of Education on the whole question of the extension of facilities in Catholic Training Colleges.[38] Numbers would remain under 300 until 1953. Meanwhile two things occurred in 1948 which were the fruit of careful promotion by Dr Shannon and Fr Cronin. 'This was first year in which Divinity was offered as a subject at the Certificate examination by our students, twelve of whom took the Advanced Course and one hundred and one the Ordinary Course.'[39] For a Catholic college this improved status of Divinity was of the utmost importance. Hitherto religion and religious education had been an unpaid function of the Vincentian priests. The repute of St Mary's in this field had been added to by the work of Father J. Thompson who had greatly contributed to the development of the Westminster Syllabus and Father Cronin had added to this by his influential book, *Teaching the Religion Lesson*.[40] Now there was the possibility of expansion in the Divinity Department in which Vincentians were to play a major role in the coming years and the employment was made possible of lecturers from a wide field of experience. Another development in the same area would come in 1950 when a supplementary course in religious education for qualified teachers was established.[41]

The second event of 1948 was the admission of the college,

provisionally, as a constituent college of the University of London Institute of Education. Two years later, after a visitation to the College by the Institute of Education, St Mary's was admitted a constituent college without limit of time. The policy of the Principals, over a 30-year period, was bearing fruit.

Yet even as these fruits of Vincentian administration were achieved, the beginning of an alternative shape to the college was inaugurated. In 1949, after considerable negotiation and discussion, Mr R.E. Mills was appointed Vice-Principal, 'being the first layman to hold that position in the history of St Mary's College'.[42]

By the mid-1950s Father Cronin was established as a leading figure in the world of teacher training. In 1955 he represented the Catholic Education Council on the Training Colleges Salaries Committee under the chairmanship of Lord Percy.[43] In response to the increasing shortage of specialist teachers in Catholic secondary schools, Father Cronin proposed to establish degree courses at St Mary's in Mathematics and Physical Education in addition to Divinity. The Instrument of Government of the College also required renewal and he was involved in settling difficulties which had arisen due to the divided control of the college between the Catholic Education Council and the Congregation of the Mission.[44]

The decade from 1959 to 1969 saw greater changes in St Mary's than any previous one. In 1959 the Ministry indicated that 12,000 new places were needed in the teacher training colleges. Some 10 per cent of these places would go to Catholic colleges. The Ministry wanted existing colleges to expand to 400 or 500 places and it was indicated that 'small colleges, while being allowed to continue for the time being, could not be sure of their future'. The rhetoric of small and intimate was to be replaced by large and less expensive to run. The Catholic Education Council agreed to the expansion of St Mary's to 500 places at an estimated cost of £138,702.00.[45]

With considerable prescience Father Cronin saw what these developments would mean for the Vincentians. In a letter to his Provincial, Father Christopher O'Leary, in January 1959, he teased out the problems of the present and the future.

> The staffing of these larger colleges presented a further problem. At present a training college staff numbers some twenty or thirty lecturers. In the Catholic colleges a sizeable percentage of these has always been drawn from the religious order that runs the college. In our case of a staff of thirty-four we have twelve Vincentian priests.

Once our student population is nearly doubled our staffing problem will be acute. One possible way of dealing with it would be to
recruit some members of other religious orders onto our staff . . .
This sort of mixed staffing has, however, never been attempted . . .
we have no way of estimating the problems, if there are any, that it
would present.[46]

He searched in the Spring of 1959 for answers and models in the
United States of America.

For the next three years Father Cronin worked with his architects to
create for St Mary's an ambiance that reflected the Catholic character
of the college. A new chapel, modelled on the Cathedral of Albi, with
its fifteen stained glass windows representing the Mysteries of the
Rosary, would be at the centre of the campus, a physical proclamation
of everything the college stood for since its beginning. He sought the
best. His architect was Sir Albert Richardson, president of the Royal
Academy; his creator of stained glass, Gabriel Loire, curator of the
stained glass of Chartres Cathedral.[47] Not only were new buildings put
in place, but the old buildings were refurbished and the Walpole
mansion decorated with sensitivity. Finance was a major headache, but
Father Cronin was able to call on the resources of the Vincentians for
a key loan of £45,000.00 at low interest rates.[48] The main part of the
new buildings was ready for use at the start of 1962, the chapel and
library in the following summer. At the same time the large houses
bordering the college on Waldegrave Park were purchased one by one
and refurbished to serve as student hostels.

No sooner was this stage of expansion complete than it became
desirable to expand St Mary's to 1000 places, and Father Cronin was
faced with the then revolutionary decision for a Catholic college to
take women students and become a mixed college.[49] In connection
with this Father Cronin sought unsuccessfully to have new hostels
opened by the Daughters of Charity of St Vincent de Paul so that the
twin congregations could work together in the college. He argued
that this would be a less expensive option.[50] The expansion went
ahead, and by 1964 with 800 students on campus Father Cronin was
for a period head of the largest teacher training college in the
country. In this year he also achieved another academic ideal when
the Robbins Committee advocated the four-year BEd degree for
teachers – new territory for Catholic colleges.

The target figure of 1000 students was reached in 1966 with the
buildings ready for that number. The costs of the building programme had risen considerably. To support the Governors in

providing their share in the increased costs Father Cronin imaginatively undertook to provide profits from the letting of the college buildings during vacations.[51]

In the 1960s St Mary's appeared to be on the crest of a wave. The new chapel, reflecting the encouragement and vision offered by Father Cronin to his architect, seemed to symbolize St Mary's as a leading Catholic college. The Vincentian Community was at its largest, with some fifteen priests in the resident community. Returning past students enthused in the reflected glory. But change was coming rapidly. Maybe the most significant change for Vincentians had been in the 1950s when the office of Dean ceased to exist. A single dean supervising the day-to-day activities and discipline of the student body belonged to the life of a small enclosed college, more akin to a secondary boarding school or a theological seminary. The single dean was enormously influential. The memories of students of the period make this quite evident. He played a larger role in their lives than did the Principal and the choice of suitable men for this post was a major responsibility for the Vincentian Congregation. The Board of Education's Report of Inspection for 1936–7 referred to the dean in these words: 'Dean or House Tutor to whom the College owes more than is realised. The Principal and the Dean are responsible for the instruction in Religion and their personal contact with the students has a deep influence.'[52] But it was not the form of tutelage which was deemed appropriate in the 1950s when teacher colleges were moving formally into the university sector. Moreover, the expansion of the college made it impractical for one dean to be responsible for all student discipline.

The Vincentian Principal functioned effectively because he had the dedicated support of his community. His relationship to these was perhaps affected by personalities, but it was both more demanding and more at ease than with members of staff not tied to him by a religious bond, whether or not such people saw themselves as career people or as bearers of a vocation. When it became clear that Vincentians could no longer function in the pivotal administrative roles of the college, when there ceased to be a Vincentian Dean and Bursar (1965) and Vice-Principal (1983), the original purpose for which the Vincentians were appointed to the college would become more and more difficult.

In another area, too, Father Cronin felt the limitation of numbers in the Vincentian staffing. In a statement for the eyes of his Provincial in 1956, when he was about to lose a Vincentian member of the Education Department, he wrote:

> There are three full-time lecturers in Education, of whom two are confreres [i.e. Vincentians]. This preponderance of confreres in the Department of Education has always appealed to us here . . . as it is in effect the guarantee that the training of the students has a positive Catholic and religious and Vincentian stamp . . . [The alternative is an] educational philosophy that . . . [is] substantially the secular and non-religious philosophy of the official text-books.[53]

With the support of his community, Father Cronin was the ideal person to head St Mary's in a period of expansion. He was forced, however, into decisions which would make a Vincentian principal-ship impossible to maintain in the future. Just a year before he retired from the principalship, honoured since 1962 with the CBE, the first hints of trouble ahead came with a report that the Depart-ment of Education was planning to 'rationalize' the Colleges of Education provision in units of not less than 750 or 900 students.[54] There was no threat to St Mary's in this policy, but it did hint at a ruthless drive for economy, retrenchment and efficiency which over the coming years would ensure the end of many colleges of educa-tion and the loss of independence by others.

Father Cronin's successors would operate in a more oppressive climate. Since the late 1960s the powers of the Principal had been considerably restricted, his room for independent action or even to rely on his community reduced, by the institution of the Academic Board with right to consultation and decision. Until that time the Principal, provided he was secure in his relations with the Governors and with the Catholic Education Council, was able to deal with the internal affairs of the College according to his personal judgement, limited only by the routine of consultation with his Domestic Council of senior members of the Vincentian community.

In his report to the AGM of the Catholic Education Council in 1972 Father Thomas Cashin (Principal 1969–76) reminded the Council that if the James proposals for the first two years of the course were adopted to any extent, the College would have to face up to the question of whether they were prepared to go into the field of general higher education divorced from teacher education. His reading of the situation was that the years to come would show more people qualified for higher education who could conveniently be catered for in the present colleges.[55] What he faced was as new in the

Catholic teacher training world as the move to mixed colleges had been six years before. The White Paper on teacher training of 1973 proposed a substantial broadening of function for the great majority of colleges of education that would involve them in much closer assimilation into the rest of the non-university sector. It was recognized that some of the smaller colleges were inconveniently located for development into general purpose institutions. It was proposed to reduce the intake of teacher students by 10 per cent in 1974, increasing the reduction in the following years.

There followed a few years of tension as the College, under Father Cashin's guidance, sought to find its feet in a new world. In 1974 there was a serious proposal that St Mary's would unite with Maria Assumpta College. Faced with an unyielding expectation from the negotiators of that college that a union would involve the disappearance of St Mary's as a separate entity, Father Cashin insisted that in any union St Mary's would be the dominant element, expanding by absorbing the smaller college. After prolonged negotiations and exchange of correspondence with the Department of Education and Science, the Secretary of State approved the proposal of St Mary's College to remain a free-standing institution catering for 1200 to 1250 students.

Up to this period the Vincentian community by its numbers within the staff made it clear that the purpose of the College was to be a Catholic college. This was symbolized by their presence. As student numbers increased the presence of the Vincentian community impinged less on the student body, and its influence declined. This was made more obvious when the effects of Vatican II on the Catholic Church came in the mid-1960s. The Anglo-Irish Province of the Vincentians lost some 10 per cent of its members within a few years. More serious still, its sources of recruitment dried up. Ordinations after 1965 were much fewer than in the previous period. To this must be coupled a crisis of identity among younger priests which made some unwilling to be involved in academic life. Moreover, the ability of a small religious congregation of priests to continue to provide staffing with appropriate academic qualification was limited. By the mid-1970s it was clear that priest staffing could not be maintained at the level of earlier years and by the early 1980s it was clear that the traditional role of the Vincentians could not be sustained. With surprising rapidity the weighting of the Vincentians in the academic, social and pastoral life of the college evaporated. Since the ending of the office of Dean in the 1950s, Vincentian priests had acted as residential wardens of student hostels and so had close involvement in student life. Age and numbers were making this impractical, and with the retirement of Vincentians from the executive Vice Principalship with responsibility for student affairs in 1983 something of the *raison d'être* of a religious congregation in St Mary's would come to an end.

Meanwhile, the problems of that post-Vatican II period explain in part divisions among the Governors about the continuance of St Mary's under a Vincentian Principal when Father Cashin, already seriously ill, retired in 1976. The Instrument of Government permitted either a closed appointment restricted to the candidates submitted by the Vincentian Provincial, or an open appointment which might lead to the appointment of a non-Vincentian Principal. The situation was now very different from 1948 when Father Cronin was appointed. In the end it was decided not to break with tradition on this occasion and Father Desmond Beirne (Principal 1976–92) was appointed.

The Colleges of Education lived uneasily on the edge of the university world. The crisis of the early part of Father Beirne's principalship was the decision of the University of London Institute of Education, announced at the beginning of the 1980s, to shed its constituent colleges. The Institute of Education was willing to validate courses in education, but not the wide range of academic departmental courses which the colleges were now running. Within a six-month period the colleges were forced to find new validator, a university preferably, alternatively CNAA. With other colleges also in the same situation, the range of options open to St Mary's was limited. Decisive action had to be taken by Father Beirne and his administrative team. Competing with other colleges with a similar mission, they visited universities spread over a wide area, though obviously a university in the South East had much to commend it in terms of convenience. The universities were in a position to choose and make demands. In the end St Mary's College forged a link with the University of Surrey. The pattern of academic life which had grown in the familiar connection with the London Institute of Education was replaced by a new broom and one not always sympathetic to the traditions of St Mary's. A new set of relationships had to be fostered at the cost of anxiety among staff members. Not until the two years after the end of Father Beirne's principalship was the college able to call itself St Mary's University College,[56] a constituent college of the University of Surrey.

In a small college, buffeted by change, much of the skill of leadership lies in riding the storm. The real struggles of these years were generated by two interrelated things, finance and numbers. Growing costs and restricted finance meant that the wide range of departments and subjects that were the outcome of the expansive years had to be looked at carefully. Small departments were not viable in this atmosphere. Repeatedly Father Beirne had to make hard decisions to close departments in the interests of the survival of the whole College. Not all decision were his own. The 1980s saw the control of finance passing more firmly to the Board of Governors, whose new control meant that they could set priorities which a Principal had to accept. The other problem, the need to increase recruitment of students, was only solved satisfactorily when St Mary's became one of the UCCA-listed colleges in 1990, bringing larger numbers of applications and students with higher qualifications.

It has been noted already that the administrative role of the Vincentians was technically in the hands of the Principal alone. His pastoral effectiveness, however, depended on the outreach of key members of the community. One of the features of Father Beirne's principalship was the emergence of a new Vincentian contribution in the form of a college chaplain. Until the 1960s there had been no college chaplain. All the priests gave their service and were available for whatever church duties the college needed. The social functions of a chaplain were also covered by them and partly by the Dean. Gradually the need for an office more specifically dedicated to the religious welfare of students emerged. This was, of course, a commonplace in colleges not endowed with a priest community. In the new chapel built in the 1960s Father Cronin had included a flat for a chaplain, later absorbed into the expanding Library. The first chaplain doubled as head of the Divinity Department. For many years the Vincentian community maintained one of its priests as unsalaried chaplain until, in the 1980s, the chaplain became a formal official of the college. By 1992, with more women than men in the College, progression was made to a chaplaincy team with a priest and a woman chaplain. It was both an obvious development and a necessary one as the time came for the Vincentians to withdraw from the role that had begun in 1899.

Father Desmond Beirne retired from the principalship in 1992. The Vincentian Provincial did not put forward Vincentian candidates to succeed him. Since that time the number of Vincentians on the staff of St Mary's has declined from three in 1992 to one member of academic staff as the century comes to an end. A place on the Board of Governors allows the Vincentian Congregation to continue in a small way to share its accumulated experience. The series of ten Vincentian Principals had nursed St Mary's from a small primary teacher college of some 50 students, catering for a poor section of the education system, to a Catholic college delivering university degrees and catering for the education of teachers in a campus enriched by students of many disciplines, where Catholic students can integrate into the broader culture of the country as a whole.

NOTES

1   V. Revd E.J. Cullen, Principal of St Patrick's Training College, *The Origins and Development of Irish Vincentian Foundations, 1833–1933* (Dublin: privately published, 1933), pp. 140–1.

2   Minutes of Provincial Council, Vincentian Archives, Dublin.

3   Letter in Vincentian Archives.

4   Letter sent on 27 July 1899 from Norfolk House, St James Square, Vincentian Archives.

5   Letter in Vincentian Archives, Dublin.

6   Ibid.

7   Original Agreement in Vincentian Archives, Dublin.

8   Agreement signed on 13 January 1900.

9   Annual Report of the Catholic School Committee 1900 (London: Printed for the Catholic School Committee), p. 23–4.

10 Report of the Catholic Education Council for England Wales and Scotland and Annual Report of the Catholic School Committee (London: Printed for the Catholic Education Council) 1905, p. 36.

11 Annual Report of the Catholic School Committee 1900 (London: Printed for the Catholic School Committee), 1900, p. 23.

12 Provincial Council Records, Vincentian Archives, Dublin.

13 Report of the Catholic Education Council for England, Wales and Scotland and Annual Report of the Catholic School Committee (London: Printed for the Catholic Education Council) 1908, p. 29.

14 Catholic Education Council Annual Report 1908, p. 20.

15 'Fr Moynihan was not present at the opening of the Council and in his absence it was agreed that his name should be submitted to the Catholic School Committee . . . for the vacancy in Hammersmith.' Minutes of the Provincial Council, 12 November 1908, Vincentian Archives, Dublin.

16 *Centenary Record of St Mary's College: Hammersmith 1850–1925, Strawberry Hill 1925–1950* (London: St Mary's College, 1950), p. 31.

17 Vincentian Archives, Dublin.

18 Copy of letter in Vincentian Archives, Dublin.

19 Catholic Education Council Annual Report 1916, p. 33.

20 Catholic Education Council Annual Report 1915, p. 18.

21 Catholic Education Council Annual Report 1919, p. 31.
22 Documents in Vincentian Archives, Dublin.
23 Letter from Father J. Walshe, Provincial, to Anderton, 12 February 1918, Vincentian Archives, Dublin.
24 Minutes of Provincial Council, Vincentian Archives, Dublin.
25 Catholic Education Council Annual Report 1922.
26 Catholic Education Council Annual Report 1926, p. 53.
27 Catholic Education Council Annual Report 1926.
28 St Mary's College Centenary Record, p. 92.
29 Catholic Education Council Annual Report 1929, p. 22.
30 Catholic Education Council Annual Report 1928, p. 43.
31 Catholic Education Council Annual Report 1929, p. 31.
32 Catholic Education Council Annual Report 1930, p. 32.
33 Ibid.
34 Quoted in Catholic Education Council Annual Report 1929.
35 Catholic Education Council Annual Report 1933, p. 19.
36 Letter from Board of Education quoted in Catholic Education Council Annual Report 1939, p. 18.
37 Catholic Education Council Annual Report 1944.
38 Catholic Education Council Annual Report 1946, p. 14.
39 Catholic Education Council Annual Report 1949, p. 36.
40 Kevin Cronin, *Teaching the Religion Lesson* (London: Paternoster Press, 1952).
41 Catholic Education Council Annual Report 1951, p. 29.
42 Ibid., p. 30.
43 Catholic Education Council Annual Report 1955, p. 33.
44 Catholic Education Council Annual Report 1955, *passim.*
45 Catholic Education Council Annual Report 1959, pp. 13–14.
46 Letter in Vincentian Archives, Dublin.
47 Colloque, *Journal of the Irish Province of the Congregation of the Mission*, Autumn 1992.
48 Catholic Education Council Annual Report 1961, p. 13.
49 Catholic Education Council Annual Report 1963, p. 15.
50 Ibid., p. 23.
51 Catholic Education Council Annual Report 1966, p. 12.
52 Board of Education: Full Inspection Reports on Training Colleges, No. 52, July 1937. (Report of Inspection of Strawberry Hill, St Mary's Training College, Middlesex, held in the session 1936–7. Inspector Mr H. Allsopp, H.M.I.) Published by HMSO.
53 Vincentian Archives, Dublin.
54 Catholic Education Council Annual Report 1967, p. 21.
55 Catholic Education Council Annual Report 1972.
56 Note from Editors: Following the introduction of the Teaching and Higher Education Act 1998 the title 'University College' is now restricted to institutions with taught degree awarding powers.

6

ST MARY'S COLLEGE HAMMERSMITH: ITS EARLY DEVELOPMENT IN THE CONTEXT OF MID-NINETEENTH-CENTURY TEACHER TRAINING

Noreen Nicholson

INTRODUCTION

AS A Catholic foundation originally intended for the training of religious teachers, St Mary's College at Hammersmith had its own distinctive character. Its development nevertheless formed part of the great expansion of teacher training in Britain in the mid-nineteenth century, and it is in this context that various aspects of the college's early years will be considered: who its students were, their daily life, what they learned, how and by whom they were taught, and what they went on to do. Before turning to these it may be helpful to sketch in the background of teacher training in general and of the situation in the Catholic community at the time the college was established.

The idea that teachers should receive preparation for their work was not new, but only began to take practical shape on a significant scale in the UK in the nineteenth century. Early initiatives were based on the monitorial systems devised by Lancaster and Bell, and combined training in teaching techniques with some instruction in basic subjects. Training was limited to a few months, most recipients were adults and many were already engaged in teaching. It took place in model or central schools established by two voluntary societies, the National Society for the Education of the Poor in the Principles of the Established Church and the British and Foreign School Society, and by a number of Church of England dioceses. The monitorial system also prevailed in Ireland in the teacher training institutions of the voluntary Kildare Place Society and, from the early 1830s, the National Board of Education.

Growing dissatisfaction with the monitorial system, both on educational grounds and because of its perceived lack of moral content, led some of those concerned with popular education to look at methods in use in European countries, particularly with regard to training teachers of very young children, the combination of personal education with vocational training and the stress laid on character formation. Two important foundations of the 1830s influenced by the new trends were the Home and Colonial Schools Society's establishment in London, providing short periods of training in Pestalozzian methods for governesses and infant teachers, and David Stow's Glasgow Normal School, where students were trained in collective methods of teaching and four model schools offered experience of different ages and social groups.

Initially, provision of schools for the poorer classes came about through voluntary efforts inspired by a range of motives. While many supporters of popular education sought to improve the moral and physical condition of the children and some to foster the development of their abilities, others were more interested in securing social stability. All but a handful of radical thinkers, however, were united in one belief – that education must be firmly grounded in religion. The churches and the educational societies were wary of intervention by the state which might compromise their independence, and opposed to any proposals for secular schooling or the non-denominational system operating in Ireland. Their influence, especially that of the Established Church, ensured that the government subsidies first given on a limited scale in 1833 were channelled through the voluntary societies.

The victory at school level was extended to the training of teachers after the defeat in 1839 of a plan put forward by Dr James Kay (later Kay-Shuttleworth), Secretary of the newly established Committee of Council on Education, for a Normal School based on Christian principles but respecting the rights of conscience, that is to say a non-denominational foundation. Funds set aside for the building of Normal and Model Schools were then allocated to the two major voluntary societies.

From that time onwards the number of institutions dedicated to teacher training grew rapidly and residential colleges offering longer courses began, in England and Wales, to replace earlier forms of training. In Ireland training of teachers remained based on model schools, and in Scotland was mainly non-residential. The new-style colleges catered for younger people as well as experienced teachers, and offered a curriculum which included considerable elements of personal and social education. The majority were connected with the Church of England through the National Society or diocesan Boards of Education, while a few represented the Evangelical tendency within the church. The British and Foreign School Society continued to train teachers at its institution in Borough Road, London, which combined a residential college with large model schools, and colleges were in due course established by the Catholic, Wesleyan and Congregational communities. Two attempts to provide training specifically designed for Poor Law school teachers were short-lived. St John's College at Battersea was founded as an independent venture in 1840 by Kay and his former colleague at the Poor Law Commission, Edward Carleton Tufnell; despite obtaining grants, it could not pay its way and was handed over in 1843 to the National Society. The second, Kneller Hall, which was founded in the late 1840s and whose Principal, Frederick Temple, later became Archbishop of Canterbury, closed after a few years.

Battersea and two National Society institutions opened in 1841, St Mark's and the women's college Whitelands, both in Chelsea, were among early colleges able to accommodate a large number of students; so too were the diocesan foundations at Chester and York, and the non-denominational Borough Road. Large colleges of later foundation included the Evangelical Cheltenham, the Wesleyan college at Westminster and the Catholic colleges at Hammersmith and Liverpool. In the few colleges which catered for both men and women contact between the two sets of students was restricted.

The early foundations had an experimental flavour, often reflecting the personalities and convictions of their Principals who, though they might technically be answerable to Committees or Boards of Governors, at institutional level had managerial responsibility and a large measure of discretion. In Church of England men's colleges the Principal was normally a clergyman, and this was the case in many women's colleges also, the chief female officer – the Lady Superintendent – acting as a domestic rather than an academic manager. Most Principals undertook a teaching role and, particularly before the period of government contribution to running costs, often carried out a very substantial part of the instruction. Many of them had previous experience of teaching, though rarely in elementary schools for the poor.

A number of the early Principals were men whose academic abilities were complemented by strong personalities. They had a clear vision of what they wished to accomplish, and the strength and self-confidence to mould their colleges in accordance with it. While it is not possible in this context to consider in detail the Principals of non-Catholic colleges, reference can be made to a few of the most influential. Among these must surely be classed Kay who incorporated into his management of Battersea in its first crucial years many features he had admired in the idealistic educational communities of Vehrli and others in Switzerland, and the schools of teaching Brothers in France. Of the Church of England clergymen who headed colleges, two long-serving pioneers particularly deserve mention. Dr Rigg, Principal of Chester College from 1839 to 1869, had previously been Senior Mathematical and Philosophical Master at the Royal Institute in Liverpool; a devotee of scientific and technical education, he combined his duties at the training college with the Headship of a Commercial and Agricultural (later Science) School on the same site. The Revd Derwent Coleridge, Principal of St Mark's from 1841 to 1864, had been Headmaster of Helston Grammar School in Cornwall; at St Mark's he continued the grammar school tradition of teaching the classics. He believed in broadening the social and intellectual horizons of the students, and the course offered at the college in the early days was designed as useful training for potential clergymen as well as teachers. Non-denominational Borough Road had two distinguished Principals in the period covered by this chapter: James Cornwell and Joshua Fitch, both of whom had received training at the college. Cornwell worked for the Society in a number of capacities including inspector before his appointment as Principal of the college in 1846, while Fitch served as an assistant teacher in the model school and was appointed Headmaster of Kingsland Road School in London in 1844. Having taken external London University BA and MA degrees, he joined the staff at the Borough Road college, became Vice Principal and then Principal on Cornwell's retirement in 1855. He subsequently became an HMI.

During the early period of state grants, which were for building only, there was minimal official intervention in the conduct of the colleges, thus allowing Principals freedom to shape them in accordance with their ideals. After a good deal of resistance and negotiation of terms, church authorities and voluntary societies agreed to inspection of schools and colleges as a condition of aid, but the control was very light; inspectors were observers and advisers, rather than judges or examiners. The balance began to change, in the schools first and subsequently in the colleges, with the establishment in 1846 of a government-funded scheme of apprenticeship in schools and of scholarships to the colleges, which also began to receive aid with running costs. Designed to enhance the numbers and educational attainments of recruits to teaching, the scheme brought with it closer official oversight of colleges and, ultimately, a considerable measure of intervention including prescribed syllabuses, oral tests conducted by the inspectors, and examination papers set and marked centrally.

The Revised Codes of the early 1860s, following on the Newcastle Commission's enquiry into the state of popular education in England, led to a narrowing of the colleges' syllabuses and to stricter controls over funding. Capital grants had already been discontinued in 1860; subsequently a ceiling was placed on running costs and grants earned for individual students were delayed until two years' satisfactory service in one school had been certified. These measures, coupled with a temporary decline in the number of pupil-teachers, made the situation very difficult for a number of colleges, with several threatened and a few actual closures. In 1870 the voluntary principle was breached in respect of elementary schooling when School Boards were set up to fill any gaps in provision. The colleges, however, while in many cases supplying teachers to the new type of school, continued as voluntary aided institutions retaining their church connections. They were supplemented, but not supplanted, towards the end of the nineteenth century by day training colleges linked to universities.

The rapid growth of population in the first decades of the nineteenth century and its increasing concentration in urban and industrial areas had heightened public awareness of the need to extend and improve popular education. All denominations were affected, but Catholics faced particular difficulties in making provision for the schooling of their poor children. A steady stream of immigration from Ireland since the beginning of the century meant that the Catholic community on the mainland had grown more quickly than the population as a whole, and it contained a disproportionate number of the poorest members of society, many of whom lived in crowded and unhealthy conditions in the large towns. Voluntary initiatives on the part of the clergy and of lay people of every social class had, since the relaxation of the penal laws in the late eighteenth century, resulted in the establishment of a considerable number of day and Sunday schools; nevertheless many children remained without any form of schooling or were drafted into Ragged Schools which were perceived as potential agents of proselytization.

A problem already serious was made more acute with the massive flow of Irish immigration during and after the famine years.

The shortage of schools was one cause of concern, another was the uneven quality of teaching. Precise figures are not available but it is likely that the majority of teachers of Catholic schools in the 1840s were not qualified, either through training or by virtue of their own education, to carry out their work to an acceptable standard. Some teachers had received training in Ireland: both lay men and women instructed in monitorial methods in the model schools and members of religious communities such as the Irish Christian Brothers and the Sisters of Mercy. Religious orders in England also provided training on a small scale: Sisters of Mercy at Birmingham, Nottingham and Derby, Sisters of Notre Dame at Northampton, Sisters of St Paul at Banbury and Sisters of the Holy Child Jesus at Derby and later St Leonard's. A few men were trained at the Rosminians' Ratcliffe College in Leicestershire.

The issues surrounding the extension of government aid to the Catholic community are considered elsewhere in this volume. Here it is sufficient to say that the ecclesiastical authorities, through the agency of the Catholic Poor School Committee (henceforward referred to as CPSC) which they established in 1847, availed themselves of it to facilitate one of their prime aims, the improvement of the moral and educational standards of schools through the provision of teachers qualified for this task. The clear preference of the church was for religious teachers, who were the principal educators of all classes of society in the Catholic countries of Europe and had traditionally taught English Catholics of the upper class, abroad in penal times and in England once again since the turn of the century. Earlier hopes of setting up a monastic training college were reinforced by resolutions at public meetings of Catholics in London and York in the spring of 1848 and the CPSC quickly took action to promote teacher training, giving financial assistance to existing convent projects and preparing for the establishment of a male college by sending to Ploermel in Brittany a group of young men to be trained in the methods of the teaching order founded by the Abbé Lamennais. It was intended that they should form the core of an English institution, and this was established in Hammersmith at the end of 1850 when the first Brotherhood students returned from France. Brook Green House, purchased by the CPSC to house the new venture, had been built as a boarding school in the late eighteenth century; a chapel, refectory and large lecture room were added, and subsequently a large Practising School with dormitory accommodation for college students above it.[1]

Training of novices as teachers continued through the 1850s but it was clear almost from the start that the numbers coming forward would be insufficient to make the institution viable either in financial terms or as a significant provider of teachers for boys' schools. In view of this shortage, and the supply of potential recruits opening up as pupil-teachers completed apprenticeships in Catholic schools, it was decided to open a lay department at the college, which received its first intake in January 1855. Two religious orders of women already engaged in preparing teachers volunteered to conduct training on a larger scale, the Sisters of Notre Dame establishing a college under government inspection at Mount Pleasant in Liverpool, and the Sisters of the Holy Child Jesus at St Leonard's in Sussex. Catholic girls were able to compete for Queen's Scholarships in December 1855, for entry to the colleges in 1856.

The men and women who took charge of the Catholic colleges[2] were dedicated educationists, with a clear vision of the spiritual and moral values they wished to communicate to the students in their charge. The women were especially notable in that, within the boundaries set by their orders and by government regulations, they had a degree of independence which was surely envied by their Protestant contemporaries. At Liverpool, Sister Mary of St Philip was effectively in charge of teacher training from the establishment of the college until her retirement in the 1890s; the college was outstandingly successful in the religious and secular training it gave to current students, and innovative in its continuing advice and support to those it had trained. Mother Cornelia Connelly, the American convert who established the Order of the Holy Child Jesus and headed the college at St Leonard's for most of its short life, brought to her work a belief in the ability of young women to grapple with difficult academic subjects which was rare at this time; she sought to cultivate judgement and understanding in her students, giving these faculties priority over memory.

The first Principal of St Mary's was the Revd Brother Melaine, who accompanied the small group of students travelling from Brittany to the newly established college at Hammersmith in 1850. He was recalled to France within a year and was succeeded by the Revd John Glenie who took up the post in November 1851, having spent some time at Ploermel studying the Abbé Lamennais' methods.[3] A convert and graduate of Oxford, he had been Head of a Catholic Middle

School in London and a lecturer at Oscott College. As Principal he was very active in teaching, in the establishment of the Practising School and in the development of the lay department at the end of 1854. He received high praise from HMI Marshall for what he had accomplished virtually unaided in his first year of office;[4] of the Practising School it was reported in 1853 that it 'owed almost all its most pleasing and valuable features' to Glenie's 'sound judgement and affectionate supervision'.[5] In 1856 Glenie accompanied HMI Stokes on his official inspector's tour through parts of Scotland and Lancashire,[6] thus familiarizing himself with schools of the kind from which his students were drawn and in which they might seek posts when trained.

Glenie was succeeded in 1861 by the Oratorian Father James Boon Rowe, a Cambridge graduate; he had first-hand knowledge of schools for the poor and the sort of conditions which his students would meet in their work through his involvement with the foundations at Drury Lane. Unusually for the Principal of a residential college he did not live on the premises but travelled daily from central London. Rowe took over at 'an unexampled point of depression'[7] when the college had considerable debts and the intake of students in January 1861, due to a high failure rate in the scholarship examination, was only eight. He put great effort into increasing the number of students and keeping the college on a sound financial footing once the existing debts had been cleared by the CPSC. He allowed the students greater autonomy,[8] and broadened the range of teaching staff.

Thomas Graham, a former Brotherhood student who had subsequently been ordained, became Principal in 1869 having served as Vice Principal since 1861. His period of service, most of which falls outside the scope of this chapter, is remarkable on many counts, not least for its length – 30 years – and the stability which this gave to the college through a period of change and difficulties. His influence over generations of Catholic schoolmasters was profound, leading his obituarist to write 'Who shall measure his work? Ask the army of teachers who owe most of what is good in them to the beautiful teaching of his great example.'[9]

The detailed consideration which follows of the functioning of the colleges in the period to 1870 draws extensively on the annual reports of the CPSC and of the government inspectors of Catholic schools and training colleges: T.W. Marshall, S.N. Stokes, J.R. Morell and J. Lynch. The personal interest in and commitment to the development of Catholic education of these inspectors, who had often known college students as pupil-teachers or even as school-children, are clearly evident in their official reports.

THE STUDENT BODY AND ITS RECRUITMENT

Who were the students at St Mary's in its first years? Unfortunately, little information is available about the earliest entrants, and even the number who passed through the religious department is uncertain. In his report to the education authorities following a visit of inspection in December 1852 Marshall recorded that

> the number of students actually in the house at this time is twenty-five. The greater part of the work in the house and garden being, however, performed by a few of the number, they cannot all be regarded as regular students.[10]

The CPSC's Annual Report for 1854 refers to the college having had under its care about 26 subjects and having sent out about seven teachers; all of the 'subjects', however, may not have been trainee teachers.[11] St Mary's Centenary Record lists the sixteen Brotherhood students whose names could be traced.[12] Of these, it is known that twelve had received their initial training at Ploermel;[13] two of the others were Thomas Graham and Thomas Capel, to whose future careers reference is made in other sections of this chapter. The students' names indicate an Irish provenance in many cases, and both Graham's and Capel's families had come from Ireland to the mainland. Graham himself was born in Scotland, while Capel was born in Waterford and brought up in Hastings, where his father served with the Coastguard.

It is likely that many of the postulants came from modest families unable to afford the full entrance fee of £25; the Conditions of Admission to the Novitiate made provision for partial or total exemption,[14] while in some cases the fees may have been met by a patron. Such arrangements would be in line with the position in a number of other colleges where, before the institution of Queen's Scholarships, many students were maintained by patrons or aided by exhibitions. A report of 1841 on Battersea refers to pupil-teachers being placed there by patrons who contributed £20 a year towards their expenses, and to older students being trained for the schools of gentlemen known to the promoters. At Chester in 1844 eight students were paying their own fees, eighteen were paid for by parents, nine by patrons, and fourteen held exhibitions, while at Cheltenham Governors were asked to make a financial contribution and in return could recommend students.[15]

In these early years the students in the colleges covered a wide age range. Battersea had its two groups, pupil-teachers 'of little more than 13 years of age', and a mature group, mostly between 20 and 30, at Chester in 1844 the range was from 17 to 37, St Mark's accepted students as young as 15 and at Whitelands in the 1840s the youngest students were 16, while some were over 25. The 1852 Conditions of Admission to St Mary's specified the most suitable age for entry as between 17 and 25, but the first group going to Ploermel had included both younger boys and an experienced teacher in his forties.[16]

The establishment of a system of government-funded apprenticeships and scholarships meant that colleges acquired a natural, though not always sufficient, source of recruits. Private students could still enrol and non-pupil-teachers sat for Queen's Scholarships, but the bulk of entrants to teacher training came to be drawn from those completing apprenticeships in inspected elementary schools. The system, which imposed a measure of standardization in respect of the age and minimum educational attainments of student teachers, applied to the lay department at St Mary's from its opening at the end of 1854. From that time on fuller information is available to us, from the annual reports of the CPSC and of inspectors' visits, and from a Register of Students preserved at the college. The dates of birth and of entry to St Mary's of students in the new department were recorded in the Register, together with the places they came from, previous occupations and classification in the certificate examination. In many cases their careers after leaving can be traced for several years.

As St Mary's was the only college training male teachers for Catholic elementary schools, its catchment area embraced all of England, Scotland and Wales. Other colleges which recruited widely were those run by the large educational societies and those of the smaller Protestant denominations, while the diocesan colleges for the most part drew on their own localities. For female Catholic pupil-teachers geographical situation seems to have been the main factor influencing choice, but some opted on the basis of familiarity with the order conducting the college, the majority of pupil-teachers from the Holy Child Jesus schools in Preston, for instance, going to St Leonard's.

Of the first six secular students who entered St Mary's in January 1855 two had been pupil-teachers in Edinburgh, two in Bolton, one in Stockport and one at the Swinton Industrial School near Manchester, a Poor Law school where there had been some difficulty in having his apprenticeship confirmed by the inspector.[17] Scotland and the North of England, particularly Lancashire, continued to be very well represented in the student body, reflecting the considerable Catholic populations of these areas and the high standards of those schools which had been among the first to apply for pupil-teachers and to put masters forward for the certificate examination. Encouragement from Stokes, the inspector for Catholic schools in the Northern District in the mid-1850s, who as Secretary of the CPSC had been involved in the foundation of St Mary's and retained a close interest in its progress, may well have caused some potential recruits to overcome anxieties about going so far from home, while the CPSC's assistance with travelling expenses helped to remove the major deterrent of cost. Stokes did, however, repeatedly urge the wisdom of establishing a male training college in the North of England; he suggested Manchester, but would have been content with 'some accessible part of Lancashire'; he pointed to the flourishing condition of the Liverpool women's college, in the midst of an immense Catholic population.[18]

In the early years schools in and around London sent few students to St Mary's; the first, in January 1857, was from the college's own Practising School. Later in the decade London's representation was increased, with pupil-teachers from schools in Fulham, Wapping, Poplar, and Commercial Road succeeding in the scholarship examination; in the East London schools, according to Marshall, almost all of the scholars belonged to the humblest rank, 'some so destitute as to regard shoes and stockings as an impossible luxury'.[19] In considering the relatively small numbers from London in this period, it should be remembered that some of the largest and most successful Catholic boys' schools were conducted by the Irish Christian Brothers, who did not wish to enter the government system of subsidy and inspection, while some schools in the poorest districts did not have the resources to qualify for aid, being unable to meet the standards laid down for accommodation and equipment.

As already hinted, the pupil-teacher system did not provide St Mary's with a steady supply of suitable candidates, and there was continuing concern about both the small number coming forward, and the often disappointing standard of attainment which led to a substantial proportion of failures in the scholarship examination. Able to accommodate 70 students, the college was never full during the 1850s. A further problem was the fluctuation in numbers, which had implications for staffing and for funding; for instance, after the satisfactory results of the scholarship examinations held at Christmas in 1858 and 1859, when 25 and 30 candidates respectively passed, in 1860 only eight were successful.[20]

Concerned at the number of vacancies in the college, Rowe, the recently appointed Principal, took steps to rectify the situation by opening a preparatory class in 1861.[21] The first of these groups attracted 27 students, of whom 23 passed the scholarship examination at Christmas; together with successful candidates from pupil-teachers completing their apprenticeship, these made up a first year of 41 students in 1862.[22] Though never again attracting such high numbers, the preparatory class helped boost recruitment to the college, and in the late 1860s measures were taken to encourage schools to put forward more and better prepared candidates through the offer of gratuities to the masters who had taught them and to the successful applicants themselves. The classes widened the recruitment base to teaching, bringing in young men with a range of previous experience; there were a number of cotton spinners, factory operatives, clerks and warehousemen, a printer, a farmer, a shipwright and a bookseller.[23] Several of the Xaverian Brothers who worked in the college also gained scholarships.[24]

Shortage of applicants was not confined to St Mary's; in 1856 the Education Department's report made reference to there being about 300 unfilled places out of the 1900 available in residential colleges;[25] these were unevenly distributed, some colleges being oversubscribed and others having a number of vacancies. There were differing opinions on the extent to which vacancies were due to overprovision, to the unwillingness of pupil-teachers to apply for places, or to their inability to pass the scholarship examination. Asked in 1855 to report on wastage, the inspectors generally concluded that most pupil-teachers who stayed the course either went to a training college or found employment as untrained teachers. When the issue was considered by the Newcastle Commission, the figures supplied by Lingen, the Secretary to the Education Department, indicated that wastage was not a major problem. They show that 12.68 per cent of pupil-teachers failed to complete their apprenticeships due to death, failure of health, misconduct, or failure in attainment; the rest successfully completed their apprenticeships and over three-quarters of all pupil-teachers became candidates for Queen's Scholarships, which most had been 'pretty sure of getting'.[26] The difficulty, it seemed, must lie with the ratio between college places, which had been expanding rapidly, and the number of pupil-teachers and other potential recruits.

These overall figures did not, however, reflect the position with regard to Catholic boys' schools and to St Mary's, where the shortage of entrants was extremely serious. Without them the college could not fulfil its crucial role of providing the teachers to improve standards in schools and thus increase the number of potential recruits to the profession. Contemporaries identified several reasons for this shortage, starting with the difficulty of getting able boys to take up apprenticeships in view of competing employment opportunities and the extreme poverty of many parents. As Marshall wrote in 1857

> It seems indeed a kind of delusion to suppose that boys, the children of necessitous parents, who can earn from 4/- to 7/- a week, and often much more . . . will accept the munificent bait of 3/10 a week, paid at the end of the year and subject to the fulfilment of stringent conditions.[27]

Among other reasons given for the shortage of Catholic candidates for training were the inadequate tuition given to the male pupil-teachers and the inability of these, because of their social background, to make the best use of what was provided. Marshall regretted the lack of candidates for apprenticeship who might be 'susceptible to polish', making it necessary to accept the 'rude and coarse'.[28] In this respect, a contrast was drawn with pupil-teachers both in the schools of other denominations and in Catholic girls' schools; with regard to the latter, the CPSC Report for 1858 noted that in general the boys were 'drawn from a ruder class of society than the other sex'.[29] The difference, it was thought, was largely attributable to so many inspected girls' schools being conducted by religious, who were well-educated and cultivated women. Consequently, their schools drew on families from a wider social range than most of the boys' schools and parents, feeling confidence in the character and qualifications of the mistresses, willingly offered their daughters for apprenticeship. In addition to the emphasis on class, which tends to grate today, the instruction given to female pupil teachers was thought to be of a higher standard than that available to their male counterparts. Contemporaries do not seem to have considered a possible further reason for the greater success of girls in obtaining scholarships in the 1850s, namely that the requirements for female candidates, particularly in Mathematics, were less academically rigorous.

In the 1860s the effects of the Revised Code were felt on the recruitment of pupil-teachers, and thus of potential teacher trainees. This difficulty was partly met by lowering the standard of entrance to the colleges, by establishing preparatory classes as at St Mary's, and by financial incentives to teachers and pupil-teachers. The pass rates of applicants to St Mary's continued to fluctuate in the 1860s with only nine gaining entry in January 1866 and six in 1867; in the more successful years, however, the college was able to stand comparison, in terms of the success of candidates for entrance, both with the Catholic women's college and with the men's of other denominations.[30] Other colleges also experienced difficulties, one example being the old-established Borough Road where the number of male students dropped annually from 95 in 1862 to a low point of 61 in 1867; it then shared in the general recovery of the late 1860s and early 1870s, reaching 105 in 1871.[31]

Those who were successful in the December examinations embarked in January on what for most students was a two-year course, often a long way from home – not the most propitious time of year to adapt to the new world they encountered. The sections that follow will look at the course undertaken by teachers in training and their life at college.

THE COURSE OF STUDY

Students today, accustomed to a large measure of control over their lives and learning, would no doubt find the strict regimes of the residential Victorian training colleges alien and unacceptable. Not only were classes compulsory and periods for study strictly regulated, but the whole day's activity was mapped out with times set for rising and lights out, prayers, meals and recreation. In some colleges the concept of free time was barely recognized, useful work taking up any slack in the schedule.

In the early days the curriculum was left to the discretion of the colleges, and while some confined themselves mainly to subjects of direct usefulness in elementary school teaching, in others the offer was wide-ranging and sometimes unconventional; subjects listed included Optics, Ornithology and Navigation.[32] Not surprisingly, given the educational background of those in charge of the majority of the colleges, considerable attention was given to such subjects as Latin, Mathematics and Church History. The Minutes of December 1846, which established the system of Queen's Scholarships and annual examinations of students in training colleges, stated that 'The standard of acquirement shall not be so ordered as to interfere with the studies pursued in any Normal School, but shall be adapted to those studies.' The only standardization imposed was to require 'efficiency in a sufficient number of the studies pursued', so that students at all colleges would have 'an equal incentive to exertion'.[33]

When St Mary's was first established the range of subjects offered reflected the need for some students to concentrate on fairly basic elements. As the Principal explained to the visiting inspector in 1852, a considerable number of them, who had embraced the calling of teachers solely from religious motives, were rather commencing than completing their education. The timetable reproduced in the inspector's report indicates that the subjects allocated most time were Religious Instruction, Arithmetic, English Grammar and Literature, Geometry and Mensuration, and Music, each of which was taught for three hours weekly. Three further hours were allotted to the group of Geography, Popular Astronomy and Natural History, while Education Theory and Practice, History, French and Drawing were given two hours each. Shorter periods were devoted to Writing, Physics and original composition. Additionally, students spent time in the Practising School. The timetable made no reference to Latin, which one might expect to have been included.[34]

In the 1850s, as the number of students in training and hence the amount of government funding increased substantially, there was a move towards standardization of the examination syllabus. Lingen told the Newcastle Commission in 1859 that originally papers had been set in every subject offered anywhere; subsequently, the education authorities, wishing to 'restrict the field over which candidates might be examined', consulted the college Principals and in 1854 published a syllabus of examinations for male students.[35] In line with others, St Mary's conformed to the prescribed syllabus, which had been 'cordially accepted by officers of the College'.[36] Bearing in mind that revisions were made from time to time, it may be of interest to reproduce here the syllabus for the December 1858 examinations.[37]

First Year

Reading: To read, with a distinct utterance, with
                    due attention to the punctuation, and
                    with a just expression, a passage of Mr
                    Warren's Set Extracts from Blackstone's
                    Commentaries.

Penmanship: To write an example of the
                    penmanship used in setting copies:
                    1.   A line of large text hand.
                    2.   A passage in small hand.

Arithmetic: 1.   To prove the usual rules from first
                         principles.
                    2.   To compute with precision and
                         accuracy.
                    3.   To make (with a knowledge of the
                         principles) simple calculations in
                         Mensuration.

Mechanics: 1.   To describe the mechanical
                         powers, and the most common
                         method of applying them.
                    2.   To make simple calculations on
                         the work of mechanical agents.

School Management: 1.   To answer in writing questions on
                         the expedients to be used for the
                         purposes of instructing in reading,
                         spelling and writing.
                    2.   To draw up timetables for use in a
                         school under given circumstances.

English Grammar: 1.   Its principles.
                    2.   To parse a passage from the
                         Chapter on 'The Modern
                         Tenures' in Warren's Extracts
                         from Blackstone.
                    3.   To paraphrase the same passage.

Geography:	1.	To be able to describe the outline maps of the four quarters of the Globe.
	2.	To be able to describe the map of each country in Europe.
	3.	To be able to draw outlines of the above maps from memory.

History: The outlines of the History of England – to be known thoroughly.

Euclid: First four books.

Algebra: As far as quadratic equations, with problems.

Drawing: Any two of:
1. Drawing freehand from flat examples.
2. Linear geometry by aid of instruments.
3. Linear perspective.
4. Shaded drawing from objects.

Vocal music: Not set down.

Second Year

Reading: To read, with a distinct utterance, with due attention to the punctuation, and with a just expression, a passage from Milton's 'Paradise Lost' or from Shakespeare.

Penmanship: As in first year.

Arithmetic:
1. The use of logarithms.
2. Compound interest and annuities.
3. Methods of teaching Arithmetic generally.

School Management:
1. To teach a class in the presence of the Inspector.
2. To answer questions in writing on:

| | a) | The different methods of organizing an elementary school. |
| | b) | The form of, the mode of keeping, and of making Returns from School Registers. |

English Grammar and Composition:	1.	To paraphrase a passage from Milton's 'Paradise Lost' (Book II) or Shakespeare (*Richard II*).
	2.	To analyse the same passage (according to Mr Morell's work).
	3.	To answer questions on the style and subject matter of the work, or part of work, named.

Geography:	1.	Physical	The areas to be
	2.	Political	covered are not
	3.	Commercial	specified. The syllabus for 1859 says 'of the British Empire'.
	4.	Popular Astronomy	

History:

Paper of questions which can be answered from perusal of any one of the standard Histories of England (Hume, Lingard, Pictorial, etc.). The paper will be divided into five sections, each containing not less than five questions. These sections will reach to (1) the Battle of Hastings; (2) Battle of Bosworth; (3) death of Charles I; (4) death of Queen Anne; (5) 1815. No candidate will be examined in more than one section. The object of the second year's reading in History should be to deepen and quicken some specific part of the first year's reading.

| Drawing: | 1. | Freehand drawing from flat examples. |
| | 2. | Linear geometry by aid of instruments. |

3.   Linear perspective.
4.   Shaded drawing from objects.
5.   Drawing objects from memory.

Vocal music: Not set down

Alternative subjects of the Second Year – one only for examination:

1.   Physical Science: Chemistry, rudiments of electricity and galvanism.
2.   Higher Mathematics and Mathematical Physics, including Euclid Book Six, trigonometry, land surveying.
3.   English Literature: Three Shakespeare plays (*Macbeth, Julius Caesar, Winter's Tale*); Bacon's *Advancement of Learning*; History of English Literature: Chaucer to Milton.
4.   Latin: To the end of Yonge's *Eton Grammar*. An easy passage of Latin prose and another of Latin poetry to be translated into English and simple grammatical questions will be founded thereon.

A standard syllabus for women followed in 1858. This lacked some of the more rigorous mathematical and scientific elements of the men's version, for which were substituted Needlework and Industrial Training, that is to say, domestic work.[38] The latter was a pet project of Canon Cook who inspected the Church of England's women's colleges, the inspectors of other denominations being rather sceptical about it. Marshall, reporting on St Leonard's in 1858, expressed unease; while he did not deny the importance of such instruction for female students, he felt that it would be unjust if results in this area affected the position of candidates in the class list. It should not absorb so much of students' and their teachers' time as to compromise the primary objects of the training colleges which were, surely, intellectual and moral training. Stokes, in respect of the Liverpool college, felt that a certain amount of domestic work was beneficial and healthy, but that it was not the purpose of training colleges to train laundry maids or cooks, while Matthew Arnold and Bowstead, reporting on the training of women at Borough Road and the Wesleyan college at Westminster, respectively, made similar points. Arnold referred to the reluctance of students to sacrifice a portion of intellectual instruction which was, above all, what they came to obtain.[39]

Subsequent revisions to the examination syllabus were generally in the direction of narrowing and simplifying the requirements for a certificate and making the work of the colleges more directly related to the elementary curriculum. The concept of a liberal education, never wholeheartedly accepted by the education authorities, lost ground to that of utilitarian, vocational training aimed at restricting the professional and social horizons of elementary teachers. The intention was made clear in the Education Department's Report for 1862 which stated that currently:

> the subjects relied upon for training in Normal Schools are identical in kind with those which it is the business of elementary schools to teach, and are not more advanced in degree than marks the interval by which the teacher ought to precede the scholar ... These subjects, in the hands of able instructors, may be invested with an interest of their own, and made to stimulate an honourable ambition to excel within, instead of beyond, the circle where the service of trained teachers is required.[40]

The introduction of Economy into the syllabus in the early 1860s met both a recommendation of the Newcastle Commission and the widely expressed demand for teaching of useful knowledge; the syllabus covered the subject's political aspects and also more practical topics such as sanitation.

Together with changes in funding, which delayed payments to colleges until certificated teachers had been employed continuously and satisfactorily in elementary teaching for two years, the intention was to prevent wastage of expensively trained masters and mistresses. The changes must have gone some way to satisfy those who shared the view of the former Principal of the Durham Diocesan Training School that 'Too many and too advanced subjects are taught ... Hence superficial acquirements, conceit and discontent on the part of those trained.'[41]

It remained possible for colleges to extend the range of subjects offered beyond the official syllabus, an instance being the series of lectures on legal and constitutional history given at St Mary's by a Catholic barrister in the winter of 1860.[42] But the pressure of examinations and constraints of time led to the dropping of subjects which were not examined – in 1861 French and Latin were no longer taught to the Queen's Scholars at St Leonard's.[43] It is not known whether it had been possible to maintain the college's policy of encouraging students to read widely, for instance supplementing the dry Geography syllabus with books of travel.[44]

The syllabus reproduced above contains no reference to Religious Instruction; for this subject the official syllabus was mandatory only for colleges connected with the Church of England. Religious education was omitted from the government inspection of Catholic schools and colleges, the ecclesiastical authorities being responsible for its provision and the maintenance of an acceptable standard. The freedom from government interference was regarded as a positive factor and, indeed, an essential prerequisite to the acceptance of aid by Catholics. There was nevertheless a danger, remarked on in the CPSC 1858 report, that students might consider religious instruction as of less importance than secular, as success and credit in the public examinations were not dependent on it.[45]

Mindful of this danger, the Catholic bishops determined on the appointment of diocesan inspectors of religious education to cover both schools and colleges. The aim was to engraft an increased religious character on Catholic schools, while

> the class of pupil teachers now looking to HM Inspector and to scientific acquirements for promotion would learn to look upon their spiritual superiors and to their own moral conduct as the only safe and sure grounds of being one day entrusted with the all important charge of educating the rising generation.[46]

The envisaged system was developed in the mid-1850s, the first dioceses to carry out inspections in schools being Westminster, Salford and Southwark.[47] In the colleges the first examinations of candidates for scholarships and students in residence took place in December 1857. Those at St Mary's were presided over by Dr Errington, coadjutor to Archbishop Wiseman, and conducted by Father McMullen, the inspector for the Westminster diocese, and the Oratorian Father Knox. The examination took two days, *viva voce* tests on one day, and written papers on catechism and scriptural knowledge on the second. Six prizes for good performance in the examinations were offered at St Mary's and St Leonard's, and twelve at the larger college at Liverpool.[48]

The scholarship candidates examined at St Mary's in December 1858 were set the following papers, with the indication that all the questions might be answered:[49]

Catechism

1. What is the meaning of the word Creed, as used in the Catechism; and what are the existing Creeds of the Church?

2.   Describe the effects of Baptism on the soul.
3.   State the four ends of the Holy Sacrifice of the Mass: what is meant by a Sacrifice?
4.   Give an accurate statement of the doctrine of the Holy Trinity.
5.   Give a similar statement of the doctrine of the Holy Eucharist.
6.   What is the connection between the doctrines of Purgatory and Indulgences?
7.   What is meant by Spiritual Communion?
8.   What is Concupiscence? Is it Sin? if not, in what sense does the Apostle Paul call it Sin?

Holy Scripture

1.   Name the books of the Pentateuch and of the New Testament.
2.   Give a short account of the life of Saul.
3.   What circumstances in the life of Abraham prefigured Our Lord?
4.   State what you know of the life and character of Balaam.
5.   Who were Moses, Josue, David, Solomon, Elias, the Machabees?
6.   Which of the Gospels was written first and which last?
7.   Give a short account of the birth, life and death of St John Baptist.
8.   Show from Scripture the time of the institution of the Sacraments of Baptism, Penance, Holy Eucharist and Holy Orders.

It is probably in relation to this examination that McMullen reported that he and his fellow examiner had found

> that the knowledge of a large proportion of the young men on the simplest and most elementary points of Christian doctrine was most inaccurate and unsatisfactory, and that for the most part no special provision had been made by the managers of their several schools for their instruction in religion during the long years of their apprenticeship.[50]

Several hours a week were devoted to Religious Instruction at the three Catholic colleges, the value of the classes being demonstrated in improving examination results; these were particularly good at Liverpool.

Reference has been made in the introductory section to the considerable contribution to teaching made by most college Principals. In addition, colleges usually had a Vice-Principal, and all had a number of teaching staff, known as masters or lecturers in the male colleges and governesses in the female. Past students were often employed, either immediately on qualification or after they had taught for some time in an elementary school. Of St Mary's it was reported in 1852 that Glenie was assisted by masters; these may have been part-time visiting tutors, since the inspector considered the teaching force to be inadequate, especially in its lack of a Vice-Principal.[51] In the latter half of the decade the teaching body was expanded with the appointments of Capel as Vice-Principal and of several lecturers including an Oxford graduate.[52] Rowe introduced a series of visiting lecturers from the Oratory, and also employed students trained in the lay department; the first, in 1861, was Stephen Johnson who was subsequently ordained and taught at Oscott College. Others in Rowe's time were John Green, Charles Regan and James Murray, who had commenced his training as a pupil-teacher in the Practising School. Additionally, some of the Belgian Xaverian Brothers who undertook the running of Brook House took the certificate examination and taught in the college. A former Battersea student taught for a short time in the late 1860s; another appointment of this period being that of James Enright, trained in Dublin. In this decade the college had a varied and well-qualified group of staff but, with the fluctuation in numbers and uncertainty about the college's future, there was a lack of stability which Stokes noted with regret.[53]

In fact, the situation was about to change, the majority of staff appointed in the late 1860s and the early 1870s remaining at St Mary's for many years. The appointment of Enright, which had caused Stokes initial concern because he 'lacked acquaintance with British arrangements',[54] proved most successful and lasted for over 30 years. Past students appointed at this time who served the college for long periods were Thomas Livesey, the author of a series of manuals on the teaching of various subjects, Thomas Flannery and Edward Mooney. The Revd Jeremiah Canty, Graham's successor as Vice-Principal, served in that capacity for twelve years.

With generally between three and five teaching staff in addition to the Principal, Vice-Principal and visiting lecturers, St Mary's enjoyed a more favourable staff/student ratio than larger colleges such as Chester and Cheltenham.[55] Nevertheless, full-time staff were required to cover more than one subject area, for instance in 1864 Regan was teaching History, Geography and Euclid.[56]

There was a ready source of well-qualified governesses for the Catholic women's colleges in the communities which ran them, both of which had the further asset of experience of conducting schools for the poor. Liverpool did not recruit governesses from its past students in this period[57] although a private student in the first intake, Louisa Pottinger, became Head of the Practising School. The college enjoyed stability in its teaching force, the same names appearing in inspectors' reports year after year; it would seem that as at St Mary's under Graham the continuity provided by a long-serving Principal encouraged staff to remain in post. At St Leonard's too, the teaching staff altered very little from year to year and, as at Liverpool, the governesses had obtained the teacher's certificate. The inspectors were impressed by their calibre, Morell referring to the teaching force as 'powerful and able', and Stokes as 'strikingly powerful and effective'.[58] In contrast to Liverpool, a number of past students taught at the southern college.

Not surprisingly in a new and rapidly growing system, with only a small pool of qualified and experienced people on which to draw, the practice of employing past students was common, and there was also interchange between colleges. Early graduates of St Mark's seem to have been particularly sought after, the college having by 1852 supplied others with two Principals, three Vice-Principals and a number of normal masters and tutors.[59]

The main method of instruction in the training colleges was the lecture, which often took the form of dictation of notes. Students were expected to 'get up' answers from these and from textbooks; little was expected of them in the way of independent thought or research – which would in any case have been hampered by the lack of well-stocked libraries. The lecture headings of the course on Method taught by Capel at St Mary's in 1859 illustrate the meticulous guidance given to students.[60]

First Year's Course: On Method

1. On method in general, and its fundamental laws.
2. On special methods: (a) analytic and synthetic; (b) interrogative, elliptical, and expository; (c) individual and simultaneous.
3. On the comparative advantages of oral and book instruction.
4. On the art of questioning.

5. On the means of securing attention.
6. On the use and abuse of illustration and apparatus.
7. On the notes of lessons.
8. On the relative importance of the various branches of elementary instruction.
9. On the use and abuse of object lessons.
10. On the manner of conducting a class.

Second Year's Course: On School Management

1. On school organization in general; its object, its characteristics, the principles on which it is based.
2. On systems of teaching: (a) individual; (b) collective; (c) mutual and monitorial.
3. On the plans of organization proper to each of the above systems, illustrated by diagrams.
4. On classification; its true basis, the number, shape and arrangement of the classes.
5. On timetables.
6. On the economical distribution of teaching power, and the personal contact of the master with each child daily.
7. On the manner of arranging, by anticipation, the amount of work to be done weekly and quarterly.
8. On school apparatus.
9. On school registers.
10. On the playground, and its uses.
11. On securing regular and punctual attendance.
12. On the government, teaching and training of pupil-teachers.
13. On the master's duties towards managers and parents.
14. On the means of perpetuating relations with children after they have left school.
15. On school libraries.
16. On industrial schools.
17. On night schools.
18. On the systems of instruction followed by Jacotot, Père Girard, Pestalozzi, Stow.

Some student exercise books of the early 1860s, preserved in the college archives,[61] contain notes on several of the subjects in the official examination syllabus, and on Sacred History and Religion. The notes, which are for the most part written in a very small hand

and with excellent spelling, may have been copied from the board or taken down from dictation; in the absence of another set covering the same material, which could have been compared, this must remain conjecture. Examples of the topics included are: Geography: the coastlines, boundaries and main physical features of European countries; History: a wide range of topics including several from the Civil War and Restoration periods, and a series of brief biographies of personalities ranging over the centuries from King Alfred the Great to members of the Restoration 'Cabal' and the Duke of Marlborough; Sacred History: The Creation, Paradise, The Fall; The Four Evangelists; Miracles; Prophecies alluded to in the Gospels; School Management: under the heading Reading, three systems of teaching are listed, Look and Say, Alphabetic and Phonic, with Principles, Advantages and Disadvantages given for each. Students were urged to take care that the children understood what they read, and to make them adopt the tone and emphasis used in conversation. There are also a few completed test papers in Grammar – paraphrases of scenes from Shakespeare's *King John*, followed by syntactical analysis – and in History, where essays were required on James II and on the Popish Plot.

The lists of textbooks in use at St Mary's in the later 1850s[62] show that many texts had been prepared by lecturers in the training colleges or by people associated with them in other capacities, such as the government inspectors. Thus for Arithmetic, the authors included the Borough Road Principals Cornwell and Fitch, and Tate, a master at Battersea, whose works on Mechanics and Geometry were also used. J.D. Morell, who inspected British and Wesleyan institutions and was a cousin of the Catholic inspector J.R. Morell, provided Grammar textbooks and Moseley, the first inspector of Church of England training colleges, who had been a professor at King's College, a book of Lectures on Astronomy. The newness of the field and the lack of quality textbooks are shown in regard to the area of Method and School Management where next to the name of the book is noted 'for want of a better'. The college used the work of a Catholic historian, Lingard, for History and for Religious Instruction the books in use were in the first year, *Abridgement of Christian Doctrine, Poor Man's Catechism, Catechism of Perseverance* and *Catechism of the Diocese of Paris*, and in the second Capes' *Bible History*, Dolman's edition of the Bible and Burns' *Church History*. Students were asked to bring with them the books prescribed for the first year, or £2 with which to buy them.

Assessment of most subjects was through written examinations. It was customary for colleges to set regular, often weekly, tests; these were useful for revision, and as preparation for the annual ordeal of a succession of three-hour papers. It appears that the order of these was not revealed to candidates, since inspectors were instructed in 1854 to be careful 'not to announce at the end of each sitting what is to be the next paper'. This was one of a number of measures intended to prevent cheating, which was 'not so uncommon as they would willingly have supposed'.[63] The papers were set centrally and 'revised' by inspectors, who classified them on a scale ranging from Excellent through Good, Fair and Moderate to Imperfect and outright failure. Numerical marking was introduced at the end of the 1860s to obtain greater consistency among examiners, the previous system being retained to the extent that marks were added and the totals converted to grades at the Education Office. Cowie indicated that students obtaining over two-thirds of the available marks in a subject would merit classification as Excellent or Good.[64] An earlier modification of the examination system was the setting of different papers for candidates of different years; this was introduced for men in 1854, but Cook thought it unnecessary for female candidates at this time. Separate papers were set for them only in School Management; second-year students were, however, given greater freedom in selecting questions to answer.[65]

Consideration of results over a number of years[66] shows a good deal of fluctuation in the standards reached at St Mary's in different subjects. The most consistently successful were School Management and the practical test in Teaching; History improved noticeably during the 1860s. St Mary's was not among the best performing male colleges, which included the large colleges at Battersea, Borough Road and Westminster. Both the Catholic women's colleges did very well, with Liverpool students being particularly successful. Other top performers were, as with the men, the metropolitan colleges – Borough Road (the women's section of which had migrated to Stockwell in 1861), Whitelands and Westminster – and the Norwich diocesan college.

Reading was tested orally by the inspectors, and reference has already been made to the use of *viva voce* examination in Religious Instruction. A further important feature of assessment was the practical test of teaching ability. This was done during the year by means of criticism lessons involving judgement by lecturers and fellow students, although peer criticism seems not to have been in use at St

Mary's where, Bowstead noted in 1873, it was 'thought liable to create bad feeling' and students were seen privately by the Normal Master.[67] The formal assessment for qualification consisted of conducting a class in the presence of the inspector. Both types of test were normally carried out in the schools used for teaching practice.

The Practising School

Although it was generally agreed that a good Practising School was a fundamental requirement for every college, there was no prescribed model for these. Some colleges had schools incorporated into the main fabric or built in the grounds, some used local schools, and a number combined both systems. The Practising Schools in most cases offered elementary education to poor children, but some were middle schools catering for better-off families. At St Mary's the additions to Brook Green House completed in the early 1850s included school premises consisting of one large, lofty room with a tiered gallery for collective teaching, and three classrooms – one each for music and drawing, and one for general purposes. The rooms were adorned with religious pictures and generally presented an aspect of cheerfulness and cleanliness.[68]

This new Practising School absorbed the Boys' department of the Hammersmith mission school, which had been under inspection since 1849 and had at that time some 50 boys aged between seven and fourteen; absenteeism was noted as a problem, many boys from poor families taking time off at intervals to work.[69] It had been among the first Catholic schools to have pupil–teachers, and Marshall noted approvingly in 1852 that the apprentices were accommodated within the college.[70] Over the years numbers at the school were augmented by the establishment in the locality of two Catholic children's homes, St Vincent's and St Joseph's, the latter being under the direct management of the college until 1867.[71]

The school was at first taught by members of the Brotherhood and later on by lay masters trained at the college. It was consistently praised in inspectors' reports, 'the pains taken to cultivate gentleness and docility of character, and by religious and devotional practices to form definite and vigorous religious habits' being particularly noted.[72] The education, though elementary, was 'solid and good' and had prepared a number of boys to compete successfully in examinations for entrance to training for the priesthood.[73] In the 1860s some boys of the 'richer class' attended, attracted by the reputation of the school.[74]

While no fault was found with the effectiveness of the teaching and discipline in the school, there was concern on the part of the inspectorate as to its suitability for practice, because of its small size and the youth of the majority of the scholars. Stokes, used to the large urban schools in Lancashire where his work was concentrated from the mid-1850s, considered that the training offered at Hammersmith was not a sufficient preparation for the difficulties to be encountered in them.[75]

It was suggested by some members of the CPSC that St Mary's might broaden the students' practical experience by using neighbouring schools in addition to the Practising School as was done at Liverpool, but the Principal did not favour this course of action. He considered that there was no real parallel with the women's college, where the religious order in charge had many schools in the town; consequently, the mistress of Method attending with her students would find similar methods in use in all of them. St Mary's had nothing like this to draw on; to send students to schools in no way under the control of the college authorities would be inconsistent with the welfare of both the school and his students. In a letter to Charles Langdale, the CPSC Chairman, setting out these views, the Principal also cited the importance of the college's retaining control over the school as a reason for not requesting financial contributions from the Hammersmith mission or the managers of St Vincent's beyond the one penny weekly fee.[76]

Liverpool students were able to develop practical skills in teaching not only infants and junior girls but also, in due course, pupil-teachers and night school students.[77] St Leonard's, on the other hand, had greater difficulties than St Mary's, being sited in an area where there were few Catholics of the poorer classes. The school there was made up largely of very young children, and had a number of middle-class girls.[78]

Arrangements for practice seem to have varied considerably from college to college and at different periods, reflecting lack of official guidance on the time to be allocated to it, uncertainty with regard to the teaching of pedagogy and, in relation to the pupil-teachers who formed the bulk of entrants, varying estimates of the utility of their previous experience. In 1852 Marshall reported of St Mary's that:

> The higher division of students spend the whole of each Tuesday – the lower division the whole of each Thursday – in this school. They partly listen to the lessons given, receiving at the same time appropriate instructions and suggestions, partly assume the charge of the

classes . . . On the two days named the Principal catechises in the presence of the students, and gives instructions to the children to prepare them for approaching the sacraments, and in the practice of devotional exercises.[79]

At a later period he noted that the second-year students were given responsibility in turn for the whole school, while four of the first years were appointed as 'quasi pupil-teachers' in the four classes. The senior students gave model lessons in each class,[80] no doubt basing their practice on the precepts of Capel's lectures on Method. In the early 1870s Bowstead, reporting on all the men's colleges, contrasted the system at St Mary's where students spent half a day in the school every week with the block practice customary elsewhere.[81]

Conduct of a school involved not only oversight of teaching and discipline, and record keeping, but also – as was the experience of St Leonard's second-year students placed in charge for the entire school day – seeing pupils in and out, dealing with latecomers, admitting and examining any new scholars, and even testing various methods for giving out bonnets at home time.[82]

The inspectors' standard way of testing students' teaching ability was the gallery lesson, a carefully prepared mini-lecture interspersed with questions to the children. Topics might be taken from the curricular subjects, or 'common things', for instance animals, plants or various objects familiar in everyday life. Stokes questioned the value of this form of test, which seemed to him artificial. Furthermore, because of the special conditions of a Practising School, the ordinary subjects of gallery lessons were likely to have been exhausted, leaving the student a choice between reducing the lesson to examination, or 'selecting ambitious matter for his display'. He favoured a method of assessment which more closely replicated conditions in an ordinary school, and to this end in his report for 1860 proposed an hour-long test based in one class and divided into four periods. During two of these the student would conduct 'quiet' lessons, such as Writing or Arithmetic on slates; one of the other two 'attended by more vocal effort' should always be Reading, the second selected at the inspector's discretion from Mental Arithmetic, Grammar, Geography and History.[83] The suggested method was put into practice at St Mary's in the following years, and judged to have worked well.[84] Although the numbers to be tested at St Mary's were often small – in 1861 there were twenty and in 1862 only six final-year students, one can only feel intense sympathy for the recipients of the lessons delivered by a succession of nervous candidates.

COLLEGE LIFE

What of students' lives when they were not engaged in study? Marshall wrote of St Mary's in the Brotherhood period:

> Strict silence is observed everywhere throughout the day, except in times of recreation. All the meals are taken in common in the refectory in silence. The Lives of the Saints, or other spiritual books, are read aloud at dinner and supper by one of the students. They serve at the meals in turn, make their own beds, clean their own shoes, and sweep the lecture room, classrooms, dormitories, etc. They also work, from time to time, in the garden. On Sundays, days of obligation and other feasts, study is not obligatory; but special religious instruction is given to the students bearing upon their peculiar vocation and future duties.[85]

On weekdays, eight hours were allocated to lectures and study, three to spiritual exercises, one to music and drawing and four to meals and recreation. Since four meals were taken, breakfast at 8.15 a.m., midday dinner, tea and supper, very little time must have been available for recreation. The institution of half holidays on Wednesdays and Saturdays, when students had to be back in college by 7 p.m.,[86] dates from a later period and may have been part of the slight relaxation of the regime introduced by Rowe.

Apart from those aspects reflecting its religious nature, such as the silence at meals and the vocational religious instruction, the picture of life at St Mary's presented in the inspector's report does not differ greatly from that of other colleges at this time. Early rising was the norm – at 5 or 5.30 a.m., and students then engaged in prayers, lesson preparation, household tasks and in some places outdoor work before the first meal of the day. The end of the activity-crammed days also came early; at St Mary's prayers at 9.30 p.m. were followed by lights out at 10 p.m. in the large dormitories divided into cubicles, while at some colleges bedtime was even earlier.

Religious instruction and observance were an integral part of life in the Victorian colleges, most of which were linked with particular denominations and were until 1870 training teachers for schools which were essentially religious foundations. Apart from the time-tabled hours of study of religious subjects, college students attended morning and evening prayers and in many cases daily church services in the college chapel. The Catholic colleges set time aside for meditation and spiritual exercises. On Sundays students attended services in their chapels or local churches, and were often in demand as Sunday School teachers.

While at most colleges students helped with the chores, others expected considerably more of them in the way of manual labour, the best-known examples being Battersea when Kay was in residence, and Chester under Rigg. At Battersea the younger students did most of the housework while all worked in the garden and tended the livestock: two cows, goats, pigs and poultry. The regime was designed to instil habits of industry, promote health and pare expenses.[87] Chester students also undertook manual labour, working with wood, metal and glass to fit out the chapel which they also helped to build, and in printing and book binding. The 1844 timetable shows two daily periods earmarked for industrial pursuits, after breakfast and before the one o'clock dinner.[88]

The way of life for college students was spartan but apparently healthy, and if the 'dietary' was frugal, it was no doubt superior to what many had previously known. Kay was concerned to improve the physical fitness of the boys and young men in his charge at Battersea, by introducing them gradually to outdoor work and providing meals featuring fresh produce from the college grounds. He was delighted with the results. St Mary's also had a large garden with fruit trees, and kept some livestock. Health was a major concern to the authorities at the training colleges and it was a regular item in inspectors' reports; there are references to students having to leave because of a break-down in health, and there was an ongoing fear of epidemics.

Not all of the students' time was taken up with study, religious observance and work in house and grounds; some relaxation was allowed though it too was often organized by the authorities. Kay took his students for long country walks, generally with an educational focus, while Borough Road students visited the British Museum and the Zoological Gardens.[89] It was common practice for female students to be taken for chaperoned walks; those at St Leonard's went on excursions, and enjoyed being close to the sea. Men's colleges had some facilities for sporting activity; in common with others, St Mary's had gymnastic apparatus, it also boasted a bowling alley, and rented a field locally for cricket.[90] The small numbers during a good deal of this period must have hampered the ability to recruit teams for competitive sports, but in later years the college participated in inter-college cricket and football matches. St Mary's was among the men's colleges providing exercise in the form of military-style drill.[91]

On the cultural side, college students took part in concerts and theatrical performances; examples from the Catholic women's colleges include a St Patrick's Day concert at St Leonard's, and dramatic productions there ranging from Shakespeare to lighter works such as *Whittington and his Cat*.[92] At Liverpool, Sunday soirées took place with singing, recitations and play readings.[93] Cheltenham's male and female students came together for choral singing, under strict surveillance.[94]

Contact with students' families was often very limited, both because of distance and through deliberate policy. At Liverpool, where many students came from the local area, parents might visit their daughters once a month, but students were not allowed to go home.[95] Students kept in touch with families and friends through letters; there are copies at St Mary's of letters exchanged in the early 1860s between a current and past students from the same Scottish town.[96]

With such determined supervision it is difficult to see how students could go astray, but some cases of misconduct did occur. The records at St Mary's indicate that the main causes of expulsions were copying at examinations, repeated insubordination and drunkenness. In 1868 Rowe reported to the CPSC that a small group of first-year students apparently thought that because the government of the college was confiding and paternal, the liberty allowed could be used in an insubordinate and undisciplined manner. After several warnings three students had been expelled.[97]

Newly-qualified teachers, usually barely into their twenties, left the protective atmosphere of the colleges and in many cases immediately assumed responsibility for schools of a hundred or more children. The next section considers the future careers of some of them.

FUTURE CAREERS

As with their background, little is known of the work undertaken by the majority of Brotherhood students on leaving the college. In an article published in 1876 the former Principal, Rowe, wrote that they had almost without exception persevered in the course of life they had chosen, and that many of them had become priests.[98] With regard to individuals, it is known that one of the first to gain a certificate, John Corbett, took up a teaching post in Manchester and both William McNamara and William Eden taught for some time at the Practising School. The distinguished careers of Thomas Graham and Thomas Capel, to whom reference has already been made in other sections, are a matter of public record.

Both joined the Brotherhood after it had been established at Hammersmith, gained certificates in a short space of time and then taught at the college, Capel specializing in Method and Graham in Mathematics and Science. Both served as Vice-Principal, Capel under Glenie and Graham under Rowe. Both were ordained priests in the diocese of Westminster. Subsequently, their careers diverged. Capel, suffering ill health, left England for the south of France, where he served as chaplain to the English-speaking Catholics at Pau until 1868. On his return to England he became well known as a public lecturer and is thought to have been the model for Monsignor Catesby in Disraeli's novel *Lothario*. He renewed his connection with St Mary's, acting as Spiritual Director for some years. In the 1870s he established a Catholic public school and also served as Principal of the short-lived Catholic university in Kensington. He died in 1911, having served for many years as a priest in California.

Thomas Graham remained based at St Mary's where he became Principal in 1869, staying in the post until his death in 1899. He took a London University degree in 1872; in 1879 Pope Leo XIII conferred on him a doctorate in Divinity, and from 1893 he was a member of the Westminster Chapter. His long experience at the college made him, in 1886, a valuable witness to the Royal Commission on the Working of the Elementary Education Acts. He was also involved in the work of several charities, served on the Mansion House Committee and gave university extension lectures.

A combination of the Education Department's wish to see a return on its considerable investment, the Catholic community's urgent need for trained teachers and the Victorian fascination with statistics, led to careful tracking of students completing their training at the Catholic colleges from the mid-1850s. Data on first destinations were included in the CPSC's reports, and in those for 1862 and 1869 summaries were published of the number of past students engaged in teaching and in other occupations. Additionally, the earlier report provided information on the first and current appointment of each student, the later one on length of service and mobility.

The figures for the three Catholic colleges, covering students who had passed the certificate examination by the end of 1862 were as follows:[99]

Hammersmith: of 102 certificated past students there were:

employed in teaching poor schools	65
teaching in private schools	7
dead	8
Brothers of Charity (teaching)	4
out of a situation	7
in ill health	1
given up teaching	10

(There is no separate reference to those teaching at the college, who may have been included in the first category.)

Liverpool: of 183 teachers trained there were:

teaching schools	149
withdrawn from the profession by death	8
withdrawn from the profession by marriage	5
private governesses	4
going through a course of religious training	7
recruiting their health for a time	2
seeking a situation	3
(leaving 5 unaccounted for)	

St Leonard's: of 85 teachers trained there were:

employed in teaching	56
dead	4
married	6
private governesses	7
incapacitated by bad health	3
in religious training	4
seeking situations	4
at home	1

While some of those leaving the Catholic colleges returned to the schools where they had been apprenticed, there is no evidence of a general expectation that they would do so and many, particularly the young men, took up posts a long way from their place of origin. Those young women who entered the religious life were in due course appointed to schools of the orders they joined.

In 1869 it was reported[100] that of the 205 teachers trained at St Mary's since 1855, 33 had died or had emigrated. Among the 163 students who had responded to a circular, 127 were teaching in inspected schools, three in prisons and two in middle schools, while one was an inspector's assistant. Three were priests and three Brothers of Charity. Other occupations included the civil service, business and clerical work; one past student was studying medicine and one had joined the army. Of 356 trained at Liverpool, 267 were teaching in elementary schools and others in schools of various kinds, some of them overseas. The largest group lost to the profession were the 33 who had married and ceased to teach; 23 had died. Figures for St Leonard's, which had withdrawn from inspection, were not given. As to mobility, the 1869 Report showed 44 Hammersmith men still in their first posting, five of these having served for over ten years, and a further seventeen for five. Only a handful had really itchy feet. A similar pattern can be discerned for Liverpool trained teachers, with perhaps a greater tendency to stability among the women.

Training in the colleges was intended to produce teachers for the poorer classes, and in respect of the Catholic colleges this intention seems largely to have been fulfilled. While it is not possible to judge precisely from the figures available, it would seem that in 1869 approximately two-thirds of the men and four-fifths of the women held posts in elementary schools. How many of these were the Principal or sole teacher, and how many the assistants who were increasingly employed in the 1860s, is not known.

Official concern about wastage of teachers trained at St Mark's, an institution less concerned than its fellows to limit student aspirations, was expressed in Cowie's 1864 inspection report; he felt that the aim the retiring Principal had had in view was not exactly that which the Parliamentary votes contemplated.[101] Although Coleridge had responded to the Newcastle Commissioners' enquiry as to whether the trained teachers were content with their posts and position in life that they possibly 'too little desired change and advancement' and that their satisfaction with their calling was 'evinced by the fact that the number of those who seek to quit it is quite inconsiderable',[102] figures taken from the same Principal's final report appear to bear out the inspector's concern. These indicate that of 708 students who had completed training between 1841 and 1864, only 329 were employed in National Schools, with a further 48 in other schools for the poor and 14 in colleges; 49 were due to begin work in 1865. As many as 99 were employed in middle schools or as private tutors, and 43 in educational or missionary work in the colonies.[103]

Chester's Principal did not keep exact records of destinations[104] but certainly in the early years students undertook to teach for the Diocesan Board for at least four years, or incur a financial penalty.[105] Most dioceses, according to Lingen's evidence to the Newcastle Commission, had the advantage of a moral understanding that the students trained in their colleges would take at any rate their first appointments in the diocese in which they had been trained.[106]

The relatively low pay offered to teachers taking up appointments in Catholic elementary schools may well have been the cause of some loss to other employment in the 1860s; in the 1870s the situation was aggravated by the competitive pay offered by the new Board Schools, which were, additionally, comparatively well resourced in terms of accommodation and equipment. Catholic teachers would naturally prefer to remain within the voluntary school system, but some were tempted away; in 1880, for instance, six teachers trained at St Mary's and ten from the Catholic women's colleges were employed in London Board Schools.[107] Salaries of male teachers there were around £100 per annum compared with the £75 to £90 offered by Catholic schools in the 1870s.[108] For secular women teachers an additional incentive may have been the better opportunity of a Headship in a Board School.

To us in the late twentieth century the most shocking cause of wastage was the death rate, which for both men and women seems tragically high; it was in fact remarked on at the time, Stokes referring to the loss by death of several valuable teachers in one year, while others had been forced to give up teaching because of impaired health.[109] The death toll by 1862 included the two Edinburgh pupil-teachers among the first entrants to St Mary's lay department in January 1855. Data in the Catholic Schools Committee's Report for 1894 indicate that by that time at least one-third of the men trained by 1862 had died – while the survivors would be in their fifties.[110] In 1886 Graham attributed the high mortality rate chiefly to consumption, the result of the unfavourable conditions in which the teachers lived and the heavy demands of their work.[111]

While some observers expressed doubts about the effects of employing college-trained teachers, who were thought to be proud and liable to neglect the needs of younger children in favour of the more advanced scholars, others took an encouraging view. The Principal of St Mark's told the Newcastle Commission that the qualifications of school masters, 'whether regard be had to attainments, power of teaching, or zeal in the exercise of their calling', were immeasurably higher than they were before the establishment of the colleges. The proof of this was that the services of men so trained were, he said, in steady demand for posts connected with popular education, not only in England, but throughout the British Empire.[112]

The tenor of inspectors' reports on the work done in the Catholic schools by men trained at St Mary's was generally very positive. In 1858 Morell commented on the improvement in the class of teachers, many of whom had been students in the training colleges; in 1859 Stokes praised the Glasgow Boys schools, 'conducted by Hammersmith men, judiciously selected and liberally paid', and Marshall noted that many of the male schools in which sensible progress had been made were taught by masters trained at Hammersmith. In 1868 Lynch wrote that the male training school 'under many disadvantages and discouragements, has sent to my district several teachers of whose success it may well feel proud, and very few whose career has been attended with discredit'.[113]

Comments on the Catholic women teachers were also laudatory, for instance, Marshall reported that many St Leonard's students were teaching in large and difficult schools; he referred to the remarkable influence which they exerted over the pupils and on their religious earnestness of motive. In 1860 Stokes reported that he had seen 42 former students at work in their own schools and classed 24 as 'Good' schoolmistresses and 17 as 'Fair'; there was only one case of comparative failure in which health had played a part.[114] We should remember that 'Fair' had then a more positive connotation in the marking system than we might now read into it.

A number of St Mary's past students continued to work in the field of education, although not in elementary schools. One such was Michael Harden, who so impressed Stokes with his work at the night school in Stockport[115] that he had him appointed as his inspector's assistant, a post Harden continued to hold when Stokes was transferred to London as a Senior Inspector in the non-denominational system established after the 1870 Education Act. Harden had also spent a year in charge of St Mary's Practising School. As already mentioned, several past students were employed as lecturers at the college, some very briefly, a few for many years. Two students of the early 1870s made their mark in teaching overseas, Daniel Fallon became a professor in Malta and Tim Donovan head of a Catholic college in Bangkok. In the field of politics, one early student, Michael Conway, became MP for an Irish constituency, North Leitrim in 1886.[116]

CONCLUSION

Although teacher training remained in the hands of religious bodies and voluntary organizations after 1870, inspection of the colleges lost its denominational basis. Previously, inspectors had visited schools and colleges of a particular kind, and their appointments had been subject to the approval of the relevant church or voluntary body. With the implementation of the Education Act this ceased to be the case, existing postholders being redeployed to cover all inspected schools in a certain area, whether voluntary aided or the new Board schools. For teacher training the system of specialist inspectors was extended from Church of England institutions to embrace all colleges in England and Wales; the current inspectors for men's and women's colleges – both clergymen – remained in post, but when Cowie retired in 1872 his successor was Bowstead, a former 'British' and Wesleyan inspector. Academic inspection of the Catholic colleges continued to be limited to the secular curriculum so that, accustomed as they were to the exacting standards of Stokes and his colleagues, they had little to fear from the new regime. They did, however, lose the Catholic inspectors' understanding of the circumstances of the community, and their close connection with the schools from which the students were drawn and in which they would subsequently work. For those interested in the development of the Catholic colleges the substitution of brief accounts of individual colleges for the very full reports of earlier years is to be regretted, though the overall perspective presented is valuable.

Cowie made a number of comments on the system of teacher training as he observed it in 1871 and 1872. The colleges were, he considered, doing 'good and honest service' and endeavouring to produce the best they could when 'the material on which their energies are expended is not equal to what they would desire to have'. They were sending out a 'supply of teachers fairly qualified for their duties' who had gained much commendation from the district inspectors; their superiority over untrained teachers was uniformly recognized. As to the course of study in the colleges, he was aware of complaints that it was 'too cramped and confined', but did not himself agree with this view. He did, however, suggest that colleges might adopt 'specialties' in, for instance, Mathematics, Physical Science and Literature. In his second general report he expressed the hope that more students would follow the example of those who were preparing for London external degrees.[117]

In this report he also noted that most colleges were currently full, and that many candidates were unable to gain entrance; a number of colleges had that year expanded their accommodation to meet the demand, and had done so without government aid. The country was, he thought, getting a bargain by using the denominational colleges; the system was economical, and at the same time 'fairly contrived to avoid conflict with existing religious susceptibilities'.[118] Both Cowie and his successor noted the general similarity in the organization of the colleges connected with the different religious bodies and societies, Bowstead referring to their residential nature and the common syllabus and examinations which were, as we have seen, the result of a series of governmental measures. The inspectors were aware of differing standards of attainment in the institutions, Bowstead pointing to the superiority of the large metropolitan colleges which commanded the elite of candidates.[119]

From today's point of view Cowie's view of the syllabus appears narrowly complacent, and the lack of opportunities given to students in training to mature – by exercising judgement and taking responsibility for their own lives – short-sighted, even wrongheaded. Gradually, changes were made, both in discipline and the course of studies, the curricula of the later nineteenth century becoming wider and putting greater emphasis on preparation for the examinations of the Science and Art Department. Increased provision for the education of pupil-teachers, particularly in urban areas where they could be gathered together for classes, had a beneficial effect on the standard of entrants to training, and this was reinforced in due course by the wider availability of secondary schooling.

Judged by the standards of the time, the colleges represented a great step forward, producing a class of teachers which, Moseley had claimed as far back as 1854, were the best in the country, being the only ones who had as a class made teaching the subject of special and systematic study.[120] As we have seen, the system which developed in the middle decades of the nineteenth century was based on compromises; the first major experiment in government-aided post-school education depended largely on voluntary initiatives and resources, and the training itself took elements from different traditions – craft apprenticeship, and grammar school and university education. This lack of clear definition applied also to the status of teachers, on whom much responsibility was placed, but who nevertheless faced a long struggle to achieve recognition as a profession.

To take an instance, acknowledgement of their expertise as teachers of elementary schools did not extend to considering trained and experienced headteachers as suitable candidates for the inspectorate. The factors militating against them were to a considerable extent social; Temple, former Principal of Kneller Hall and for a brief period an inspector of training colleges, told the Newcastle Commission that he did not think teachers would make good inspectors at all. In his view, they would not feel sufficiently on a par with school managers to deal effectively with them, and would not have the sort of self-reliance required in an officer of that kind.[121] In the 1860s some teachers were appointed as inspectors' assistants to help with the routine conduct of examinations under the Revised Codes; the later breakthrough to full inspector status was helped by the establishment by School Boards and local authorities of inspectorates to which teachers were appointed.

The Catholic colleges had much in common with those of other denominations, but differed from them in religious ethos and teaching. The body of certificated Catholic teachers also had distinctive features deriving from the character and needs of the community they served, the most significant being that so many women teachers were members of religious communities, and thus accorded a respect and status which elementary teachers generally were not able to command. Notable too, and linked with the above, is the preponderance of women in the Catholic teaching force from an early date. When government aid first became available to them, Catholic schools followed the pattern of other denominations in having more certificated masters than mistresses. As the system developed, however, with the numbers of children in aided Catholic schools increasing from just under 30,000 in 1855 to 63,000 ten years later and 95,500 in 1870, the proportion of women teachers grew rapidly. They overtook the men before 1860 and certificated women teachers outnumbered men by approximately five to two in 1870, at which time numbers of men and women were roughly equal in Church of England schools and men still predominated in British and Wesleyan schools.[122]

In part the differences reflect the siting and nature of schools, and the age of their pupils; for instance, very young children, who formed the bulk of the Catholic school population, were taught by women in the many infant departments, often attached to girls schools, established in the 1850s and 1860s. Infants formed a smaller proportion of the pupils in British and Wesleyan schools, which generally catered for parents of a better-off class who could afford to keep their children at school for longer. Catholic women, however, also took on teaching roles usually assigned to men; the tendency to substitute female for male teachers in mixed all-age schools in Lancashire, on which Stokes remarked in 1860[123] seems to have arisen from the lack of suitably qualified male candidates prepared to accept the salaries offered, together with the willingness of two communities, the Sisters of St Paul and the Sisters of Mercy, to take on mixed schools.

It is against this background that we take a final look at St Mary's. Faced with many difficulties not of their own making, the college authorities, with moral and financial support from the CPSC, worked hard to attract young men into teacher training and to help them gain the combination of spiritual qualities and secular knowledge required in successful educators of children. Evidence of the quality of those they sent out can be found in the inspectors' reports already cited; as to quantity, the numbers trained slowly increased. In 1871 for the first time every place at the college was filled – a remarkable recovery from the nadir of 1866 and 1867 – and while this level of entry was sustained only briefly, the very poor figures of earlier years were not repeated.[124] Gradually, too, St Mary's supplanted Dublin as the main source of male teachers in Catholic schools. Whereas in 1861 only a little over one-third of certificated masters had been trained at the college, by 1870 the proportion had risen to well over half, and in 1886 Graham told the Cross Commission that most male teachers in Catholic schools had passed through the college.[125]

It is possible that, as Stokes thought, a male college in the North would have attracted a greater number of candidates. There is no doubt that the Liverpool college benefited from its situation amongst a large and concentrated Catholic population, but there were, as we have seen, other factors involved in its success; the attraction of teaching as a career for women was such that by the early 1870s the demand for places warranted the opening of a second college. This was established in 1874 by the nuns of the Sacred Heart and based initially in their convent at Roehampton, moving later to Wandsworth.

The situation was different in the case of young men, and the problem of filling even one college with trainees of the right calibre was a recurring theme of these early years. In 1855 the CPSC,[126] exhorting priests to find suitable entrants to the Brotherhood, had pointed out that Brook Green was not a pool of Bethesda, capable of miraculously restoring faculties or multiplying numbers, but only 'a school wherein labour, humility and self-denial may be expected to produce the ripe fruit of Christian teachers in those who have received an adequate primary instruction'. This expectation the college amply fulfilled.

NOTES

Two sources used extensively in preparing this chapter are the annual reports of the Catholic Poor School Committee and those of Her Majesty's Inspectors. References to the former are made in the form CPSC, followed by the year of the report and the page number; for the latter the abbreviation CCE (Committee of Council on Education) is used throughout, although responsibility for publication passed to the Education Department during the period covered. (S) after the year of an HMI report signifies that the inspector was reporting on schools rather than training colleges.

Biographical details on college Principals and others have been taken from the *Dictionary of National Biography* (Oxford: Oxford University Press) and other works of reference including R.E. Aldrich and P. Gordon, *Dictionary of British Educationists* (London: Woburn Press, 1989).

1   CCE, 1852, p. 343.
2   A note on the names of the Catholic colleges: both the reports of the government inspectors and those of the CPSC referred to the women's colleges by their location, Liverpool and St Leonard's, and this usage has been followed here. HMI generally called the men's college Hammersmith while the CPSC reports referred on different occasions to St Mary's, Brook Green and Hammersmith. Except where contemporary sources are quoted, St Mary's is used here, indicating the continuity of the college's history.
3   J.A. Britton, 'The origin and subsequent development of St Mary's College, Hammersmith, 1847–1899', MA (Education) thesis, University of London, 1964, p. 74.
4   CCE, 1852, p. 347.
5   CCE, 1853 (S), p. 1195.
6   CCE, 1856, p. 797.
7   CPSC, 1861, p. 9.
8· According to the college timetables reproduced in the inspectors' reports, a

substantial allocation of hours for private study was introduced in 1861, Rowe's first year in office. In his report for 1868, p. 467, Stokes noted that the treatment of the students had been 'so far modified as to make the training school attractive to youth'.

9   *The Tablet*, 17 June 1899.

10 CCE, 1852, p. 344.

11 CPSC, 1854, Appendix F, p. 79.

12 Centenary Record of St Mary's College, published by the College, 1950, p. 135. Additionally, the CPSC Report for 1854, Appendix E, p. 78, lists three first-year students who may have been members or potential members of the Brotherhood.

13 CPSC, 1849, p. 20.

14 CPSC, 1852, Appendix E, pp. 39–40.

15 Reference for Battersea: 'First Report of the Training School at Battersea to the Poor Law Commissioners' (presented by James Kay and Edward Carleton Tufnell in January 1841), reproduced in J. Kay *Four Periods of Public Education*, (Brighton: The Harvester Press, 1973), p. 311. The book was first published in 1862. Dr Kay added his wife's family name of Shuttleworth to his surname on his marriage in 1842. For Chester: J.L. Bradbury, *Chester College and the Training of Teachers* (Chester: the Governors of Chester College, 1975), p. 106. For Cheltenham: C. More, *A Splendid College: An Illustrated History of Teacher Training in Cheltenham 1847–1990* (Cheltenham: Cheltenham and Gloucester College, 1992), p. 8.

16 For Battersea: Kay, pp. 310–11; for Chester: Bradbury, p. 106; for St Mark's: R.W. Rich, *The Training of Teachers in England and Wales during the Nineteenth Century* (Cambridge: Cambridge University Press, 1933), p. 86; for Whitelands: F.A. Widdowson, *Going up into the Next Class* (London: Hutchinson & Co., 1980), p. 221; for St Mary's: Britton, p. 54.

17 CPSC, 1849, Appendix R, p. 159.

18 CCE, 1857(S), p. 623; 1858(S), p. 195 and p. 204; 1859(S), p. 215.

19 CCE, 1859(S), p. 206.

20 CPSC, 1862, p. 21.

21 CPSC, 1861, p. 8.

22 CPSC, 1862, p. 21.

23 The information on the previous occupations of students is taken from the Student Register preserved in the college archives.

24 CPSC, 1861, p. 11.

25 CCE, 1856, p. 5.

26 'Report of the Royal Commissioners appointed to inquire into the State of Popular Education in England', 1861, (henceforward referred to as Newcastle Report) vol. VI, p. 30.

27 CCE, 1857(S), p. 617.

28 CCE, 1857(S), p. 618.

29 CPSC, 1858, p. 22.

30 In the Christmas 1864 examinations, for instance, 21 of the 25 candidates for entrance to St Mary's were successful, 58 of 65 Liverpool candidates, and 303 of 341 candidates for entrance to Church of England men's colleges (CCE, 1864, p. 304); the standard attained by the male Catholic candidates was thus

not much below that of the other categories. In 1869 they outperformed them, the figures being, respectively, 34 successful out of 36, 42 out of 59 and 366 out of 427 (CCE, 1869, p. 414).

31 G.F. Bartle, *A History of Borough Road College* (Isleworth: West London Institute of Higher Education, 1976), pp. 31–2.

32 The examples are taken from J.L. Alexander, 'Collegiate teacher training in England and Wales', PhD thesis, University of London, 1977, p. 294.

33 Minutes of the Committee of Council on Education, 21 December 1846, reproduced in Kay-Shuttleworth, p. 538.

34 CCE, 1852, pp. 344–6.

35 Newcastle Report, vol. VI, p. 48.

36 CCE, 1858, p. 356.

37 The syllabus for 1858 was reproduced in CPSC, 1857, Appendix I, pp. lxxi–lxxiv.

38 The subjects of the women's syllabus were listed in CPSC 1858, Appendix H, pp. lxii–lxiv.

39 CCE, 1858, pp. 364–5 (Marshall); pp. 370–1 (Stokes); p. 343 (Arnold); pp. 350–1 (Bowstead).

40 CCE, 1862, p. xii.

41 Newcastle Report, vol. V, p. 132.

42 CCE, 1860, p. 379.

43 M.E. Cullen, 'The growth of the Roman Catholic training colleges for women in England during the nineteenth and twentieth centuries', MEd thesis, University of Durham, 1964, p. 76.

44 CCE, 1857, p. 807.

45 CPSC, 1858, p. 11.

46 CPSC, 1853, Appendix E, p. 72.

47 CPSC, 1856, p. 11.

48 CPSC, 1857, p. 17 and Appendix K, p. lxxiv.

49 CPSC, 1858, Appendix E, pp. xliii–xliv.

50 Report of the Diocesan Inspector for 1859, Archives of the Archdiocese of Westminster, W2/2/4b, pp. 5–7.

51 CCE, 1852, p. 347.

52 Information on staffing in the Catholic colleges is taken from the reports of the CPSC and the government inspectors; for St Mary's the lists published in the Centenary Record have also proved very helpful.

53 CCE, 1867, p. 576.

54 Ibid.

55 Based on information in Bradbury, p. 103 and More, p. 31. At Chester, in the early days at least, a considerable part of the teaching was undertaken by the Principal and Vice-Principal, and staff were shared with the Science School.

56 CCE, 1864, p. 400.

57 M.P. Linscott, 'The educational work of the Sisters of Notre Dame in Lancashire since 1850', MA (Education) thesis, University of Liverpool, 1960, p. 200.

58 CCE, 1862, p. 278; 1861, p. 360.

59 Rich, *The Training of Teachers*, p. 155.

60 CCE, 1859, pp. 415–16.

61 There are several notebooks in the college archives, identified as being those of Charles Quinn, a student from Scotland who was at the college in 1861 and 1862.

62 The books in use at St Mary's were listed in the CPSC Reports each year between 1856 and 1860. The reference to the cost to students is taken from CPSC, 1860, Appendix F, p. xlviii.

63 CCE, 1854, p. 123; Letter to HMI conducting examinations.

64 CCE, 1871, p. 157.

65 CCE, 1854, p. 33 and pp. 63–4.

66 The information on the results of assessment is taken from tables printed in the CCE annual reports of the 1860s.

67 CCE, 1873, p. 255.

68 CCE, 1853 (S), pp. 1194–5.

69 CCE, 1849 (S), pp. 540–1; 1850(S), p. 830.

70 CCE, 1852, p. 344.

71 CPSC, 1867, p. 28.

72 CCE, 1853 (S), pp. 1194–5.

73 CPSC, 1865, p. 14.

74 CCE, 1866, p. 510.

75 CCE, 1858, p. 357.

76 Register of Letters 1862–1872, Archives of St Mary's College; Rowe to Langdale, 26 June 1866.

77 CCE, 1862, pp. 288–9.

78 CCE, 1860, p. 382.

79 CCE, 1852, p. 347.

80 CCE, 1859, p. 413.

81 CCE, 1873, pp. 254–5.

82 CCE, 1861, Appendix to Stokes' report, p. 367 (paper on use of the Practising School, furnished by the College).

83 CCE, 1860, pp. 383–4.

84 CCE, 1861, p. 361; 1862, p. 279.

85 The information in this section about St Mary's in the Brotherhood days has been taken from the full and interesting report made by Marshall after his visit to the college in December 1852; CCE, 1852, pp. 343–8.

86 CCE, 1871, p. 183.

87 Information on the way of life of students at Battersea during Kay's superintendence of the college has been taken from the previously cited Report to the Poor Law Commissioners in 1841, Kay-Shuttleworth, pp. 312–19.

88 Bradbury, p. 104 and p. 106–7.

89 Bartle, p. 23.

90 CCE, 1860, p. 375.

91 There are references in St Mary's Centenary Record to inter-college matches; Mr Austen, the Drill Sergeant, was on the staff for almost 30 years from 1862. Giving evidence in 1886 to the Royal Commission on the Working of the Elementary Education Acts (Cross Commission), the Principal said that he encouraged fixtures against other training colleges in and near London (Cross Report, 1, p. 452).

92 Archives of St Leonard's College at Mayfield Convent, MS 10 and 12.

93   A. Wall, 'The supply of certificated teachers to the Roman Catholic elementary schools of Britain, 1848–1870', MPhil thesis, University of Lancaster, 1983, p. 259.

94   More, p. 25.

95   CCE, 1856, p. 801.

96   Archives of St Mary's College – typed copies of letters among miscellaneous papers; Charles Quinn, whose notebooks are in the archives, seems to have been a recipient of some of them.

97   CPSC, 1868, pp. 20–1 and annotations in St Mary's Student Register, *passim.*

98   J.B. Rowe, 'Elementary education and the Catholic Poor School Committee', 1876, p. 10 (reproduction in pamphlet form of an article in *The Month*).

99   CPSC, 1862, Appendix E, pp. xlvi–lvi.

100   CPSC, 1869, pp. 27–8 and p. 31.

101   CCE, 1864, p. 333.

102   Newcastle Report, vol. V, p. 139.

103   Rich, p. 108.

104   Bradbury, p. 124.

105   Rich, p. 82.

106   Newcastle Report, vol. VI, p. 40.

107   Management Committee Reports of the School Board for London, returns for the six months to 25 March 1880, pp. 151–277; these show *inter alia* the colleges at which teachers had trained and the salaries they received. Graham told the Cross Commission in 1886 that a number of ex-students were teaching in Board Schools in direct opposition to the wishes of the Catholic authorities (Cross Report, 1, p. 451).

108   The St Mary's Student Register has annotations showing the salary paid in respect of some of the teaching posts to which students were appointed on qualification.

109   CCE, 1862(S), p. 112.

110   Catholic Schools Committee Annual Report for 1894, Appendix V, pp. 61–74 (the word Poor had by this time been dropped from the Committee's name).

111   Cross Report, 1, p. 454.

112   Newcastle Report, vol. V, p. 138.

113   CCE, 1858 (S), p. 206 (Morell); 1859 (S), p. 210 (Stokes); ibid., p. 198 (Marshall); 1868 (S), p. 312 (Lynch).

114   CCE, 1858, p. 363 (Marshall); 1860, p. 381 (Stokes).

115   CCE, 1860 (S), p. 194; 1862 (S), p. 120.

116   St Mary's Centenary Record, *passim.*

117   CCE, 1871, pp. 154–5 and p. 158; 1872, p. 308.

118   CCE, 1872, pp. 308–10. According to Bowstead (CCE, 1873, p. 241) the number of available places for men in 1873 was 1424 (i.e. *c.*700 per year), of which 1378 were taken up.

119   CCE, 1871, p. 154 (Cowie); 1873, pp. 241–3 (Bowstead).

120   CCE, 1854, p. 300.

121   Newcastle Report, vol. VI, p. 362.

122   The figures for school attendance are taken from tables in the CCE annual reports; they include all the day scholars in inspected Catholic schools in

England, Scotland and Wales who were present at the annual inspections/ examinations. The statements regarding the balance between male and female teachers are also based on CCE statistics; the published tables show an increasing proportion of women teachers in all types of school in England and Wales, with a much slower change in Scotland.

123 CCE, 1860 (S), p. 201. In his report on schools in the North Western district, Stokes listed those conducted by religious communities of women. The Sisters of St Paul had ten mixed schools and the Sisters of Mercy three, mainly in villages and small towns.

124 Graham told the Cross Commission that the college had admitted 236 students in the last ten years (Cross Report, 1, p. 453). He also referred to a marked improvement in the candidates.

125 In 1861, 46 of 118 certificated masters in Catholic schools were St Mary's trained; in 1869, at least 127 out of 208. These figures are taken from CPSC, 1861, p. 15 and 1869, pp. 27–8 and CCE, 1869, p. 491. Graham's statement paints a more optimistic picture than his reply to another question, which indicated that in 1884 240 out of 314 Headmasters of Catholic schools had been trained at the college (ibid.).

126 CPSC, 1855, p. 11.

7

PROPAGATION OF THE FAITH: ST MARY'S COLLEGE AND THE TRAINING OF CATHOLIC TEACHERS, 1944–72

Michele Dowling

> Simmarians can remember with pride that the religious traditions of their College have enabled them to consolidate the Faith of countless thousands of children who have passed through their hands. That, in essence, is what Simmaries is for, and explains what we are.[1]

THIS CHAPTER looks at the way in which St Mary's was presented as an institution for the training and education of Catholic teachers for the Catholic schools of England, Wales and indeed further afield, in the period 1944–72. The material is devised from a larger study of teacher education in the post-war period and, where appropriate, comparisons and contrasts are drawn between St Mary's and the other colleges in the study. This period witnessed great changes in teacher education generally. St Mary's was no exception. By the time the James Report[2] was published in early 1972, the colleges had changed completely from the institutions which had been in place after the Butler Act almost 30 years before. Evidence has been drawn from documentary sources, from college archives, from a postal survey distributed to former students of the colleges, and from interviews with a number of former staff and students at the colleges between 1944 and 1972. College papers tend to give the official view of what the college attempted to do. It is there in the statements, the issues of concern raised at meetings, and the discussions carried out in committees. But words are just part of the picture; silences too are important and it is interesting to compare the issues of concern in one college with the absence of concern in another.

College magazines and newsletters are particularly informative in presenting the college's self image, and in this case *The Simmarian Newsletter* and *St Mary's College Centenary Record* have been especially useful. The image presented in these publications has a dual purpose of being promotional and affirmative, the one directed at the outside world, the other directed towards the self, or the internal world of the college community. The survey and interviews offer a slightly different perspective. Yet even here there is a sense in which the college's affirmed self-image was accepted and thus further affirmed. There are some exceptions, but in general respondents who took part in this project were contacted through the college. These former students had maintained links with their college over maybe forty years or more, and thus were very positive about their experiences at college. This is not to say there were not complaints about aspects of college life, but I am aware that the images given to me of the colleges by former students are possibly less balanced than those offered by a sample drawn from a broader section of the former student body.

The focus of this chapter will be on St Mary's, but it is useful to remember that the college was not situated in a vacuum, but rather in a period of huge changes and negotiation in teacher training generally. Forces at work in society at large had an impact on all the training colleges at this time.

In 1944 St Mary's was still the only Catholic training college for men in England. As such, it attracted men from all over the country as well as from Northern Ireland which did not have a Catholic training college for men until 1948. Catholics believed that it was important for their children to be taught by Catholic teachers as is made clear in the following piece written by Father G.J. Shannon, CM who was Principal at St Mary's between 1941 and 1948:

> For Catholic parents . . . education is a temporal manifestation of God's eternal providence; it is the formative and directive Providence of the Creator applied to these little ones. Education of children must be the most important, most absorbing, most universal function in life . . . Catholic schools and Catholic teachers are demanded by the divine plan for the human race.[3]

Shannon regarded the training of Catholic teachers as the keystone in what he called the educational arch. Catholic education, he felt, would be assured as long as there was an adequate supply of Catholic men and women coming from the colleges 'to set before children the vision of the universe in Faith and the model of supernatural progress in their Catholic lives'.[4] The Faith is what sets the Catholic teacher apart from other teachers, that and the teacher's holistic approach to education. The Catholic teacher presented knowledge to children as a part of a holistic view of the world: God and Providence are not separated from the lesson on maths or English, but rather are present in the bearing and approach of the teacher. Shannon wrote that this is because:

> When a Catholic teacher looks at his pupils in the light of the Faith he sees the choirs of angels and the hordes of hell circling in expectation round the soul of every child ... The light of Faith picks out each individual child as an end in itself, the term of the processes of all the ages. In each child the redemptive act of Christ's Sacrifice finds its completion; and every generation of redeemed children who come before the Catholic teacher is seen by him as equi-distant from eternity. Catholic teachers are the only teachers to whom the adjective 'progressive' may truthfully be applied, because they know and work in the knowledge, that in every class taught the aim of all human progress must be attained.[5]

These sentiments were expressed before the great upheavals of the 1950s and the 1960s in particular, but similar ideas appear again and again in the writings of the Principal and other members of staff in the college. *The Simmarian Newsletter* is a ready source of such views. This had been moribund for some time and was revived by Father Kevin Cronin, CM who became Principal in 1948. It was effectively a way in keeping in touch with former students of the college. Each issue contained a letter from the Principal and also from the President of the Simmaries Association – a national association of past pupils established in 1950. It also gave a report of the college's sporting activities, the clubs and societies active at the time and the activities of branches of the Simmaries Association in various parts of the country. One of the most active members of the association was its first president, Terence Quirk.[6] Quirk agreed with the importance of providing a Catholic education for Catholic children and he regarded St Mary's as playing a crucial role in this. Towards this end he said of the college:

> This must be a unique community bound together by the Faith, by our desire for service to a great cause – the education of Catholic children in Catholic schools by Catholic teachers enjoying what we must strive to secure – real equality for our future citizens, based on the justice of our claims and without constraint of conscience or financial penalty.[7]

For Quirk, then, the Catholic teacher was engaged in more than merely ensuring the transmission of a particular religious message – he or she was engaged in a struggle to secure the right to recreate the Catholic community, enjoying the same facilities and access to resources as others without prejudice to their religious affiliation.

The fact that Roman Catholicism was a minority religion and not funded in a similar manner to the Church of England is one reason for Quirk's insistence of equality of treatment for Catholic schools and teachers. His arguments would also have had a basis in Pius XI's encyclical *The Christian Education of Youth* of 1929. In this the Pontiff stressed the importance of 'man's education' as a way of preparation for what 'he must be and what he must do here below, in order to attain the sublime end for which he was created'.[8] Moreover he asserted that:

> it is the inalienable right as well as the indispensable duty of the Church, to watch over the entire education of her children, in all institutions, public or private, not merely in regard to the religious instruction there given, but in regard to every other branch of learning and every regulation in so far as religion and morality are concerned.[9]

This was not the only occasion when Quirk raised the issue of equality for Catholic schools. In a 1951 issue of the *Newsletter* he referred to two articles in *Education* in which it was claimed that LEAs refused to assist parents who wish to send their children to Catholic grant-aided schools outside the area where Catholic schools were not available. He regarded this as a deplorable injustice and called for 'fair treatment for Catholic schools'.[10]

The issue of the Catholic teacher was raised again in 1956 in Father Cronin's letter, part of which is quoted at the beginning of this chapter. In this letter Father Cronin linked the role of the teacher with the traditions of the college. The essence of the college as he presented it was bound up with the mission of the Catholic teacher which was not just to teach a child to read, write and count, but to instil in the child the essence of the Catholic Faith.[11]

This sense survived into the 1960s. Indeed, in a letter written in 1968 Father Cronin told readers of *The Simmarian Newsletter* that the Second Vatican Council gave new impetus to their role as Catholic teachers:

> The Council tells us that the laity must take up the renewal of the temporal order as their own special obligation. In the light of the decrees of the Council we must aim at being devoted Catholics and dedicated teachers. Our Simmarian activities can help us considerably in our work of drawing souls to Christ.[12]

These were the most obvious examples from the *Newsletters*, but the religious tone which permeates them all is unmistakable. This is mirrored in the college in general. One of the most obvious ways in which the Catholic presence was felt was in the persons of the priests on the staff. The proportion of religious on the staff fell over the years as photographs show quite dramatically. However, for the period under discussion here the Principal and Vice-Principal were always members of the Vincentian Fathers, and they could veto the appointment of staff members. Much of the writing in the *Newsletter* was done by clerical members of the staff, thus ensuring a religious tone to the publication. In addition to the Principal's letter, notes on student life and accounts of events in the college were frequently written by clerical members of staff. Students tended to come from Catholic families, and in general they had also been to Catholic schools. Thus they were accustomed to a Catholic atmosphere. This was made clear in interview with former students. One respondent who had attended the college in the 1950s told me that he never noticed a heavy emphasis on religion, but that in his case it would have been preaching to the converted in any case. He said that he and his fellow students felt that 'their purpose was to prepare more Catholic teachers for Catholic children', although not all of them went into Catholic schools either on teaching practice or after-wards.[13] Indeed, there is evidence of some tension between students who did their teaching practice in non-Catholic schools and the school authorities concerning morning prayers and assembly. In December 1963 a school informed the college that it might refuse to accept students from St Mary's in future as they had refused to attend assembly. The Hierarchy's instructions in this case was that students may attend assembly in a passive capacity but that ultimately each student was to satisfy his own conscience.[14] Other respondents from the 1950s and the late 1960s also commented on the Catholic presence in the college. They felt that it was bound up with its ethos. Students varied in their recollection of how overt the presence was. In answers to the postal survey some remember an explicit emphasis on the role of the Catholic teacher being mentioned in lectures, others do not mention this. In general, however, students agree that they remained conscious of Catholicism throughout their time at St Mary's.

In the early days this was manifest in the presence of Vincentian priests on the staff who wore the soutane and were highly visible within the community. Later the new chapel, an imposing building close to one of the major entrance gates, proved a physical reminder of the spiritual presence.[15] Within the college morning prayer was said daily. The regulations were changed in 1963 to allow for a minute's prayer in the classroom at 9 a.m. and the Angelus was to be said at the end of the 11.30–12.15 period rather than at 12.00. Morning Mass had been compulsory until 1948 when the rule was changed in recognition of the greater number of older students, some of them married, who had entered the college after a period in the forces. Mass continued each day on a voluntary basis but on one morning each week a period was kept free to enable all members of the college community to attend should they wish – this was in addition to Sunday Mass which was also voluntary.

It is also interesting to note that in the 1950s at least, religion was entwined in the rituals of another important part of life at St Mary's – rugby.[16] One student I interviewed mentioned the fact that the rugby team used to go spontaneously to the church before a match. This was done regardless of an individual's personal feeling about religion – it was part of the ritual. In the respondent's words:

> every time before a rugby match, in the first year I played for the second fifteen, the second year I played for the first fifteen, every time before you went out on the pitch you were in the chapel and say a prayer together. I don't know what we were praying for – probably for the total destruction of the enemy but it was quite odd, we always did that and I don't think it was a rule it was simply a practice which we decided we were going to do . . . maybe like the New Zealanders doing their Hakka Dance on the pitch, same kind of thing, I don't know.[17]

The religious presence was also evident in other ways, for example, the motto of the college. *Monstra te esse Matrem*, which translates as 'Show thyself to be a Mother' comes from the Marian hymn, *Ave Maris Stella*. This was the college hymn, sung at Mass in the College chapel. According to the Principal, Father Cronin, 'in the context it [the motto] implies that we, as Simmarians, rely far more on heavenly grace and aid for the success of the work we do than on our own natural gifts and ability'.[18]

This came from a piece on mottoes written for *The Simmarian Newsletter*, which began with the college motto and moved on to consider two other mottoes which are prominent in the college as it now stands. These are the motto of the Waldegrave family who owned the 'Old House' between 1812–78 and a motto inscribed by its original builder, Horace Walpole, on the ceiling of the library. The first of these is *Calem non animum*, or 'the skies not the mind' which Father Cronin felt was 'an admirable motto for a Catholic Training

College ... spiritual values, not merely academic ones! The motto could have been made for us'.[19] The second motto, Walpole's, reads *Fari quae sentiat*, translated as 'say what you think'. Cronin commented:

> It pleases me to regard Horace Walpole's motto as eminently suitable to us, for the particular reason that we have always had in our College a well-developed tradition of liberty, and in particular of liberty in the expression of different points of view.[20]

He finished his piece by expressing his hope that 'we trained you to think aright, and I hope too that you have gone on uttering those things that you know to be good and sound'.[21] This is indicative of the way in which the message of spirituality was transmitted in an indirect way, that is in a way that involved musings on general aspects of life at the college rather than merely overtly in the lecture room or tutorial.

However, lecture notes from 1959–60 show clear evidence of the Catholic influence. This is most explicit in the 'Seven aims of Catholic education' which the student had noted. These were:

To produce:
1.   intelligent Catholics
2.   spiritually vigorous Catholics
3.   cultured Catholics
4.   vocationally prepared Catholics
5.   socially minded Catholics
6.   healthy Catholics
7.   good citizens[22]

These could apply to the aims of education generally, but they were presented to the students as specifically Catholic. In addition, until the mid-1960s the Head of the Education Department was a Vincentian priest and all of the lecturers teaching in Education in 1959–60 also were priests.[23] From my study of all the colleges, I conclude that the orientation of the subject in question depended very greatly on the interests and values of the lecturer. There was no central curriculum and departments were able to choose the texts used by their classes. The tone of the lectures and the emphases laid on questions, issues and authors could also vary according to the personal preferences of the lecturer. In this context one would expect a Catholic tone to overlay the Education theory taught at St Mary's. There were some examples of this in the notes, less explicit than that quoted above. The stress on virtue and the importance of self-control for example, and the need for character formation to triumph over natural inclinations and instincts.

Beyond the College, St Mary's promoted the Catholic cause by helping to instigate the campaign to secure benefits for clerical students who were not entitled to the same state support as lay students. In 1961 students from St Mary's took a motion to the Association of Catholic Teacher College Students (ACTS) calling for a full investigation of the financial position of religious sisters and brothers taking courses in higher education to establish what reasons, if any, could justify the fact that they did not receive the grant available to other students.[24] This set in motion a series of meetings between the National Union of Students and relevant bodies including the Ministry of Education. The campaign to secure full rights for student religious continued into 1962. By late summer Bishop Beck and Dr H.M. King, MP were also involved in the campaign. In July 1964 the Ministry announced a grant of £150 for religious sisters and brothers attending institutions of higher education. The action of the NUS was the catalyst for the campaign, but the original impetus had come from St Mary's.[25] ACTS joined NUS in 1962. This was seen as important in linking the Catholic colleges to NUS. ACTS was also affiliated to the Union of Catholic Students. The actions of ACTS in this case, and proceedings from conferences over the 1960s show that St Mary's students played a prominent role. Thus they not only accepted, but actively pursued their part in the image of the college's as being to the fore in Catholic education.

Issues relating to the Catholic teacher and Catholic education continued throughout the 1960s. Indeed, in the early years of the decade they seemed to gather a new impetus as the question of the value of Catholic schools was raised in the Catholic press. Initially the greatest concerns voiced in the press had been the growth of the Catholic school population and the almost certain shortage of places for Catholic children in Catholic schools. This was soon overtaken by a feeling among many Catholics that Catholic schools were a poor investment. Great concern was voiced at the levels of leakage, that is the numbers of children who were lost to the church during their school careers. Letters to the Catholic press during 1963 and 1964 in particular highlighted these worries.[26] Among those criticizing the system of Catholic education, the greatest fear was that the schools were being expected to operate in a vacuum. They were not helped by investment in parish life or indeed, by a vibrant home life which consolidated the child's religious belief. In this situation leakage was felt to be inevitable, and the question was asked repeatedly – is the school bill worth it? In an interview in July 1963 with Hugh Kay, who favoured a reform of the present system of Catholic education, Bishop Beck of the Catholic Education Committee defended the system. Beck considered that Roman Catholic children being taught by Roman Catholic teachers was a great strength. He replied that leakage rates were difficult to assess, and that while there were undoubtedly bad areas, there were also good areas. He also pointed out that in the case of non-practice the attitude of the home was of crucial importance: the school could not replace the home but it could help enormously. For this reason alone the schools should be open to all whether they were practising Roman Catholics or not.

The idea that the school should compensate for inadequacies in the home in the teaching of religion reappeared in a number of sources.[27] It was one of the themes in a piece by Archbishop Heenan in the *Catholic Teacher's Journal* in July 1963 and led to a huge response. One woman teacher who wrote to the *Catholic Herald* rejected this claim that the school take over what was fundamentally the role of the home and family. The family was the unit of Catholic society, she stated, thus any suggestion that the school should supplant the family was surely contrary to church teaching on the family. If there were perceived inadequacies in the home, she continued, the church should tackle those and not try to pass on the problems to the school. This effectively brings us back to the question of the use of church funds – so much was being spent on schools there was not enough to finance other activities in the community. Thus problems at home and parish level were allowed to go unchecked.

St Mary's soon came to the fore in this debate. It appeared in several of the early issues of the journal *Catholic Education Today* which was based at St Mary's. The first issue was in 1967 when the question had been further complicated by the moves towards ecumenism initiated by the Second Vatican Council. This raised the question whether it was a good idea to segregate children of different Christian denominations. This particular viewpoint was evident in an article by Terry Eagleton in the first issue of the journal in January 1967.[28] He closed his article thus:

> we are coming to reject the idea of Catholic schools and parishes as structures closed to the world, and demand that they should be open and dynamic; the real questions, however, aren't whether a particular structure is open or closed, but whether it is the right

kind of structure at all – whether there isn't something inherently closed about the whole sort of institution?[29]

This was a challenge to more than just Catholic education. However, this article set the scene for a number of articles which appeared over the years in this journal. A reply in the same issue from A.C.F. Beales entitled 'The Schools Debate' dismissed Eagleton's arguments as 'inconsequential and inconclusive'. Beales argued that the Catholic schools were in the schools system, albeit in a particular way, and that the impact of the Catholic schools in Christianizing the nation was small. Beales further rejected that there was anything exclusive about the way in which the Catholic Teachers' Federation had considered the place of the Catholic teacher, which was one of the criticisms made by Eagleton as damaging to the overall education of the child.[30] The debate continued in 1968 in an article which looked at the same question from a different angle. In 'The social dimension of Catholic education', Charles Boxer opened his article by suggesting that Catholic educationalists were confused as to the nature of the society they were teaching their children to enter, and how to reconcile this with the specific traditions from which they come. He argued for a broader notion of Catholic thinking to move beyond the institutional boundaries of the church buildings and to include a social component in its thinking and action. Unless this was done, he claimed, the schools will continue with a religious teaching which he referred to as 'a disheartening waste of time'.[31] What was needed was a new priority – social education:

> What passes for specific Catholic teaching should take second place to a system of teaching which would help our children to become responsible, happy members of society, people who have learned what it means to live in community, people who have learned something about how community can be spread, who care about human warmth, people who have learned to develop a sense for loving.[32]

Unfortunately, Boxer did not suggest how this might be done, nor indeed was he specific on what message was being passed to children in Catholic schools at that time and those aspects which he felt to be deficient.

Such discussions on religion in the schools had implications for the training colleges and St Mary's was prominent in efforts to come to terms with these challenges. One of the more common complaints was that teachers were inadequately prepared to teach religion in the schools and thus the children were allowed to lapse or at least did not receive the instruction expected from a Catholic school. In 1964 St Mary's hosted a meeting organized by the Catholic Teachers' Federation on the secondary schools, religious instruction, the work of the Catholic colleges and the opportunities for further religious education training for teachers.[33] Representatives of St Mary's continued to play a prominent role in further conferences and discussions on this issue throughout the decade. This is a reflection of the genuine concern among Catholic educators about the apparent failings of Catholic education as it then operated. It can also be seen as the affirmation of St Mary's self-image as a prominent player in the promotion of Catholic education. As such, it played a dual role in confirming its self-image internally and promoting its image externally.

At this point it is worth commenting that these debates took place in the context of a developing notion of child-centred education which gained acceptance after the war. In this view of education the teacher is less the fount of all knowledge, the authority who dictates to the class, and more the guide, the nurturer who enables each child to fulfil their own potential. This idea of the teacher and of education had been gaining ground at varying rates in the colleges since the Second World War. By the mid-1960s it was the accepted way of approaching teaching. It was officially endorsed in 1967 with the publication of the Plowden Report, *Children and their Primary Schools*.[34] The tenor of several of the above pieces indicate that the authors are trying to come to terms with more than merely a religious orientation in the schools. It is strange in some ways that this concern was raised so late, as there seems to be little radical change in what is going on in the colleges following Plowden – in all the colleges I have examined, Plowden is the endorsement of methods and approaches already in place. These changes had been coming since the early 1950s at varying rates, and to varying degrees. In many colleges the 1950s seem to have been a transitional period in which teacher educators were trying to come to grips with new methods of education. This was also the time before Piagetian psychology which really only began to make inroads in the 1960s. St Mary's, like the other colleges, adopted the new methods, although it seems to have been slower to accept the newer methods than some of the other colleges I have studied – particularly the women's colleges. I suspect this is because St Mary's was a men's college and that it came from a tradition of training secondary teachers, whereas the new methods were more appropriate to primary classrooms.[35]

In a more general sense, religion was going through a period of attack from a more permissive society. All the voluntary colleges I have looked at express concern at the declining numbers attending church or chapel services, as well as the problem of moral standards in the colleges. This was raised in a 1961 memorandum to the colleges by the then Minister for Education, David Eccles. He was concerned that as the schools had an influence on the children they educated, it was necessary to consider those institutions which influenced the teachers that went into the schools. He considered that, 'We should begin at the beginning and look to the Training Colleges as a centre of influence among the whole profession.' In particular he stated that, 'what I should like to know is the extent to which students will now have more time to hear, read and think about morals and religion'.[36] This memorandum resulted in a series of replies from Principals to the Minister. A 'Digest' of these replies is held in the Whitelands College archive.[37] The Principals commented that they were concerned at the lack of in-depth understanding of religion among students. Concern was also expressed at the 'new' moral standards which promoted sexual promiscuity, the loosening of religious commitment, and smoking and drinking as acceptable behaviour. In addition to this there was also the overwhelming defence of the Christian ethos of the colleges. This was most evident in the church colleges where the 'community of purpose is seen to spring, rightly and inevitably, from the religious foundation'. However, it was also indicated in replies from LEA College Principals. One actually commented that it was a handicap not to have a chapel which could serve both as a point for worship and 'as a visible sign that the college community is firmly rooted in the Christian community'. The colleges also felt it wrong to abandon systems of care whereby students were given clear guidance of the sort Eccles felt might be lacking. The colleges protested that they were in a far better position to care for their students, to offer adequate pastoral and tutorial systems and to foster a sense of responsibility and integrity than the universities whose structures and functions did not enable them to carry out that role to the extent the colleges could.[38]

In this context it is interesting to read what the Anglican Bishop of London, speaking as the Chairman of the Church of England Training Colleges, had to say about Whitelands College in 1964.

> [Our first aim] is to send out from Church Colleges 'good teachers and good men and women'. It is no longer our aim to produce teachers only for church schools but to send out to both county and

church schools responsible teachers, prepared to help in the work of Christian education. To this end we try to provide opportunities for students to grow in responsibility and insight so that they may become balanced persons with powers of independent judgement and decision and an enlightened concern for the children and young people they will teach.[39]

The meeting at which the Bishop was speaking felt that the particular contribution of a church college was the experience of living in a Christian community, in the sense that they are aware of the need to be members one of another with a true concern for all in their own community and in the schools. The religious and sacramental life of the college and the chapel, and the underlying sense of unity and purpose which the Christian basis and traditions should give, were thought to offer students the opportunity to experience this sense of community more than students in secular colleges. It was also hoped that students would come to a more mature and complete understanding of their own faith through courses in religion and Christian doctrine.

The teaching of religion was one area in which the church colleges differed from LEA. Religion or Divinity in the church colleges was a compulsory course and often lasted the entire three years of the student's college career. During the 1960s there is some evidence that students in the colleges felt that this was an unnecessary burden on them and that it diverted their attention from subjects which they felt were more important. Whether Divinity courses should be optional was one of the questions raised at the meeting with Principals at the ACTS conference in 1964. In 1968 the Standing Conference of Church Colleges was told that students across the country were unwilling to teach religion in the schools, feeling unsure of their ground and inadequate.[40] At Bede College in 1965 the House Committee considered the suggestion that the three-year obligatory course in religious knowledge should be curtailed to improve standards in the four-year BEd. This was rejected as the Committee agreed that religious education was crucial in a church college.[41]

The debate continued at other levels too. In one men's Church of England college there was a discussion as to whether prospective teachers should not be expected to assume higher moral standards than their contemporaries. This college too constantly reiterated the special position of the church college as opposed to the secular LEA college. This seems to increase during the 1960s. Students were asked to ponder on the obligations that came with being members of a church college. It was also important for the voluntary colleges to justify their existence in the face of expansion and the expectation after the Robbins Report that the average college would be of 750 students and over.[42] Various strategies were pursued by the colleges to ensure that they would manage to grow to a figure that would ensure their survival. Colleges in the 1960s not only needed large student bodies to cope with the demand for teachers in the schools, but they also needed larger student bodies to enable them to increase their staffs and so improve the depth of specialization in the colleges at staff level. The smaller colleges which were the norm up to the 1950s may have been intimate and familial institutions where staff and students could live in a tight-knit community, but they were also often academically challenged by the fact that staff were expected to cover several subjects. As the 1960s progressed and particularly with the introduction of the BEd. in 1965–6, these colleges could not compete. Some pooled their resources or amalgamated with neighbouring colleges to extend their teaching potential; some managed to expand as a single institution and keep pace with the required standards; others developed new courses and specialisms to attract students; still others were forced to close their doors.

St Mary's was at this time one of the larger colleges in the voluntary sector. By 1968 there were 1150 students on the roll, so her future as a viable institution must have seemed safe. The greater numbers had been helped by the admission of women to the college in 1966. In 1963 there had been 621 students on the roll, but the Ministry had already accepted plans for a building programme which would allow for expansion to 1000 students including 300 women.[43] However, while the college might survive as an institution, there was no guarantee that the ethos of the college would survive the growth in numbers and the change from a relatively select group to a much larger institution. This was a fear expressed in other voluntary colleges at this time too. It was recognized that the changes of the 1960s would radically alter the character of the institution as much as it had altered its physical appearance. Thus the debate on the nature of Catholic education and the role of the Catholic teacher can also be seen in the context of a general feeling in the voluntary colleges that they were losing some of the control over the college as an institution with a particular ethos.

One of the interesting omissions in St Mary's files, when compared to Bede, for example, is the sense of crisis and that the ethos of the college was under threat. The Bede files bear testimony to an expression of fear that students did not realize what being members of a Christian community was – that a church college brought with it certain obligations which students do not seem to appreciate. The Principal frequently raised the issue of attendance at chapel, and indeed it is mentioned in some annual reports.[44] In his talk to students in 1962 'The importance of an adult acceptance of the obligation of chapel attendance' is one of the four points he intended to make to the student body.[45] There were no similar remarks in the files in St Mary's. There were some fears that the introduction of women to the college in 1966 might disrupt the established style of life in college but these were put aside as unfounded within months of the admission of women.[46] However, there were no records of the sort of concerns aired in Bede. This could have been because the issue was seen to be a non-issue – students knew that they were expected to attend weekly Mass and other services were available for those who wished to avail of them. As mentioned above, compulsory morning Mass was abolished to cater for a more adult student body after the war, and it can be surmised that adults were expected to know what was required from them under the tenets of their Faith. It is also possible that this apparent lack of concern with religiosity in the college was symptomatic of a more general complacency within the Catholic Church in Britain at the time. Unlike the other Christian churches, the Catholic Church had not yet experienced a large loss of adherents or the loss of confidence which accompanied this.[47] Another possibility is that issues concerning religion and morality were discussed but not minuted. I asked former staff members about this and in general they did not remember any great discussion about religion or morality in the college. Female students felt that they were guarded more closely and were more regulated than their male colleagues, and this may have been the college's way of ensuring certain moral standards. However, it was felt that by the late 1960s a new way of behaviour was accepted as the societal norm. Students were now adults and were to act according to their own consciences. By this time respondents felt the ethos of the college was changing for a number of reasons in any case. Religion still had a presence, but it was not as evident as it had been. To begin with, the number of religious on the staff had declined continuously and by the late 1960s the Vincentians no longer held the positions of Bursar or of Head of Education.

(However, the Principalship remained in Vincentian hands until 1992 when a lay man was appointed to the post.)

Indeed, the only place that I found where the issues of religion, change and the problems that these might pose were discussed was among Catholic students attending the eighth annual ACTS conference in April 1963.[48] One group discussion was dedicated to 'Apathetic Catholics in the Colleges'. The group felt that this was a serious problem and felt that a decline in religious observance might be part of a rebellion against what were regarded as the petty rules and regulations which were imposed on students. Rebellion was against the order or the authorities of the church college rather than religion itself. Indeed, it was reported that where students were given the right to organize their own religious life, attendance at services had risen, or at least was not in serious decline.[49] From the papers from St Mary's it appears that the college was one of those where students were given the freedom to practise or not as they chose. If this is the case, and if the college adhered to the pattern observed above, it is possible that attendance at services was not seen as a problem worthy of note at staff level.

ACTS is an interesting group, as it tackled what it saw to be a number of issues affecting Catholic students during the 1960s. In 1964 the annual conference included a meeting with Principals of the Catholic colleges. ACTS had conducted a questionnaire survey in which students were asked if Divinity courses should be optional and whether all students at Catholic colleges should be expected to teach religion. The students surprised Principals by pointing to a level of religious apathy in the colleges which they said they were unaware of. However, they agreed that it was a serious problem and that the question of student apathy should be taken further. The Principals also pointed out the global nature of the problem and warned students not to get it out of proportion in the colleges in England and Wales. However, it is interesting to see that students perceived this religious question to be more serious than the staff in the colleges. The issue was raised again in a different form in 1966 in a piece in the *Catholic Herald* which reported that ACTS which had a membership of 6600 was seeking changes in the teaching of religion in Catholic schools.[50] They pointed out that if the changes were to be effected, co-operation of teachers would be essential. They also complained that students were not adequately prepared to teach religion. They were dissatisfied with certain other points: the lack of sociological and psychological information with which people could

supplement their religious teaching; the lack of a nationally co-
ordinated syllabus, examination and assessment for the teacher's
certificate; the low examination results in some Catholic colleges of
education in Divinity, which was often coupled with a low lecturer–
student ratio, and finally they complained at the system of Catholic
education resulting in a large number of unqualified Divinity teachers in schools.[51]

In this chapter I have attempted to show that St Mary's prided
herself as having a crucial role in the propagation of the faith
through trained Catholic teachers in Catholic schools. I have also
attempted to put this in the context of the role of other religious
colleges and to consider the way in which all of the voluntary colleges
rose to the challenges posed by the changes in education and in
society during the 1960s.

A push from the Ministry to produce more teachers led to the
expansion of the colleges during the 1960s in particular. During
these upheavals a good reputation helped to promote St Mary's in a
competitive market-place. The same is true for colleges such as
Whitelands in London and Bede College in Durham. Many of the
traditional structures and organizations of these institutions were
changed beyond recognition during the 1960s. They were transformed from being small, mono-technic institutions, often also
single sex, with students and at least some staff members in residence, to larger establishments. Students lived out in lodgings or in
privately rented accommodation as well as in college. Staff no longer
accepted residence as part of their position. In many colleges new
arrangements for teaching practice meant that the entire student
body was not together in college at any one time. Further changes in
the 1970s meant that new courses were added to the syllabuses
offered in the colleges. With diversification teacher training is no
longer the only course offered at St Mary's, or indeed at the other
voluntary colleges.

Other changes were brought about by changes in expectations of
young people generally. Student representation, the lessening of rules
and regulations, particularly those relating to visiting hours and the
entertainment of guests, dress codes and meal organization all feature
in the debates and discussions taking place in the colleges at this time.
The advent of a more permissive attitude in society in general and the
increasingly open secularization of society posed another challenge
for the colleges and for the church colleges in particular. With these
changes came a new moral code which challenged more traditional

notions of sexual propriety. There also seemed to be a culture of negotiation in which participants sought to redefine traditional boundaries. This had an effect on all of the colleges as students moved towards more freedom and responsibility in the everyday workings of the college. This resulted in student representation on college Academic Boards, governing bodies and various internal committees. Student Unions also became more active and looked for more autonomy from college authorities. Changes in attitudes and what young people considered acceptable behaviour also led to questions on what was appropriate behaviour for intending teachers. For church colleges there was an added issue as they were concerned not only with the training and education of teachers, but with passing on a particular Christian message which would be disseminated through the teacher in the schools. As institutional religion came under attack, what would that mean for them and for the special ethos that they held as their *raison d'être?* However, these changes did not undermine the sense of tradition in the institution. This sense of tradition seems to live on in all of the older training institutions which I have looked at, and for the voluntary colleges religion is at the heart of this tradition. In this context perhaps we should let Father Shannon have the last word. On the occasion of the centenary of St Mary's, then a men's college, he preached a sermon which he entitled 'Simmaries: the Spirit and the Mother'. The following, taken from that, sums up the sense of tradition and continuity which he saw as an integral part of the college:

> A College is built up with living stones. Simmaries is not confined to local habitations; she is not limited by Hammersmith or Strawberry Hill; she is not adequately reigned by the old buildings now abandoned to the throb of Lyon's engines or by the lawns, arches and battlements of Horace Walpole's dilettante romance. Here or there she may lodge her passing tenement, but her being is something greater belonging to a different order; it is a spiritual reality. The being of Simmaries is in her sons; she is her children, the living and the dead. She is inseparable from our predecessors. Their zeal, their faith, their charity and selfless labours have been fused into the structure of her spirit, and shape the very landscape of her soul.[52]

NOTES

1   Letter from K. Cronin, *The Simmarian Newsletter*, April, 1956. Simmaries can best be thought of as a pet name given to the college by its students and staff.

Simmarians refers to those men (and later women) who trained at the college.

2   Department of Education and Science, *Teacher Education and Training: A Report by a Committee of Inquiry Appointed by the Secretary of State for Education and Science, under the Chairmanship of Lord James of Rusholme* (London: HMSO, 1972).

3   G.J. Shannon, 'The Catholic teacher', *St Mary's College Centenary Record 1850–1950* (London: St Mary's College, 1950), p. 84.

4   Ibid., p. 85.

5   Ibid., p. 86.

6   Terence Quirk took over the editorship of the newsletter after he completed his Presidency and he remained in this post for many years. He was also an active member of the Catholic community, his contribution recognized when he was made a Papal Knight in later life.

7   Letter from T. Quirk in *The Simmarian Newsletter,* November 1950.

8   Pius XI, *The Christian Education of Youth,* from Revd G.C. Treacy (ed.), *Five Great Encyclicals* (New York: Paulist Press, 1939), p. 39.

9   Ibid., p. 43.

10   Letter from T. Quirk in *The Simmarian Newsletter,* 1951. It must be noted that he was referring to two articles which had been written in 1944.

11   Letter from K. Cronin, *The Simmarian Newsletter,* April 1956.

12   Letter from K. Cronin, *The Simmarian Newsletter,* January 1968.

13   Interview with former student, 1954–56, November 1997.

14   AC/7, Academic Board Minutes, 6 December 1963. The matter was not raised again so presumably the issue was resolved by students attending assembly in a passive capacity.

15   Commented on specifically in interview by former student (1959–60) and staff member (1969–89), 24 April 1998.

16   In interviews all former students have mentioned rugby as being significant in the life of the college; and rugby was mentioned even by those who did not play the sport and who had no interest in the scene that went with it. According to one respondent, there was a rumour in the 1950s that if you played rugby your place at St Mary's was safe. Indeed, one respondent who was both a student and served on the staff of the college suggested that when it came to screening students for admission men were looked on far more favourably if they had rugby, whereas women were screened more thoroughly on academic ability. A female respondent felt that the community atmosphere in the college was very much associated with the rugby playing crowd and the social scene that went with that. Questionnaire replies also indicate the central position of sport in the social life of the college.

17   Interview with former student, 1954–6, November 1997.

18   Letter from K. Cronin, CM, in *The Simmarian Newsletter,* November 1952.

19   Ibid. All the mottoes and their translations come from Cronin's piece.

20   Ibid.

21   Ibid.

22   From lecture notes on Education Theory, 1959–60. Privately held.

23   The owner of the notebooks which I have studied wrote the name of the lecturer on the front of all his notebooks. All of these were clerics. If there were

others involved in teaching in Education at that time he did not attend their lectures.

24   NUS files, MSS.280/ 134/4.

25   Ibid.

26   Letters on this topic continued in subsequent years, although not in the same volume.

27   It was not restricted to Catholic sources. In the Methodist Education Committee Report for 1961–2 the following comment appears: 'The need is not just for well trained teachers, but for teachers with well-grounded Christian faith. it would seem that more and more children come to the schools from homes that have not the least interest in religion or in the Church; the Christian gospel means nothing to them' (Southlands College archive).

28   Eagleton is now best known as a left-wing anti-church intellectual, but in the 1960s he was involved in a left-wing Catholic publication called *Slant*. *Slant* had come out of Cambridge in 1964 and was essentially the work of a group of Catholic undergraduates (later graduates) from a working-class or lower middle-class background. They had links with the Dominicans which ensured that the voice of *Slant* carried further than one would expect from a group with so small a following. They presented a programme of reform which was much in line with that proposed elsewhere: decentralization, a popular liturgy, acceptance of contraception, etc. *Slant* petered out in the late 1960s and its final issue was dated March 1970. It had failed to find the ground it needed for its brand of Christian radicalism.

29   Ibid.

30   A.C.F. Beales, 'The Schools Debate', *C.E.T.*, 1:2, March–April 1967.

31   C. Boxer, 'The social dimension of Catholic education', *C.E.T.*, 2:1, Jan.-Feb. 1968, pp. 13–14.

32   Ibid.

33   Reported in the *Catholic Herald*, 10 April 1964.

34   Central Advisory Council for Education (England), *Children and their Primary Schools* (London: HMSO, 1967).

35   St Mary's was forced to train almost all of its students for the primary school following a directive from the Ministry in 1960. This was to cater for the huge demands in the primary school due to the population structure at the time. However, many colleges introduced a course for Junior/Secondary which meant that students were prepared to teach in either primary or secondary schools.

36   Memorandum from David Eccles to the Principals of the Training Colleges, 6 October 1961, from the Whitelands College archive. Whether the colleges had the kind of influence on students that Eccles seemed to think they did is debatable. However, in this context that is less important than the fact that he believed them to have the most significant determining influence on intending teachers.

37   'Digest of Principal's replies to the Minister's letter and memorandum of 6th October 1961', ibid.

38   Ibid.

39   'Aims of the College [Whitelands] as agreed at a meeting of the Academic Board held on 19 February, 1964', Whitelands College archive.

40 E/ HB2/ 183, from the Principal's report on the Standing Conference of Church Colleges, 4–5 June 1968, reported to Staff Council, 19 June 1968.

41 E/ HB2/ 11, Report of the House Committee, submitted to Governing Body, March 1965.

42 Robbins, etc.

43 *The Simmarian Newsletter*, March 1963.

44 The level of chapel attendance was mentioned in the annual reports for 1948–9, 1949–50 and again in 1954–5. E/ HB2/ 50, 51 and 55.

45 E/ HB2/ 180.

46 Letter from Father Cronin to the readership, *The Simmarian Newsletter,* April 1967. He says in the letter: 'In general it is felt that the women have settled in well and have been accepted by the staff and students . . . The final characteristic of our group of women is their well developed sense of responsibility. We have always prided ourselves in Simmaries that we have treated our men students as adults, giving them a maximum responsibility to manage student affairs, and expecting everything from them in the way of sensible use of the liberties they enjoy. We find that this is one of the things that have appealed especially to the women students and that they have shown themselves equally capable of acting responsibly.'

47 See A. Hastings, *A History of English Christianity* (London: Collins, 1986), pp. 473–96, and 519–30.

48 NUS files, MSS.280/134/4, report of the eighth ACTS conference, 5–7 April 1963.

49 Ibid.

50 ACTS membership in 1966 was 6600 and it must be noted that this was a considerable proportion of the total student body in Catholic colleges. In 1969–70, for example, the total number of students attending Roman Catholic Colleges of Education was 10,500. As such, ACTS cannot be dismissed as a minority group of zealous Catholics which did not represent Catholic students in general.

51 Ibid., from the *Catholic Herald*, 30 September 1966.

52 'Simmaries: the Spirit and the Mother', sermon preached by Father G.J. Shannon at the Centenary Mass, Whit Sunday 1950 and reproduced in the *St Mary's College Centenary Record*, 1950, pp. 135–6.

8

THE CHANGING SOCIAL AND RELIGIOUS CONTEXT OF CATHOLIC SCHOOLING IN ENGLAND AND WALES

Michael P. Hornsby-Smith

THE CHANGING CONTEXT

THIS CHAPTER aims to provide a sociological interpretation of the changing context within which the Catholic school system collaborated with the state as the 'unobtrusive partner' (Hornsby-Smith, 1978) in the 'dual system' of provision in the post-war years. It will offer an interpretation of the context from which to address such questions as: how did the changing social and religious context influence the manifest and latent aims of the Catholic schools system in England and Wales over the past half century? How successful were Catholic schools in achieving these aims? In what ways have they changed? What contribution might they make in the third millennium?

The second half of the twentieth century has been a period of unprecedented change. At the end of the Second World War there were still recognizable British, Dutch, French and Portuguese empires. Fifty years later the processes of global political de-colonialization have been substantially completed and been replaced by forms of economic dependency in a global capitalist economic system. For Britain this has meant the painful process of adapting to a role as but one of a number of medium-sized nations. For years it clung to its supposed 'special relationship' to one of the two superpowers and resisted becoming entangled in the remarkable processes of reconciliation and growing social, economic and political integration which were led by France and Germany on the continental mainland of Western Europe. It took four decades for the 'iron curtain' between Western Europe and the subject countries of Central and Eastern Europe to collapse and raise the possibility of a new vision of Europe from the Atlantic to the Urals.

Exhausted after the efforts of the Second World War, Britain's long-term industrial decline continued and was exacerbated by the loss of cheap raw materials from its erstwhile empire. Its share of world trade declined steadily and the trend was given an alarming push by the oil crises of the mid-1970s. From then onwards the process of de-industrialization accelerated with massive reductions in employment in manufacturing. It was gradually realized that 'downsizing' was not cyclical but structural and was being faced by all the economies of the industrialized world.

To some extent such worrying trends in the economy and in employment were partially alleviated by the emergence of new technologies, especially in television, satellite broadcasting, electronics, computing and information technologies, e-mail and the Internet. Communications throughout the world have become virtually instantaneous; what is happening in the farthest corners of the earth can be transmitted immediately to all parts of the globe. In recent years this has dramatically altered the nature of global markets for capital. Not only does it increasingly make sense to speak in terms of processes of globalization and of a global capitalist economy, but such changes have inevitably reduced the ability of nation–states to run their economies entirely as they would wish. In a very real way, the world in which we live at the end of the twentieth century is increasingly inter-dependent.

In a world of rapid technological change it is inevitable that new problems have had to be faced. With all the promise of nuclear power came the loss of a certain level of innocence and the shocked realization that human beings had the potential to destroy not only their enemies but also the planet itself. For decades political leaders struggled to cope with this entirely new and frightening reality in their defence and security policies. People everywhere became aware of and learned to cope with the threat of nuclear annihilation. Much more recently concerns became more generalized to ecological and environmental issues which affect all life on the planet.

Among the most important of technological discoveries has been the ability to control fertility. Around the mid-1960s birth rates started to decline and the process has gone so far that many countries in Western Europe are no longer reproducing themselves. Other significant demographic changes include the steady increase in life expectancy and hence in the proportion of dependent people relative to the economically active population. The decline in the number of births led rapidly to a reduction in the demand for school places, and from the mid-1960s onwards the school system has had to adjust to this changed demographic situation. In the early post-war years the demand for labour to assist reconstruction resulted in the sucking in of large numbers of immigrants. One consequence has been that 'Britain has become irreversibly a multi-racial, multi-cultural society' (Anon, 1981: 381) and this is something to which Catholic schools have had to adapt with sensitivity.

Perhaps some of the most difficult changes to evaluate are the diffuse cultural orientations which determine the very nature of social relationships. In the aftermath of two world wars there is little doubt that authority relationships with traditional elites everywhere were subtly changed. Ordinary people were less likely to follow authority figures, including church leaders, teachers, or parents unquestioningly. The democratic imperative was experienced at every level. With this drive to make up one's own mind came, at a later stage, a strong shift in value-orientation towards individualization, 'the social and historical process in which values, beliefs, attitudes, and behaviour are increasingly based on personal choice and are less dependent on tradition and social institutions' (Ester *et al.*, 1993: 7; see also Barker *et al.*, 1992). In Britain in particular, it is likely that such a shift was accelerated during the ascendancy of liberal economics during the Thatcher administrations in the 1980s.

There is practically no evidence to suggest that Catholics in England and Wales were uniquely immune to the effects of these wider social forces in the post-war years. But, in addition, they experienced the effects of the Second Vatican Council which sought to renew the church and encourage its adaptation to modernizing forces throughout the world (Butler, 1981). Concepts such as the 'People of God', 'participation' and 'collegiality' legitimated a very substantial shift in the way Catholics saw themselves as full members of the church and in relation to the clergy. In practice, change could only take place over time and, indeed, was contested so that there were competing models of the church (Hornsby-Smith, 1987: 31–6) in a period of paradigmatic change (Hornsby-Smith, 1989: 22–44).

In sum, the second half of the twentieth century has seen some major changes in the social and religious context within which Catholic schools in England and Wales have had to operate. The rest of this chapter is divided into four sections. First, the place of Catholic schools in the period of the 'fortress church' of 'closed' Catholicism, roughly up to the end of the 1960s, will be considered.

This will be followed by a recapitulation of the evidence relating various measures of adult religiosity with Catholic schooling which was derived from the 1978 national survey of Catholics in England and Wales. Third, some reflections on the changes which have taken place in English Catholicism following the dissolution of the distinctive Catholic subculture since the 1960s will be offered. The chapter will conclude with some sociological reflections on the role of Catholic schools in a declining church as it enters the third millennium.

THE FORTRESS CHURCH

From the restoration of the Hierarchy in 1850 until the Second Vatican Council (1962–5) the Catholic Church in England could reasonably be described as a 'fortress'. The metaphor emphasized 'the defence of strong outer walls against outsiders, prohibitions of breaches in the walls, the elimination of excursions beyond them, disciplined training and absolute obedience to superiors' (Hornsby-Smith, 1987: 21). As Peter Coman (1977: 15–30) pointed out two decades ago, it could meaningfully be said that English Catholicism was a distinctive minority subculture. This was expressed by strongly held norms and values, such as a particular stress on loyalty and obedience to the Pope and the Roman authorities, and the observance of distinctive sexual and marital norms regarding contraception, divorce and abortion. Their separateness was fostered by such practices as the use of Latin in the liturgy and by abstention from eating meat on Fridays, practices which 'gain significance as symbols of allegiance simply by their lack of meaning for other cultures' (Douglas, 1973: 62; quoted in Coman, 1977: 16).

Coman has argued (ibid.: 17) that the Irish dimension and Roman allegiance induced a sense of boundary and social distance from the wider English society and tended to foster a defensiveness in the face of perceived hostility. The church leadership, fearing an erosion of the values of its members, erected a series of defensive walls against the surrounding society and promoted a policy of segregation. Thus the Catholic community constructed a British version of 'pillarization' with its own Catholic schools system, a pervasive and ubiquitous system of parishes, clubs and societies to occupy the leisure time of Catholics, and strong sanctions against those who diverged from the expected norm of marital endogamy.

There were four distinct strands which made up the English

Catholic community (Hornsby-Smith, 1987: 23–6). First, there were the 'recusant' Catholics who could claim to have retained their Catholicism through penal times from pre-Reformation days. Second, there were the converts. Third, the largest strand comprised generations of Irish immigrants and their descendants. Fourth, there were the other immigrants, including the large numbers of refugees from Europe following the Second World War. Overall, it was estimated that approximately one in eight Catholics are in each of the following categories: recusants, first-generation Irish, other immigrants, and second-generation Irish. There are around 8 or 9 per cent converts (allowing for children) and a similar number of second-generation immigrants with origins outside the British Isles. The balance of around one-third of English Catholics has a variety of other and mixed backgrounds but it is likely that the bulk of them will have an Irish ancestry which originated three or more generations ago (ibid.: 26).

At the end of the Second World War the Catholic community in England and Wales could reasonably be characterized as predominantly working class, overwhelmingly concentrated in the large urban centres, and disproportionately found in the North-West, the traditional entry point for immigrants from Ireland. The best quantitative estimates we have about the early post-war period were produced by the Newman Demographic Survey. Largely as a result of high levels of immigration from Ireland in the late 1950s, the Catholic population increased from 4.7 million or 10.7 per cent of the total population in 1951 to 5.6 million or 12.2 per cent in 1961 (Spencer, 1966: 62). It was estimated that there were three-quarters of a million Catholics, or 23 per cent of the population, in London. Over two-fifths of the population of Liverpool, nearly one-third of Manchester and around one-fifth of the populations of Birmingham, Coventry and Newcastle were Catholics (ibid.: 64). The proportion of all marriages solemnized in Catholic churches had risen from 5.5 per cent in 1924 to 12.3 per cent in 1962 and the proportion of Catholic infant baptisms as a proportion of total live births had risen from 9.2 per cent in 1924 to 16.1 per cent in 1963 (ibid.: 72).

There is a sense in which the 'ghetto' forms of the working-class Catholicism of Irish immigrants which had evolved up to 1939 continued after the war for a number of years. Thus there is a certain continuity between Steven Fielding's description of the Whit walks in Manchester before the War (1993: 74–7) and Anthony Archer's (1986) depiction of working-class Catholicism in Newcastle in the early post-war decades. Fielding describes how disciplined the Catholic walk was with children being drilled in schools for weeks beforehand and under-sevens being excluded. He explains that:

> The walk gave Catholics a chance to publicly assert their individual and collective self-importance in the midst of a society where it was usually denigrated. The singing of the hymn Faith of Our Fathers, which told the tale of persecution but eventual triumph of Catholicism, should be interpreted in this light. The widespread English Protestant view of the Catholic Church as inferior and alien was at least temporarily turned on its head. Whit also gave each of Manchester's Catholic national minorities an opportunity to express their distinct identity: Italians, Poles and Ukrainians all made their particular contribution to the parade. These ethnic groups provoked little hostility: this was not the case with the Irish contingent.
> (1993: 75–6)

Archer describes the Catholic Church of the pre-Vatican period as 'most serious about its business':

> Its defining points were clear: the Pope, Sunday Mass, marrying a Catholic and sending one's children to a Catholic school. It made demands that were exact, costly and strict. Precisely because of this, its claim to mediate the sacred was the more convincing.
> (1986: 104)

In a recent description of the experiences of a working-class Catholic family from a Lancashire mill town over three generations from the beginning of the century up to the early 1960s, Jim Ainsworth (1998) offers an interesting, presumably largely autobiographical, account of Catholic parish and school life in the early post-war years and of his progressive alienation due to the persistent anti-socialist 'propaganda' preached from the pulpit. In the early 1950s there was still the annual crowning of the statue of Our Lady and the special role of the May Queen with the boys in blue satin suits and the girls in blue satin dresses with hymns such as 'Immaculate Mary' and 'Bring Flowers of the Rarest', processing round the church grounds and the neighbouring streets observed by all the admiring relatives (ibid.: 62). It was still normal for the priest to be invited to bless the house shortly after moving in and dedicate it and the family to the Sacred Heart of Jesus (ibid.: 68–9). Religion was a major part of the school curriculum and on Mondays the ordinary attendance register was supplemented by the taking of the religious register:

> In neatly ruled columns the teacher would mark ticks or crosses

against the name of each child, under the following headings – whether they had attended Mass, or not, and at what time [The school wanted all the pupils to attend 9.00 a.m. Mass every Sunday – to go to 10.00 or 11.00 was frowned upon.], had they been to Confession on the Saturday morning or early evening, had they taken Holy Communion, and lastly had they been to Benediction on Sunday afternoon.

(ibid.: 77)

Ainsworth, through the memories of 'Eddie', a young teenager in the early 1960s, also describes the annual Mission over six days with a packed church and huge congregations and the 'Hell Fire and Damnation' Friday evening Mass.

It was a sadistic occurrence that caused youngsters, and indeed some of the more easily taken in adults, to have sleepless nights worrying about their future in the life hereafter. Eddie can remember these nights as if they were yesterday, because of the vivid descriptions given of the suffering experienced by the millions of souls over the past centuries. In the days when children would gladly sit quietly and listen to the teacher tell them a story, when radio was the most common form of home entertainment, the professional performance given by these priests on a weekly basis in the towns throughout the Diocese, was truly frightening in its effects on the captive congregations.

(ibid.: 134)

Such reflections convey something of the flavour of the church in the early post-war years when the priest said Mass in Latin, often inaudibly and with his back to the congregation, and when he was treated as a sacred figure to whom deference and loyal obedience were due. Father was the supreme leader and decision-maker. While the Mass was clearly the centre of Catholic worship, it was supplemented at the parish level by a multiplicity of devotions: Benediction, the Rosary, the Stations of the Cross, and so on. Parish clubs provided possibly the one arena where the laity expropriated some autonomy. Parish-based organizations offered not only spiritual reinforcement but also ensured that the leisure lives of Catholics were articulated in appropriately 'safe' ways, uncorrupted by the profane delights of dance halls and pubs. Yet, possibly as a result of the independence learned during the war, there were clear signs of a more confident and independent laity. John Bryden has described how in March 1948 a group of around thirty Catholic university students walked from London to Walsingham 'to bear witness to their faith in the crucified and risen Jesus, and to make reparation for the sins of students, particularly those which were contributory to the Second World War' (1998: 1). Student Cross is now more ecumenical and comprises nine different 'legs' from different starting points, each walking with a wooden cross in Holy Week to arrive in Walsingham for the Easter liturgies. Some 200 pilgrims now take part and it has just celebrated its fiftieth anniversary. In July 1948, fourteen groups of men, representing the fourteen Stations of the Cross, set out from various destinations such as Middlesbrough, Wrexham and East Grinstead, to arrive at the shrine of Our Lady at Walsingham where Cardinal Griffin led the prayers on the Feast of Our Lady of Mount Carmel. Many of these pilgrims were recently demobilized ex-servicemen concerned to heal Europe's wounds and at a time when the threat from the Soviet Union was looming large (Wells, 1998; Lyons and Furnival, 1998).

There were other lasting initiatives which originated in these years and which testify to a defiant and assertive sense of the 'lay apostolate'. The Newman Association was formed in 1942 (Cheverton *et al.*, 1992) and as a member of the international Pax Romana and following papal encouragement aimed 'to permeate contemporary thought' and contribute to 'the service of the Church' (in those days interpreted very much in terms of the hierarchical episcopacy). In the early post-war years committed young Catholics were active in apostolic organizations such as the Young Christian Workers and the Jesuit-run cell movement. Charles Walker records that in 1950, the YCW had nineteen full-time organizers for boys and seven for girls and that more than 5000 young people were attending regular meetings (Walker, 1994: 107) but that by 1992 the national team had shrunk to five organizers, three for boys and two for girls (ibid.: 127). The membership of the Union of Catholic Mothers and the Catholic Womens' League both peaked around the mid-1960s (Eaton, 1999). Such figures reflected the major social changes of the post-war period, not least the expanding educational opportunities and changes in the occupational structure (see, for example, Brothers, 1964).

Peter Coman's book is a valuable reminder that the fears of a strong state and of the exercise of state power especially in the areas of education and health were initially expressed by hostility and strong resistance on the part of the Hierarchy to the legislative proposals. He reported that the future Cardinal Heenan suggested in 1942 that 'the country is in danger of becoming National Socialist

– too much is being handed over to the state!'. Two years later the Bishop of Leeds was reported to have told a rally of the Catholic Parents' and Electors' Association that 'Mr Butler must have slept with a copy of *Mein Kampf* under his pillow to have devised such a bill'. Writing in *The Tablet* in 1944 the future Archbishop Beck wrote: 'It is against the menace of the Total State that Catholics are at present waging their defensive war' (Coman, 1977: 45–6).

Other 'signs of the times' and evidence of a growing willingness on the part of informed laity to stand up against clerical direction included the demise of the Catholic Social Guild. This followed the emergence of substantial policy differences between 'traditional–conservative' Catholics (such as Fr Paul Crane, SJ, one-time secretary of the CSG who later founded the right-wing Christian Order) and those who accepted clerical leadership in all matters, on the one hand, and 'traditional–liberal' Catholics such as Michael Fogarty and Labour Party supporters of the new welfare state and those who sought to identify areas of legitimate lay autonomy, on the other (Coman, 1977: 80–4; McHugh, 1982: 47–75). McHugh's analysis goes further and attributes the demise of the CSG in 1967 and the failure of Plater (formerly the Catholic Workers') College to 'assume a privileged and enlarged presence' (ibid.: 80), to a shared 'objectivism', an uncritical attachment to natural law and 'the deductive method of social thinking' (ibid.: 199), and an unquestioning acceptance of clerical authority and leadership even on social issues. In contrast, members of the new Laity Commission of the Bishops' Conference found the natural law approach 'quite unsustainable' (ibid.: 234, footnote 157).

With the active support of Cardinal Hinsley, the Sword of the Spirit was launched in 1940 (Walsh, 1980) and has developed into the internationally respected Catholic Institute for International Relations of today. The first Catholic People's Weeks was held in 1945 (Baily, 1995) and the Catholic Housing Aid Society (CHAS) was founded on the initiative of two lay women in 1956. The Family Fast Day collections originated with the National Board of Catholic Women in 1960 and raised just under £7000 (Orchard, 1985). Two years later the Catholic Fund for Overseas Development (CAFOD) was set up as an agency of the Bishops' Conference. Voluntary giving to CAFOD now exceeds £11 million annually.

The early post-war years, then, were characterized by a combination of a triumphalist ultramontanism (Catholics were right and they had a guarantee in the Pope who was uniquely guided by God and that would increasingly become apparent) and defensive defiance in the face of a hostile society. This was expressed most fiercely in the defence of the Catholic community's interests, especially the issue of Catholic schools. The 1944 Education Act has been called 'the greatest gift to the Catholic community' but there was a perception of a great social injustice in the requirement to raise a large proportion of the capital necessary to build new schools. Throughout the 1940s and early 1950s Catholics were mobilized to lobby for the maintenance of the 'dual system' and an increase in the rate of capital grant for new capital building. This created problems for some Labour Party supporters who regretted the continuing influence of priests on local schools and saw the campaign being hijacked by the Conservative Party (Ainsworth, 1998: 40–2). The rate of grant was gradually raised in a series of increments from 50 per cent to 85 per cent. By the end of the 1960s Murphy (1971: 121–9) suggested that there was an end to 'passionate intensity' about the issue.

The growth and improvement of the Catholic education system in the first two decades after the end of the war had two, largely unanticipated, consequences. In the first place it served to generate a 'new Catholic middle class', upwardly mobile as a result of the successful achievement of those qualifications and credentials necessary for professional, technical, administrative and managerial occupations. As a result, Catholics became more socially and geographically mobile and diffused more evenly throughout the different regions, and they also moved out of the inner city parishes and their increasing numbers in suburban estates led to a rapid increase in the number of new suburban parish churches. They became more 'respectable' and this contributed to a declining hostility towards them. Within the church, they exerted increasing pressures on priests for a greater say in parish governance, notably as governors and managers of Catholic schools.

The second consequence concerns their mission towards the children of the large numbers of Irish immigrants who had come to Britain. Mary Hickman (1995) has argued strongly that Catholics schools had been encouraged by the British state because they served its interests in pacifying a potentially rebellious minority by incorporating them into British society. The Catholic Church's interest was in retaining their Catholic allegiance and it aimed to achieve this by strengthening their Catholic identity at the expense of the children's Irish identity. Thus church and state connived in the strategy of incorporation and denationalization. This is a serious thesis which deserves to be taken seriously. In my view, however, it argues too much from particular Irish communities in Liverpool and London and underestimates the extent to which there has been a considerable degree of assimilation of Irish immigrants over two or three generations.

CATHOLIC SCHOOLS AND RELIGIOUS OUTCOMES

So what difference did Catholic schools make? By the 1960s Spencer, one of the foremost critics of the policy that 'the Catholic child from the Catholic home should continue his education at the hands of Catholic teachers in a Catholic school' (quoted in Spencer, 1968: 171) was noting that there were, in any case, no places in Catholic schools for one-third of Catholic children, that Catholic undergraduates were critical of the quality of Catholic schools, and that there were no data with which to test the 'effectiveness' of Catholic schools, relative to alternative uses of the available and limited resources, such as parish-based catechetical programmes (Spencer, 1971). Using data from thirteen parish censuses between 1962 and 1965 he showed that 'the Mass attendance rates of those who never attended a Catholic school are significantly lower than those of the "always" and "partly" [attended Catholic schools] groups' (1968: 206). But he also showed that the association between Mass attendance and parental religiosity was greater than that with Catholic schooling. Even so, his conclusion that 'the empirical basis of the strategy of providing a place in a Catholic school for all Catholic children is extremely doubtful' (ibid.: 207) seems to go beyond his evidence. Indeed, a review of a number of researches, including the well-known Greeley-Rossi study in the United States, showed 'a positive, if slight, association between Catholic schools and the achievement of religious goals' (Hornsby-Smith, 1978: 31).

Similar findings were reported from the national survey of a representative sample of over 1000 English Catholics in 1978. Respondents were asked not only about their experiences of Catholic schooling but also about their religiosity as adult Catholics and that of their parents and spouses, if they were married. This enabled analyses to be undertaken of the effects of both parental and spousal religiosity and the proportion of their schooling in Catholic schools (Hornsby-Smith and Lee, 1979: 87–94, 221–2). Ten religious outcome variables were considered, including adult religious practice, doctrinal orthodoxy and church involvement scales. On nine of these scales there was a positive association with the proportion of education in Catholic schools (ibid.: 221). Using multiple regression analysis and testing a path model showed that the strength of this relationship was generally smaller than that of the religiosity of the spouse, parental religiosity, occupational status, age and gender.

The various effects appear to be cumulative. Whereas 87 per cent with both high levels of parental and spousal religiosity, all of whose education was in Catholic schools, themselves score high on the adult religious practice scale, only 11 per cent of those with low parental and spousal religiosity who had had no Catholic schooling, did so. On the other hand, only 30 per cent who came from religious homes and who had had all their education in Catholic schools but whose spouse did not score high on a religiosity scale, did (ibid.: 225). 'It seems, in other words, that the effects of Catholic education are short lived except in cases where the subsequent adult environment becomes supportive' (ibid.: 100). Finally, one might note the finding that the 'proportion of Catholic schooling is the one variable, apart from age, to have any noticeable effect on age of ceasing regular Mass attendance; an indication perhaps that Catholic schooling is at least some deterrent to lapsation' (ibid.: 91). These results are extremely pertinent, given the evidence, elsewhere in the report and subsequently, of widespread disaffection on the part of young Catholics and very high levels of 'lapsation'.

THE CHURCH IN TRANSITION

It was Harold Macmillan who coined the phrase 'you've never had it so good!'. He was referring to the results of the long post-war economic boom which had led to substantial rises in standards of living for the people of this country by the early 1960s. There is a sense, too, in which the church in this country had never known better days since the restoration of the Hierarchy in a hostile country in 1850 (Hornsby-Smith, 1989: 2–3). In the two decades after the end of the war the number of parishes increased by one fifth from 1910 to 2320 and the number of priests by one quarter from 6257 to 7808. In the early 1960s a whole string of indicators peaked: Mass attendances around two million; child baptisms around 134,000; receptions (conversions) around 15,000; confirmations around 81,000; and marriages over 46,000 with 50 per cent between two Catholics. The corresponding figures 30 years later are 1.1 million; 75,000; 6000;

46,000 (for 1985); and 17,000 (with the proportion of marriages between two Catholics around one third).

Clearly major social and religious changes were becoming apparent by the 1960s (Sharratt, 1977). The very high levels of Irish immigration in the 1950s dropped rapidly in the early 1960s (Spencer, 1966: 76). The social changes deriving from the expansion of secondary education and the occupational advancement of Catholics generally resulted in high levels of both social and geographical mobility as increasing numbers of Catholics entered the 'new middle class'. There were the religious changes, too, which focused around and derived from the great Second Vatican Council in 1962–5. These contributed to a significant shift in the ecumenical climate. Hostility towards Catholicism declined, especially during the days of Pope John XXIII, and Catholics were becoming more 'respectable' and were to be found in an increasing number of senior public positions as Cabinet ministers, Leaders of both Houses of Parliament, editors of major broadsheets, Secretary of the Cabinet, General Secretary of the Trades Union Congress, and so on. Taken together, the social and religious changes of these post-war decades totally transformed the nature of the church in this country as the boundary walls which had defended the 'fortress' church gradually dissolved. There was a decline in marital endogamy and an increase in friendships with non-Catholics (Hornsby-Smith, 1987: 183).

The process was not cataclysmic – the dramatic collapsing of the fortress walls as a result of a single explosive attack from without. Rather, it was a gradual change which had taken place over several decades as a result of the steady dissolving of the walls in the solvent of rapid external social change after the global trauma of the Second World War and the internal religious *aggiornamento* encouraged in the 1960s by Pope John XXIII. With hindsight it is clear that the process was well under way by the 1960s (ibid.: 210).

Not everyone welcomed the new openness in the church, the liturgical reforms, the easing of regulations restricting ceremonial in the case of religiously mixed marriages, and the ending of mandatory abstinence from the eating of meat on Fridays (Coman, 1977: 105). In her famous *cri de cœur*, the anthropologist Mary Douglas argued that 'Friday no longer rings the great cosmic symbols of expiation and atonement: it is not symbolic at all, but a practical day for the organisation of charity. *Now English Catholics are like everyone else*' (1973: 67; emphasis added). Indeed, they were becoming so. The 1978 survey of Roman Catholic Opinion (Hornsby-Smith and Lee,

1979) and research in four parishes in London and Preston provided the strongest evidence yet of the extent to which Catholics had converged with the rest of the population (see, e.g., Hornsby-Smith, 1987: 109, 165). What these researches demonstrated was that at least by the 1970s Catholics were heterogeneous in terms of belief, practice and morality (ibid.: 47–66). It seems likely that whereas:

> up to the 1950s Catholics differentiated relatively little between creedal beliefs, non-creedal beliefs such as papal infallibility, teachings on moral issues . . ., and disciplinary rules . . . in a strongly rule-bound and guilt-ridden Church, where notions of mortal sin and eternal damnation were strongly emphasised . . ., it also seems likely that with the 'loss of the fear of hell' from the 1960s, this is much less true today.
>
> (Hornsby-Smith, 1991: 215)

The evidence suggests that 'there is a distinct "hierarchy of truths" in the minds of most Catholics' (ibid.: 215) and an 'emergent plurality of ways in which religious authority is legitimated' (ibid.: 221–2). While there was no evidence of a generalized anti-clericalism, clerical authority was increasingly likely to be contested where it lacked credibility. Catholics were generally opposed to absolutist moral rules which failed to take account of the situational context. The 'loss of the fear of hell' (Lodge, 1980: 113–27) was particularly strong among young Catholics with the result that:

> more and more Catholics are making up their own minds on more and more things and are getting on with the everyday tasks of living their lives, bringing up their families, and coping with the everyday problems of child-rearing, earning a living and making ends meet, unemployment or redundancy, being good citizens, and so on, as best they can, with whatever support they can get, from whatever source. It would seem that the days of substantial thought-control over all aspects of social life, powerful especially in the defensive ghettos of the fortress Church, are now well and truly over. With the removal of the threat of eternal damnation, going to church has to take its chance along with all the other claims on the discretionary time, energy and interest of Catholics.
>
> (ibid.: 226–7)

The sort of Catholic doctrine which taught that 'however slight it may be . . . every direct sin . . . contrary to holy purity, whether of thought, look, word, or action, is mortal if it receives full consent' (Hart, 1918: 219–20), which was still being taught in the early post-war years, was simply regarded as nonsensical, or 'over the top', or undiscriminating and hence inadequate, by young Catholics a generation later.

What does seem to be apparent, then, is that somewhere around the late 1950s and early 1960s there was a distinct shift in the church, the causes and consequences of which we are still struggling to comprehend. Most commentators, such as Avery Dulles (1977: 1), on ecclesiological grounds, and the present writer (1989: 17), on social structural grounds, have taken the Second Vatican Council as the defining moment of change in the church since it legitimated a new and distinctly different way of looking at the nature of the church and which had significant consequences in every sphere of its activities from worship and liturgy to its relationship to the world. Bill McSweeney, however, argued that 'the year 1958 marked the end of old Catholicism-imperialist, authoritarian and totalitarian in action and intent' (1980: 86). Frank McHugh, with a sociology of knowledge approach, has also argued that the year of the death of Pope Pius XII was

> a significant watershed in Catholic Church history, on the grounds that the ideological homogeneity of Catholicism . . . may be considered to have survived until 1958 and to have begun to break up thereafter . . . as a response to a highly specific type of Catholicism in the preceding period.
>
> (1982: 12; see also 1987).

In December 1966, two years before Pope Paul VI's encyclical *Humanae Vitae* (1968), England's foremost theologian and editor of *Clergy Review*, Charles Davis, suddenly left the church saying that he did not find either a concern for truth or a concern for people in the official church. Rather, 'there is a concern for authority at the expense of truth', and that he was 'constantly saddened by instances of the damage done to persons by workings of an impersonal and unfree system' (Davis, 1967: 16; see also Hastings, 1986: 573–4). Following a sympathetic editorial in *New Blackfriars* in February 1967, Fr Herbert McCabe was promptly sacked (Sharratt, 1977: 143–5). Public criticisms from such an eminent and informed 'insider' was further evidence that all was not well and that the fortress church was imploding.

There are numerous examples of this such as the controversies over contraception (Hastings, 1986: 575–7; Sharratt, 1977: 140–3), the dispute about religious education between Cardinal Heenan and the staff of Corpus Christi College (Hackett, 1976), and clerical celibacy (Hastings, 1978). Tony Spencer wrote a controversial analysis of the 'Demography of Catholicism' in *The Month* in 1975. Using statistics provided by the Catholic Education Council and making various assumptions, for example about Irish immigration, he investigated a number of measures of 'perseverance' from Baptism to First Communion, to Confirmation and to Marriage and concluded that 'drop out (as distinct from religious practice levels below canonical norms) was marginal in the late 1950s, but had assumed massive proportions by the early 1970s (1975: 103) and averaged a quarter of a million each year between 1965 and 1971 (ibid.: 104). We might note, for example, that according to Spencer's figures, both Catholic marriages as a proportion of all marriages and the Baptism/Birth Ratio peaked in 1961 (ibid.: 100–1). In an editorial *The Tablet* (19 April 1975) observed that leakage at the rates suggested 'would virtually empty the establishment within a generation, which is absurd!'. Richard Cunningham (1975a), the Secretary of the Catholic Education Council, attempted to refute the details of the analysis and there was a further exchange of correspondence in *The Tablet* (10 and 17 May 1975). Cunningham (ibid.: 383) noted Mass attendances of 2,114,000 in 1966. Twenty years later estimated weekly Mass attendances were down to 1,135,047.

Hopes for grass-roots-led strategies of 're-formation' and 'revitalization' (Hornsby-Smith *et al.*, 1995: 204–5) at the National Pastoral Congress in Liverpool in 1980 led to the rhetoric of a 'sharing Church' (Anon., 1981: 307–28) but within eighteen months delegates reported substantial disillusionment with the outcomes at the diocesan level (Hornsby-Smith and Cordingley, 1983; Hornsby-Smith, 1987: 139–40). When the Pope came in 1982 there was a public display of support and excitement at the public recognition of him as a world leader so that, as one nun put it: 'now we can come out from under the bushes'. But by now it was clear that while Catholics thought the Pope was a great guy and while they might listen respectfully to his teachings on contraception and divorce, they were quietly going away and making up their own minds in the light of their own experiences and circumstances (Hornsby-Smith *et al.* 1983; Hornsby-Smith, 1987: 117–39).

It is clear that in the past three or four decades there has been a radical transformation in the way that religious authority has been interpreted (Hornsby-Smith, 1991). On personal matters, such as those concerned with marriage and family life, there was a growing sense in which clerical leaders were not credible so that their pronouncements, therefore, were not accorded legitimacy. There was also a growing desire for dialogue and accountability in the church. The bishops in their *ad limina* visit to Rome in 1997 raised such concerns diplomatically but Pope John Paul II replied firmly that different forms of lay participation should be fostered but 'without adopting notions borrowed from democracy and sociology which do not reflect the Catholic vision of the Church and the authentic spirit of Vatican II' (*The Tablet*, 1 November 1997: 1419–21). *In The Sign We Give*, the report of a working party on collaborative ministry (1995), the bishops attempted to respond to the changing climate but significantly there was no consultation with some of the bishops' own consultative bodies in the preparation of their statement *The Common Good* (1996).

CATHOLIC SCHOOLS IN A DECLINING CHURCH

As we enter the new millennium it is clear that much of the optimism and expectations that emerged around the mid-1960s at the time of the Second Vatican Council and later with the National Pastoral Congress and the visit of the Pope were misplaced. The notion that the fortress church of the early post-war years had given way to a pilgrim 'People of God' on the move was also mistaken in that it misleadingly suggested a unity of purpose and commitment. Even my more recent claim (1996) that the Catholic Church in this country has moved from the 'intransigence' of 'closed' Catholicism to the 'accommodation' strategy of an 'open' Catholicism seems, as we approach the millennium, unduly optimistic and, in retrospect, driven more by the categories of Peter Berger (1973) and John Whyte (1981) than by the evidence.

One senior priest observed that the 1944 Education Act had been 'the greatest gift to the Catholic community'. Quite apart from its contribution to the development of a new Catholic middle class, he saw the new grammar schools as a rich source of priestly vocations. But there were wider implications of the extra-parochial grammar schools for parishes and for priest–lay relations. Joan Brothers (1964) soon noted that priests in Liverpool were bemoaning the changed relationships with young students who had gone from the grammar schools to universities. The declining salience for them of their home parish was really an indication that the Catholic community was changing fast.

The abrupt drop in the birth rate in the 1960s led to a major contraction in the size of the Catholic education system (Cunningham, 1975b). As unobtrusive partners in the 'dual system' they also collaborated with the process of the comprehensivization of secondary education from the 1960s. Almost inevitably most attention has focused on changes in Catholic schools but the story of the contraction of the former system for the training of Catholic teachers in the teacher training colleges and hence the Catholic community's involvement in higher and further education is of first importance but remains to be told. What is clear is that it created much hardship and concerns about the decision-making procedures. (See, e.g., the letter from staff at Coloma College of Education in *The Tablet*, 12 July 1975; and the report in *The Tablet*, 10 May 1997 and subsequent correspondence, especially in the issues of 13 September and 11 October 1997 about the closure of La Sainte Union).

Concerns about the cost of the Catholic school building programme in the post-war years and criticisms of and uncertainties about the effectiveness of Catholic schools relative to other schools, and the contraction of the Catholic education system also coincided with a shift of focus. Whereas for two decades the primary concern had been to obtain a proper proportion of public funds for the expansion of the Catholic school system, there began to emerge a concern with the quality of Catholic education, with the processes taking place in Catholic schools, and with the effectiveness of the schools in attaining both religious and academic goals. Such concerns were reflected in the introduction of a regular Educational Supplement in *The Tablet* from 27 September 1975.

In this changed climate, Bishop Konstant (1981) chaired the study group which produced the report on the educative task of the Catholic community. It suggested that:

> Catholic education should be distinguished by at least four features which arise out of belief in Jesus Christ as the universal saviour: the communication of a Christian spiritual perspective of the meaning of life; a special respect for the baptised of all ages and concern for their individuality and integrity; a dedication to the pursuit of justice; and the promotion of a sense of mission.
>
> (ibid.: 138)

For possibly the first time in an official report there was a recognition that schools were not alone in this educative task and that this had important consequences for the church. Thus it concluded that:

> The effectiveness of Catholic schooling (however this can be measured) is directly and essentially related to the full involvement of the Church (that is, all the members of the Church) in other areas

of its educational mission. Our consideration of the nature of the Church's mission and of the need for the development of faith, particularly in the contemporary context, led us to the conclusion that schools cannot validly be judged in isolation. Schools must be part of a total Christian catechesis stretching through life. Unless the local Church embodies such a catechesis, into which the Catholic school is integrated, the school cannot play more than a marginal part in the growth in faith of its members. In other words, the key question is one of the co-ordination of the work of the whole Church before, during and after school.

(ibid.: 139)

The shifting concerns of Catholic educationalists is apparent in their more recent writings. Thus McLaughlin *et al.* observe that:

Increasingly, Catholics are turning their attention to the ways in which Catholic schools in this new phase of their history should respond to contemporary challenges brought about by the sweeping and wide ranging changes in the education system initiated by the 1988 Education Reform Act and developed in subsequent legislation.

(1996: 6).

One such concern is that of multi-culturalism and the proper nature of religious education in a multi-faith school or area. There is an ongoing debate about this as can be seen from the conflicting views of Bernadette O'Keeffe (1992) who favours multi-culturalism and starting from where the children are at and Edward Hulmes (1992) who argues that Catholic schools should present the unique Catholic interpretation of their faith. Following the publication of the bishops' statement of Catholic social teaching in *The Common Good* (1996), the Catholic Education Service (1997) published a commentary on the implications for Catholic schools and colleges while the Bishops' Conference (1997) issued the report of a consultation with headteachers of Catholic secondary schools in urban poverty areas.

Gerald Grace has provided an excellent analysis of the changing social and ideological context within which Catholic schools have had to survive with the ascendancy of liberal individualism as against social communalism since the 1980s and with the insertion of market forces and market values into education:

Previously insulated to a large extent from market forces by state and diocesan funding, by the historical loyalty of local Catholic communities, and by large pupil enrolments resulting from large Catholic families, Catholic schools were the possessors of a relatively autonomous zone of influence. Within this autonomous zone, Catholic school leaders could articulate a distinctive mission and set of Catholic values independently of market culture and market values . . . With [the educational reforms of the 1980s and] local management of schools, open enrolments, a more differentiated Catholic community, and a lower Catholic birth-rate, such schools have to operate in a competitive market in education. In other words, the space, identity and voice of contemporary Catholic schooling is now more directly challenged by market values than ever before in its history. In these circumstances the critical question for Catholic school leaders is, can a balance be found between Catholic values and market values, or will market forces begin to compromise the integrity of the special mission of Catholic schooling? Can Gospel values survive in the face of a more direct relationship with the market place?

(Grace, 1995: 174–5)

James Arthur has argued that the 'holistic' model of Catholic education, 'concerned with the transmission . . . of Catholic faith – its beliefs, values, character and norms of conduct' (1995: 233) – has been transformed by 'dualistic' and 'pluralistic' models and that this constitutes 'the ebbing tide' of Catholic education. Grace (1998) has pointed out, however, that Arthur's thesis was not based on any systematic research in Catholic schools and remains, therefore, at the level of a hypothesis in need of testing. In his own study of Catholic headteachers he was able to identify a number of moral, ethical and professional dilemmas which they faced as they struggled to promote the traditional 'inspirational ideology' of Catholic education with its mission of the 'preferential option for the poor' (who happened historically to be Catholics in most immigrant communities!).

In the first place, there was 'a disjuncture between official Catholic moral teaching and the mores of contemporary society' (Grace, 1995: 164). Headteachers reported that 'community, partnership and dialogue approaches' to resolving 'difficult moral and behavioural situations were being threatened by parents' more assertive use of legal procedures' (ibid.: 165). There were 'dilemmas of admission' and tensions 'between a relatively open and comprehensive policy on school admissions and an awareness that certain amounts of selectivity by faith, commitment, social class and ability level would be in the long-term interests of the school in a competitive market for schooling' (ibid.: 167). Issues of exclusion from schools with 'a discourse and an imagery of fall and reconciliation, of sin and forgiveness, and of justice and mercy' created moral and professional dilemmas where 'exclusion of certain pupils was necessary for the common good of the school' (ibid.: 168). Other dilemmas were presented by instances of drug-taking and racism. The process of applying for grant-maintained status with its financial incentives and attractions of autonomous decision-making rights conflicted with the traditional communitarian concerns for the 'common good'. The promotion of the ideology of parental power in a 'more assertive and differentiated Catholic community' resulted in headteachers having to grapple with the 'struggle between hierarchical counsel and parental assertion' (ibid.: 171). Headteachers had to resolve 'fundamental dilemmas between notions of common good and of autonomous advantage' in a situation of 'increased salience of market values in schooling' (ibid.: 173).

Part of the everyday social reality which Catholic schools have to cope with is the pluralism of the religious beliefs and commitment of their students, as Grace has pointed out. There is now a growing research base which documents this. In *Teenage Religion and Values* Francis and Kay (1995) reported on the moral, personal, social, political and religious attitudes of just over 13,000 young people aged between 13 and 15 years from 65 state schools. Just over 9 per cent of the sample were Catholics who constituted 37 per cent of weekly church attenders. The general impression one gets from the mass of data is that, on the whole, the Catholic teenage attenders do not differ markedly from their peers. Their religious beliefs are decidedly stronger than teenagers generally and they are much less likely than Free Church attenders to have a literalist interpretation of creation or believe that Christianity is the only true religion (ibid.: 137, 145). They are much more likely than other church attenders to consider 'church is boring', and to believe that the church and the Bible seem 'irrelevant to life today' and they are less likely to agree that 'Christian ministers/vicars/priests do a good job' (ibid.: 196). Similar findings were reported by Sylvie Collins (1997) in her study of 1090 teenagers from a Catholic, a Church of England and a local authority state school in south-east England and by Richter and Francis (1998) in their study of church leavers.

What seems to be quite clear is that the task of Catholic schools as we enter the third millennium is very much more complex and difficult and replete with ambiguity and moral dilemmas than was the case 50 years ago. With general social and religious mobility and the dissolution of the distinctive Catholic subculture of the embattled fortress church there has emerged a general pluralism of belief and practice within the church. With this has come a radical trans-formation of accepted notions of religious authority. More recently the rise of 'new right' ideology has been reflected throughout the education system and there has been a rise of parental power and assertions of individual rights to counter more traditional commu-nitarian views of the common good and deferential notions of the authority of priests and teachers.

In general, Catholicism has been increasingly privatized and there has been a shift from a more communally-based Catholic identity to a more voluntaristic and individually chosen identity in the 'individu-alizing society' (Ester *et al.*, 1993). Such changes are part of the more global processes of modernization. As the French sociologist Danièle Hervieu-Léger has pointed out (1993; Davie, 1996), what is sig-nificant is the 'chain of believing' or religious 'memory' which legitimates membership. Her own study (1994) of students on pil-grimage led her to detect a tension between the politico-utopian project and a cultural mobilization of memory promoted by the clerical leadership, and the ethical prophecy and emotional mobili-zation of memory attractive to young pilgrims. Without the affirming, and sometimes reinforcing contribution of Catholic schools, there is a danger that the chain of memory will become 'perilously close to breaking' (Davie, 1996: 9).

REFERENCES

Ainsworth, J. *Catholicism, Socialism, Football, and Beer* (Hyndburn and Rossen-dale Trades Union Council, 1998).

Anon *Liverpool 1980: Official Report of the National Pastoral Congress* (Slough: St Paul Publications, 1981).

Archer, A. *The Two Catholic Churches: A Study in Oppression* (London: SCM, 1986).

Arthur, J. *The Ebbing Tide: Policy and Principles of Catholic Education* (Leomin-ster: Gracewing, 1995).

Baily, P. *A History of Catholic People's Weeks: 1945–1995* (Wilprint Group, 1995).

Barker, D., Halman, L. and Vloet, A. *The European Values Study 1981–1990: Summary Report* (London: Gordon Cook Foundation, 1992).

Berger, P.L. *The Social Reality of Religion* (Harmondsworth: Penguin, 1973).

Bishops' Conference of England and Wales *The Sign We Give: Report From the Working Party on Collaborative Ministry* (Chelmsford: Matthew James, 1995).

Bishops' Conference of England and Wales *A Struggle for Excellence: Catholic*

Secondary Schools in Urban Poverty Areas (London: Catholic Education Service, 1997).

Brothers, J. B. *Church and School: A Study of the Impact of Education on Religion* (Liverpool: Liverpool University Press, 1964).

Bryden, J. *Behold the Wood: A History of Student Cross 1948–1998* (Oxford: The Student Cross Association, 1998).

Butler, C. *The Theology of Vatican II*, revised and enlarged edition. (London: Darton, Longman and Todd, 1981).

Catholic Bishops' Conference of England and Wales *The Common Good and the Catholic Church's Social Teaching* (Manchester: Gabriel Communications, 1996).

Catholic Education Service *The Common Good in Education: A Commentary on the Implications of the Church's Social Teaching for the Work of Catholic Schools and Colleges* (Chelmsford: Matthew James, 1997).

Cheverton, E. *et al. A Use of Gifts: The Newman Association 1942–1992* (London: The Newman Association, 1992).

Collins, S. 'Young people's faith in late modernity', unpublished PhD thesis, University of Surrey, 1997.

Coman, P. *Catholics and the Welfare State* (London: Longman, 1977).

Cunningham, R.F. 'Figures and facts', *The Tablet*, 229 (7034), 26 April 1975a: 383–4.

Cunningham, R.F. 'Twenty-five years of progress', *The Tablet*, 229 (7056) 27 September 1975b: 915–17.

Davie, G. 'Religion and modernity: the work of Danièle Hervieu-Léger', in K. Flanagan and P. Jupp (eds), *Postmodernity, Religion and Sociology* London: Macmillan, 1996).

Davis, C. *A Question of Conscience* (London: Hodder and Stoughton, 1967).

Douglas, M. *Natural Symbols: Explorations in Cosmology* (Harmondsworth: Penguin, 1973).

Dulles, A. *The Resilient Church: The Necessity and Limits of Adaptation* (Garden City, NY: Doubleday, 1977).

Eaton, M. 'What became of the Children of Mary? Post-war women in the Catholic church', in M. P. Hornsby-Smith (ed.) *English Catholics 1950–2000* (London: Cassell, 1999).

Ester, P., Halman, L. and de Moor, R. (eds) *The Individualizing Society: Value Change in Europe and North America* (Tilburg: Tilburg University Press, 1993).

Fielding, S. *Class and Ethnicity: Irish Catholics in England, 1880–1939* (Buckingham: Open University Press, 1993).

Francis, L.J. and Kay, W.K. *Teenage Religion and Values* (Leominster: Gracewing, 1995).

Grace, G. *School Leadership: Beyond Education Management; An Essay in Policy Scholarship* (London: Falmer Press, 1995).

Grace, G. 'The future of the Catholic school: an English perspective', in J. Feheney (ed.), *From Ideal to Action: The Inner Nature of a Catholic School Today* (Dublin: Veritas, 1998).

Hackett, D. 'Cardinal Heenan', *The Month*, 9 (1) January 1976: 23–6.

Hart, C. *The Student's Catholic Doctrine* (London: Burns Oates and Washbourne, 1918).

Hastings, A. *In Filial Disobedience* (Great Wakering: Mayhew-McCrimmon, 1978).

Hastings, A. *A History of English Christianity: 1920–1985* (London: Collins, 1986).

Hervieu-Léger, D. *La Religion pour Mémoire* (Paris: Cerf, 1993).

Hervieu-Léger, D. 'Religion, Europe and the Pope: memory and the experience of French youth', in J. Fulton and P. Gee (eds), *Religion in Contemporary Europe* (Lampeter: Edwin Mellen, 1994), pp. 125–38.

Hickman, M. J. *Religion, Class and Identity: The State, the Catholic Church and the Education of the Irish in Britain* (Aldershot: Avebury, 1995).

Hornsby-Smith, M.P. *Catholic Education: The Unobtrusive Partner: Sociological Studies of the Catholic School System in England and Wales* (London: Sheed and Ward, 1978).

Hornsby-Smith, M.P. *Roman Catholics in England: Studies in Social Structure Since the Second World War* (Cambridge: Cambridge University Press, 1987).

Hornsby-Smith, M.P. *The Changing Parish: A Study of Parishes, Priests, and Parishioners After Vatican II* (London: Routledge, 1989).

Hornsby-Smith, M.P. *Roman Catholic Beliefs in England: Customary Catholicism and Transformations of Religious Authority* (Cambridge: Cambridge University Press, 1991).

Hornsby-Smith, M.P. 'The Catholic Church and education in Britain: from the "intransigence" of "closed" Catholicism to the accommodation strategy of "open" Catholicism', in F. Tallett and N. Atkin (eds), *Catholicism in Britain and France since 1789* (London: Hambledon Press, 1996), pp. 43–65.

Hornsby-Smith, M.P., Brown, J.M. and O'Byrne, J. 'Second thoughts on the Pope's visit', *The Month*, 16 (4) April 1983: 131–3.

Hornsby-Smith, M.P. and Cordingley, E.S. *Catholic Elites: A Study of the Delegates to the National Pastoral Congress*, Occasional Paper No. 3 (Guildford: University of Surrey, 1983).

Hornsby-Smith, M.P., Fulton, J. and Norris, M.I. *The Politics of Spirituality: A Study of a Renewal Process in an English Diocese* (Oxford: Clarendon Press, 1995).

Hornsby-Smith, M. P. and Lee, R. M. *Roman Catholic Opinion: A Study of Roman Catholics in England and Wales in the 1970s* (Guildford: University of Surrey, 1979).

Hulmes, E. 'Rediscovering the roots of European unity? New opportunities for Catholic education', *Aspects of Education*, 46, 1992: 52–61.

Lodge, D. *How Far Can You Go?* (London: Secker and Warburg, 1980).

Lyons, J. and Furnival, J. (eds) *50th Anniversary of the Cross-Carrying Pilgrimage; July 1948–July 1998* (Liverpool: Mersey Mirror, 1998).

McHugh, F. P. 'The changing social role of the Roman Catholic Church in England, 1958–1982', unpublished PhD thesis, University of Cambridge, 1982).

McHugh, F. P. 'Two churches: the significance of the political', *New Blackfriars*, 68 (802) February 1987: 89–98.

McLaughlin, T., J. O'Keefe and B. O'Keeffe (eds) *The Contemporary Catholic School: Context, Identity and Diversity* (London: Falmer Press, 1996).

McSweeney, B. *Roman Catholicism: The Search for Relevance* (Oxford: Blackwell, 1980).

Murphy, J. *Church, State and Schools in Britain, 1800–1970* (London: Routledge and Kegan Paul, 1971).

O'Keeffe, B. 'Catholic schools in an open society: the English challenge', *Aspects of Education*, 46, 1992: 34–51.

Orchard, E. *The Pampered Poodles: The Origin of Family Fast Day* (London: CAFOD, 1985).

Pope Paul VI *The Regulation of Birth (Humanae Vitae)* (London: C.T.S., 1968), (Do 411).

Richter, P. and Francis, L.J. *Gone but not Forgotten: Church Leaving and Returning* (London: Darton, Longman and Todd, 1998).

Sharratt, B. 'English Roman Catholicism in the 1960s', in A. Hastings (ed.), *Bishops and Writers: Aspects of the Evolution of Modern English Catholicism* (Wheathampstead: Anthony Clarke, 1977), pp. 127–58.

Spencer, A.E.C.W. 'The demography and sociography of the Roman Catholic community of England and Wales', in L. Bright and S. Clements (eds), *The Committed Church* (London: Darton, Longman and Todd, 1966), pp. 60–85.

Spencer, A.E.C.W. 'An evaluation of Roman Catholic educational policy in England and Wales 1900–1960', in P. Jebb, *Religious Education: Drift or Decision?* (London: Darton, Longman and Todd, 1968), pp. 165–221.

Spencer, A.E.C.W. *The Future of Catholic Education in England and Wales* (London: Catholic Renewal Movement, 1971).

Spencer, A.E.C.W. 'Demography of Catholicism', *The Month*, 8 (4) April 1975: 100–5.

Walker, C. *Worker Apostles: The Young Christian Workers Movement in Britain* (London: CTS Publications, 1994).

Walsh, M. *From Sword to Ploughshare: Sword of the Spirit to Catholic Institute for International Relations 1940–1980* (London: C.I.I.R., 1980).

Wells, A. 'Taking up our crosses', *Catholic Herald*, 3 July 1998.

Whyte, J.H. *Catholics in Western Democracies: A Study in Political Behaviour* (Dublin: Gill and Macmillan, 1981).

9

CATHOLIC EDUCATION IN THE UNITED STATES: MEETING THE CHALLENGE OF IMMIGRATION

Stephen J. Denig, CM

IMMIGRATION HAS played and continues to play an important role in the history of education in the United States. Immigrants founded the first schools. In the nineteenth century the great waves of immigration from Europe brought about upheavals in public education and conflict between the church and the state. At the present time, educators, especially in the urban centres, are struggling to deal with waves of immigration from Africa, Asia, and Latin America.

This chapter will explain the impact that immigration has had on the history of education in the United States. The first part is a brief analysis of the establishment of schools in the colonial United States. The next section is an account of the struggles of the early nineteenth century between church and state on educational funding. The third part is a discussion of the influence of immigration on the struggles between the church and state on education during the nineteenth century. The final part is a look at education in the United States in the twentieth century, especially as education seeks to deal both with voluntary immigrants from Africa, Asia, and Latin America and with involuntary immigrants (African-Americans). As this story of education unfolds, the contributions of the Vincentians will be highlighted.

EDUCATION IN THE COLONIAL UNITED STATES

Prior to the founding of the American nation at the end of eighteenth century, religious congregations sponsored most of the schools in the territories that were to become the United States. These schools had a decidedly religious purpose – the salvation of souls. Parents also sponsored schools or provided tutors for their children in order to provide for a more secular education; and philanthropic groups, likewise, sponsored schools for the children of the poor. The government played little role in education, except in those regions in which the government and religious denominations were intertwined. Because the history of education differs by region, each region will be considered separately.

New England

Dissenters from the established religions of Europe emigrated to colonial New England and established schools. The Dutch Reformed Church founded the first school in the thirteen original colonies in 1633 in Massachusetts (Burns, 1908) and two years later the Boston Latin school was established. These schools were founded to continue the education of young men, ages seven to sixteen. Boys were first taught to read at home or in the home of a neighbour but when they entered school they were taught more advanced reading and writing skills. The primary texts were the Bible, the catechism, and the primer. Girls, on the other hand, were taught domestic skills, either in their own homes or in the home of a neighbour and a sampler was their only diploma.

In 1647, the Old Satan Deluder Act in Massachusetts required each town and city to establish a school, supported by public revenue. The purpose of schooling, as the name of the act implies, was to educate children to read the Bible and the catechism, and thus be able to resist the wiles of the devil. 'Throughout the seventeenth century, the leaders of New England retained sublime confidence that man's chief enemy was ignorance of Holy Scripture. The schooling called for was, in reality, to ensure the religious welfare of the children' (Pratte, 1973: 40). Attendance at school was mandatory for boys. In Massachusetts, as well as in most of New England, all government services, including education, were under the monopoly of the established church, Congregationalism (Cubberly, 1919). Congregationalists were Dissenters. The Puritans, who established the Colony of New Plymouth at Plymouth Rock in 1620, sought to 'purify' the Church of England of Romanism. They fled to the colonies in order to escape persecution in England. The one exception to the dominance of Congregationalism was Rhode Island, where Roger Williams, a religious exile himself from Massachusetts, established in 1636 a colony that granted freedom of religion. These immigrants and their children created, in most of New England, the state-supported religious school (Cubberly, 1919).

Southern States

Whereas the settlers in New England were primarily dissenters from the Church of England who sought religious freedom, the settlers in the Southern States were members of the church who came for economic gain (Cubberly, 1919). The culture was primarily agrarian and the aristocratic ideals of England dominated the culture. The plantation owners, the bankers, and the merchants preferred to send their children away to private schools or had them tutored at home by local ministers and seminarians (primarily of the Anglican faith).

This aristocratic character of the society led to very little interest being paid to the education of the poor. Their needs were largely ignored, except in the larger towns and cities, where various philanthropic societies established 'pauper schools,' which were in poor condition and poorly attended. Part of the reason for this poor attendance was that white parents were required to admit that they were paupers before they could have their children attend without paying tuition (Pratte, 1973). It was not until 1810 that Thomas Jefferson, the third President of the United States and the author of the Declaration of Independence, influenced Virginia, his home state, to set aside some public funds for the education of poor white students. However, 'the major part of this Literary Fund was directed to the support of academies and colleges, the types of school in which the ruling class actually believed' (Monroe, 1940: 212). Thus, there was little effort in the colonial South to establish schools for poor white children. There was even less effort to establish schools for the children of poor blacks.

Middle Atlantic States

Between the dissenters of New England and the aristocrats of the South were the inhabitants of the Middle Atlantic States. In these states, no one denominational sect was dominant. In most of the states, the influence, however, was decidedly Protestant. The two exceptions are Maryland and Pennsylvania. George Calvert, Lord Baltimore, became proprietary governor of Maryland in 1632, and encouraged immigrants of all religions to settle in the colony. Eight years later, in 1640, the Jesuits opened a school in Newton, Maryland. It was financed by the local Catholic laity, rather than the parish church. William Penn, who established Pennsylvania in 1681, also granted religious freedom to the settlers. Shortly after the American Revolution, in 1782, St Mary's School in Philadelphia opened with a school board of eight lay managers.

In these Middle Atlantic States, education was seen as a private and parochial function. Each denomination opened its own school in order to train children in the beliefs of its religious faith. The model in the Middle Atlantic States was the parish-supported parochial school (Cubberly, 1919). A notable exception to this pattern of parochial schools, however, occurred in Pennsylvania. William Penn argued that the state, in addition to the home and the church, had a legitimate interest in education as the foundation for responsible citizenship (Kashatus, 1995).

In summary, a variety of denominations exerted influence over the development of education in the original thirteen colonies. In the New England States, Congregationalist Dissenters from the Church of England established state-supported religious schools. In the Southern States, aristocrats saw to the education of their children, but paid little attention to the education of the vast majority of people. The parochial model remained dominant in the Middle Atlantic States. In these three regions, schools were established for the children and grandchildren of immigrants from Europe.

Spanish and French Missionaries

There was a decidedly different approach to education in the territories that were colonized by French and Spanish missionaries. The Catholic Church was the dominant influence and the schools were established for the indigenous population. The earliest schools in the area that is now the United States were those established by the Spanish missionaries. In 1531, the Bishop of Mexico, whose diocese included the Southwest of the United States, reported that each convent of the Franciscans in his diocese had a school attached to it. He noted that 600 Aztec youth were attending a college founded by the Franciscans (Burns, 1908). By 1541 the Franciscans had established a school in Quivera, Oklahoma for Native Americans. This was the first school in the territory that is now the United States. In 1606, the Franciscans opened a school in St Augustine, Florida in order to instruct the children in reading and writing and Catholic doctrine.

The school, which closed in 1753, was also a preparatory seminary (Burns, 1908).

In the early eighteenth century, the Jesuits opened schools in Lower California. Usually each mission had two schools for children aged six to twelve, one for boys and one for girls. When the Jesuits were expelled in 1767, the Franciscans, notably Junipero Serra, arrived on the return trip of the boat used by the Jesuits (Burns, 1908). These Franciscans continued the mission of education begun by the Jesuits in California.

In 1722, the French Capuchins established a school for boys in New Orleans, the capital of New France. Five years later, the Ursuline sisters opened Ursuline Academy in New Orleans. This school, which still exists, had three divisions: a traditional convent boarding school for girls of the élite, a day school for the daughters of the merchant class, and a school to teach religion to Black and Native American children (Burns, 1908).

In the Southwestern and Western regions of the United States, missionaries, primarily Catholic, founded schools for the indigenous population. In New England, the Middle Atlantic States, and the South, the Protestant influence was strong in the schools established for the children of immigrants from Europe.

Although there were secular influences on education in colonial America (e.g., William Penn), the predominant influence was religious. Schools were established so that children might be instructed in the faith of the sponsoring church. Citizenship in heaven was the concern.

CHURCH AND STATE IN THE EARLY NINETEENTH CENTURY

In the early nineteenth century, a more secular purpose emerged. William Penn had urged in the late seventeenth century that schools be established in order to promote responsible citizenship (Kashatus, 1995). The new nation required an educated citizenship that was able to participate in democracy. The purpose of education was to create an educated electorate. The Pennsylvania legislature, a century later, attempted to enact legislation providing for the support of tax-supported schools. They were opposed by several religious denominations, especially the Lutherans, who operated the largest parochial system at this time. These schools sought to preserve the religion and culture of Protestant Germany for the children of immigrants. In 1796 the Lutheran Ministerium argued that 'the design of the Pennsylvania Assembly to establish free schools throughout the State would very much injure the German schools, especially in regard to the religion taught in them, and would very likely destroy them' (Beck, 1965: 63).

This concern for an educated citizenry brought the state into direct opposition with the Catholic Church, especially with regard to the education of the children of immigrants. The state sought to integrate these children into American society, a predominantly Protestant society. The church opposed this inculcation, and sought to establish schools where the culture and religion of the immigrants from Catholic Europe could be protected and fostered.

The Constitution of the United States does not give a role in education to the federal government. The Tenth Amendment of the Bill of Rights reserves to the individual states all powers not explicitly delegated to the federal government. Because education is not mentioned in the Constitution, control of education is a responsibility reserved to each state. The federal government, however, through its power to tax and spend, can exert a considerable influence on education.

Throughout this period, even as public support for public schools increased, churches continued to establish schools. For example, in 1809 Elizabeth Bayley Seton arrived in Emittsburg, Maryland where she opened a school at St Joseph's Parish, which became a parish school and is recognized today as the foundation of the Catholic Parochial School System. As increasing numbers of single women joined her in this endeavour, she founded a religious community, the Sisters of Charity, and took the rule of the Daughters of Charity. After her death, many of the Sisters of Charity became Daughters of Charity. Both these branches of the Vincentian family, the Sisters and the Daughters, have continued the tradition of Catholic education inspired by Saint Elizabeth Seton.

The most significant conflict between the religious and the secular purposes of education occurred in New York City. In 1800, the trustees of Saint Peter's Church approved the establishment of the first Catholic school in New York (Farley, 1908). On 9 April 1805 (Laws of NY, 1806), the state legislature resolved to fund the education of the poor. By 1806, Saint Peter's School was the largest denominational school in the city (Ryan, 1935) and it sought a portion of the school in accordance with the above law. On 5 May 1806, Saint Peter's church received $1,565.78 from the educational fund (Minutes, 1917). Saint Matthew's Lutheran School in Manhattan also received money at this time from the state for the education of poor children (Beck, 1965).

In 1805, the Free School Society opened its first school. This school was opened in response to the above-cited act of the legislature providing for the 'education of the children of indigent persons who do not belong to or are not provided for by any religious society' (Laws of New York, 180b: 268). After the initial allocation of funds in 1806 and until 1813, this society was the sole recipient of public educational funds. It would be a mistake, however, to consider this school a secular school. On Tuesday afternoons various religious sects provided religious instruction to the children and on Sunday mornings the children met at the school and then dispersed to attend their respective churches (Burns, 1912).

In 1813 the state allocated funds to be used to pay teachers. Religious schools were again included in this allocation (Revised Laws, 1813: 267). In 1820, the trustees of the Bethel Baptist Church in New York City applied to the state legislature for a share of these public school funds. This occurred without incident and funds were given to the school to be used to pay the salaries of teachers. When a surplus of funds accumulated, the church asked for permission to use these funds to erect new buildings and open new schools. The Free School Society already had permission to use surplus funds in this way. Permission was granted and the church opened two new schools.

The Free School Society protested to the legislature in 1823. The legislature, after considerable debate, repealed the 1813 law and turned over control of the school fund and its distribution to the city council of New York City (NYS Laws, 1824). Bethel Baptist Church pursued its application for funding to the city council, which decided to refuse funding not only to the three schools that the church was then operating but also to any religious schools (Cubberly, 1919).

This decision that New York City would fund from state revenues only non-religious schools slowly spread throughout the country. With this spread occurred a change in the purpose of education. The primary influence on education in the colonial United States had been the churches, seeking to prepare citizens for heaven. With the birth of the republic, individual states sought to create an educated citizenry. Sectarian religious influence was diminished by the restriction of government funds to public, non-religious schools. This also marked a change in what is considered a public institution. Previously, public institutions were those that served a public need (e.g. education of youth). After this time, public institutions were those that were financed from public funds (Carper, 1998).

In general, Protestants, who were the majority of the population of the United States, supported the public schools. These schools were seen as common schools, where all citizens would receive the same instruction in American and Christian virtues. 'The common schools that Horace Mann envisaged were designed to equalise opportunity for everyone, to create a level playing field, and to bring children from all walks of life together in order to prepare them for citizenship in a democracy' (Kane, 1995: 2). Bible readings, hymns, and prayers were all part of the curriculum. These were meant to be non-denominational, and on Sundays the children were to be taught the particular tenets of their faith in their churches (Carper and Layman, 1995).

For the Protestant majority, the Bible, along with the catechism and hymns, were the foundations upon which the republic rested. These were to be taught in schools. To be opposed to the reading of the Bible was to be a traitor. In general, however, the Catholic hierarchy opposed this non-denominational approach. To many bishops, the leadership of public schools were 'Protestant gentlemen who promoted an evangelical piety which was offensive' (Dolan, 1985: 263). What they found offensive was the private reading of Scripture. The Catholic Church considered itself the primary teacher of the Bible, and did not permit Catholics to read the Bible unless the church gave its interpretation.

When the American bishops met in Baltimore in 1840, this Protestant orientation of the common schools was a major concern. They wrote:

> We can scarcely point out a book in general use in the ordinary schools ... wherein covert and insidious efforts are not made to misrepresent our principles, to distort our tenets, to vilify our practices, and to bring contempt upon our Church and its members.
>
> (Nolan, 1984: 126)

There were efforts at compromise, however. Between 1833 and 1870, Bishop John Purcell of Cincinnati, Ohio tried to co-operate with public schools by having Catholic students use Catholic Bibles. These Bibles had commentaries, explaining the church's interpretation. The public school authorities, at the urging of the Protestant ministers of the city, determined that the only sanctioned Bibles were those without commentary. The efforts of Bishop Purcell were not successful.

By 1840, many religious leaders, especially the Catholic bishops, were determined to establish religious schools. They continued to seek ways to find public funding for these schools. Some were opposed to the public schools as godless. Others thought that some compromise was possible.

THE INFLUENCE OF IMMIGRATION IN THE MIDDLE TO LATE NINETEENTH CENTURY

Immigration, especially from Catholic Europe, escalated and with it nativist reactions. In New York City alone, immigration had swelled the population from 120,000 in 1820 to over 300,000 in 1840. These immigrants were primarily Catholics. Moreover, only 2 to 3 per cent of Catholic children were attending the public schools (Ravitch, 1974).

It was a period marked by violence. In 1834 the Ursuline convent in Charlestown, Massachusetts was burned. Twelve years later two Catholic schools in Philadelphia were burned and 13 people were killed (in riots) in anti-Catholic riots in the city.

The Governor of New York, William Seward, was alarmed by the rate of immigration. He wrote to the state legislature in January 1840:

> The children of foreigners, found in great number in our populous cities and towns, and in the vicinity of our public works, are too often deprived of the advantages of our system of public education, in consequence of the prejudice arising from differences of language and religion.
>
> (Bourne, 1870: 179)

His support for public funding of religious education infuriated the Know-Nothings, a nativist party. The nativists were American citizens, predominantly white, Anglo-Saxon Protestants, who sought to limit immigration and were alarmed by the growing influence of foreigners (i.e., the Pope) in American society. The Know-Nothings, citing Seward's support for Catholic education, opposed his attempt to be the Republican nominee for President in 1860. Abraham Lincoln won that Republican nomination and, subsequently, the election to the Presidency.

After this statement by the Governor, the trustees of Saint Peter's Church immediately applied to the City Council of New York for a share in these funds, arguing that for many years they had been educating from church funds between 400 and 500 children annually (Memorial, 1840). When the City Council refused, they appealed to the state legislature. A Hebrew school and a Scotch Presbyterian school joined with the Catholics in their appeal. They were opposed by the Public School Society, whose opposition was supported by the Methodists, Episcopalians, Baptists, Dutch Reformed, and Reformed Presbyterians (Cubberly, 1919). The legislature denied the requests of the Catholic, Hebrew, and Scotch Presbyterian schools and the schools appealed.

As a result of these appeals, the New York State Superintendent of the Common Schools, John Spencer, recommended to the legislature that the government should take under its control all schools receiving public funds (Assembly Documents, 1842). As a result of this recommendation, the state legislature (Laws of New York, 1842) created the City Board of Education to regulate all schools that received public funding, including the schools formerly managed by the Public School Society. In 1842, the legislature also passed the Maclay Bill (Ravitch, 1974). This bill denied public funds to both sectarian schools and other schools teaching any sectarian doctrine.

The immigration of many Catholics into the country placed severe financial constrictions on the church, which attempted to gain funding for its schools. Although the monopoly of the Public School Society was broken, religious schools failed to achieve their goal of public funding. Tax-funded schools were to be secular (Lannie, 1968), and religious schools were to be denied funding. Religious schools, however, continued to exist.

NATIVIST ANTI-CATHOLICISM

With the passage of the Maclay Bill, Bishop Hughes gave up his effort to find common ground with public schools. Yet, his concern remained – the education of Catholic students. The problem was that the supposedly non-sectarian public schools of the country were still largely Protestant. Bishop Hughes' concern was intensified by the waves of immigrants following the Irish potato famine. In 1850 there were 660,000 Catholics in the United States. Within one decade that Catholic presence had almost tripled to 1,600,000, three-quarters of the increase being Irish immigrants. In 1850, as the first effects of the famine were being felt in New York, Bishop Hughes wrote: 'I think the time is almost come when it will be necessary to build the school-house first and the church afterwards' (Kehoe, 1865, v. II: 715).

As the Protestant influence over the schools began to lessen, the schools became increasingly secular. There was a growing bitterness on the part of many in the Catholic hierarchy towards the 'godless' public schools. Yet, to the chagrin of the hierarchy, growing numbers of Catholics supported these 'godless' schools. Five thousand Catholics attended New York City's public schools in 1840. By 1849, over half of the students in the school system were Catholics. In 1870, 22,000 Catholics were in attendance (Walch, 1996).

To some Catholics, the 'godless public schools' were a good thing. Father Edward McGlynn, pastor of Saint Stephen's Church in New York City, spoke on 17 December 1871 in favour of denying funds to any school that used Bibles, hymns, or prayers (McAvoy, 1966). Some bishops (e.g., Bishop Purcell of Cincinnati) still sought to make accommodation with the public schools. These efforts were often counterproductive. For example, as a result of Bishop Purcell's efforts to have the Cincinnati public schools make accommodations for Catholic students the Board of Education decreed in 1859 that Bible reading, religious instruction, and hymns were to be removed from the curriculum. The Protestant clergy rallied against this decision, which they saw as an attack on the Christian foundations of Americanism. In 1870 the Supreme Court of Ohio ruled in favour of removing the Bible, religious instruction, and hymns from public schools and 'placed another brick in the wall of separation between Church and State' (Dolan, 1985: 269).

The Catholic Church by the middle of the century had become the largest single denomination in the country. As Ahlstrom (1972) noted, it was suspect for a number of reasons. First, the United States historically was allied with Protestant England, whose rivals were Catholic France and Spain. Second, the strong Enlightenment philosophy on which the country was founded saw the Catholic Church as the most powerful institutionalization of medieval superstitions. Third, the growing strength of Catholicism threatened the Protestant power structures of the day. And finally, Catholic immigrants settled primarily in the cities, where they contributed to the gradual shift of power from traditional agrarian structures to urban centres.

'The fact is that no one in America worried about religious instruction in schools before Catholic immigration threatened the Protestant hegemony' (Laycock, 1992). Anti-Catholicism in the

United States continued to grow as the number of Catholic immigrants increased. The Know-Nothings were growing stronger, and sought to deny public funds to all Catholic institutions. In September 1871, President Ulysses Grant said to a reunion of Civil War veterans in Des Moines, Iowa: 'Leave the matter of religion to the family altar, the Church, and the private school supported entirely by private contribution. Keep the church and state forever separate' (McAvoy, 1966: 21).

Representative James G. Blaine, who ran for President against Grant in 1872, proposed an amendment to the US Constitution prohibiting the use of public funds to support any institution, including schools, under the control of any religious sect or denomination. This amendment passed in the House, but failed in the Senate (Peterson, 1990). Many states, however, adopted versions of this amendment in their state constitutions, and all new states added to the Union were required to insert this amendment into their constitutions.

THE VINCENTIAN UNIVERSITIES

Despite this anti-Catholic nativism, immigration, especially from Europe, continued unabated. The concerns of the bishops were to train priests for their dioceses and to educate Catholic youth, especially immigrants. This concern was not limited to primary and secondary schools. Individual bishops asked religious communities (among them the Vincentians) to establish seminaries and colleges in their diocese. One of the purposes for which Saint Vincent de Paul had founded the Vincentians in 1617 was to promote the formation of the clergy. From this involvement in seminary education flowed their involvement in college education.

In 1815, the Vincentians were invited to come to the Louisiana Territory in order to found a seminary. Saint Mary's of the Barrens opened in 1818. Financial support for the seminary was provided by the establishment of a lay college and the seminarians supported themselves by teaching the lay students. The Vincentian superiors in Paris looked askance at this mingling of clerical and lay students and tried to suppress it in 1835. Their efforts were only temporarily successful. A fire in 1866, however, brought about the closing of Saint Mary's College (Poole, 1988a).

In 1844 the lay students were transferred from Saint Mary's to Saint Vincent's College in Cape Girardeau. This college grew out of Saint Vincent's Male Academy, which the Vincentians found in 1838

and was incorporated as a college five years later. A seminary programme was added to the curriculum, and Saint Vincent's became
an apostolic school in 1910 (Poole, 1988b).

Niagara University was found in 1856 as Our Lady of Angels
Seminary. Bishop John Timon, CM, the first Bishop of Buffalo, was
concerned about the shortage of priests to pastor his rural diocese
and petitioned his confrères to open a seminary. John Lynch, CM,
later Archbishop of Toronto, became the first president (McKey,
1931). This school again used the mixed model of seminary and
collegiate education. In 1961, the seminary programme was transferred to Albany, New York. This seminary closed eleven years later,
and thus ended Niagara University's history as a seminary. The
university has continued and now is the oldest of the three Vincentian universities in the United States.

The Vincentians founded Saint Vincent's College and Seminary in
Los Angeles in 1865 at the request of Thaddeus Amat, CM, the
Bishop of Monterey and Los Angeles. Around 1886 the seminary
programme ended. In 1911, ownership of the college was transferred
to the Jesuits, who renamed it Loyola.

Saint John's University traces its origins to 1870. Many of the
immigrants crowding into New York City settled in the neighbouring
city of Brooklyn. Bishop Loughlin, the first bishop of the Diocese of
Brooklyn , asked the Vincentians to establish a school for the intellectual and moral education of the youth of his diocese. From 1891 to
1930, the seminary for the Diocese of Brooklyn was attached to Saint
John's. At the present time, Saint John's is the second largest Catholic university in the United States.

The largest Catholic university in the United States is DePaul.
DePaul was incorporated in 1898 as Saint Vincent's College. Archbishop Patrick Feehan, the first archbishop of Chicago, asked the
Vincentians to open a college on the north side of Chicago because
the population in that part of the city was experiencing a rapid
growth due to immigration. Archbishop Feehan himself was an
immigrant who had studied under the Vincentians at Castleknock.

The final college established by the Vincentians in the United
States was the Holy Trinity College in Dallas, Texas. It opened in
1907 and three years later the name was changed to the University of
Dallas, a name it retained until 1929 when it closed. The present
University of Dallas bears no organic relationship to the Vincentian
institution.

The Vincentians still sponsor three universities in the United

States: Niagara University, Saint John's and DePaul. Saint John's in New York City and DePaul in Chicago are the two largest Catholic universities in the United States.

THE INSTRUCTION OF 1875

As immigration into the United States continued in the latter part of the nineteenth century, nativist opposition grew stronger. In response, the bishops continued to support Catholic schools but did not mandate them. James McMaster, editor of the *Freeman's Journal* sought to have the Vatican deny absolution to all Catholics who sent their children to public schools. Cardinal Franchi, Prefect of the Sacred Congregation on the Inquisition, wrote a letter to the archbishops of the United States and asked them to consider whether absolution should be denied to these parents. Although there were some who agreed, the majority thought that it would be counterproductive, that it would drive Catholics from the church and would only stir up greater hatred on the part of Protestants (McAvoy, 1966).

Nevertheless, the Sacred Congregation issued an Instruction to the American bishops in 1875 urging them to do all in their power to prevent children from attending public schools and to issue a mandate that if there was a parochial school available, if the parents could afford it, and if the instruction in the parochial school was at least the equal of that in the public school, then the sacraments could be denied to those who obstinately refused to send their children to parochial schools (Walch, 1996).

In order to understand this Vatican response, it is important to consider what was occurring in Europe at the time. Higher criticism of the Scriptures led many to question the historicity of the events of the Bible. Discoveries in physics and geology and the theory of evolution challenged the veracity of Scripture, the supernatural basis on which the authority of the churches, Catholic and Protestant, was based (Cassidy, 1948). In the name of secularism, schools under the control of the church were being seized by the state, and were being forcibly made devoid of all traces of Catholicism. In 1864, after German civil authorities sought to secularize the schools in the Grand Duchy of Baden, Pope Pius IX sent a letter to the Archbishop of Freiburg stating that Catholics were conscience-bound not to attend schools where their faith was in danger (McAvoy, 1966). In Belgium, when the anti-clerical government tried to ban religion from public schools, the hierarchy created their own schools, which led so many to leave the public schools that the government collapsed. In France, the anti-clerical government suppressed all religious education in both public and religious schools. And in Italy itself, national unity had led to the seizure of the Papal Estates and to the secularization of the ecclesiastical schools (Gleason, 1987). Against the background of its own experience in Europe, it is understandable that the Vatican looked askance at what was reported to be happening in American public schools.

THE THIRD PLENARY COUNCIL OF BALTIMORE

By the time that the bishops gathered for the Third Plenary Council (1883–4) public education was thoroughly entrenched on the American scene. Efforts to foster a non-denominational Christian education through the public schools had met with initial success, but then failed due to opposition from Catholics who believed that non-denominational was synonymous with Protestant and anti-Catholic. Publicly funded denominational schools had periodically emerged, to flourish for a while and then wither. The Catholic bishops knew that the time was not ripe to seek funding for Catholic schools. The question before them was whether to promote cooperation with the public schools or to promote the building of Catholic schools.

Armed with this Instruction, the supporters of Catholic schools sought to have the Council mandate Catholic schools in every parish and to force Catholic parents to send their children to these school by threatening to withhold absolution. There was strong support at the Council for Catholic schools, led by Archbishop Michael Heiss of Milwaukee and Bishops Joseph Dwenger of Fort Wayne and Bernard McQuaid of Rochester. There was also strong opposition from Bishop Edward Fitzgerald of Little Rock, Archbishop Ryan of Philadelphia, and Archbishop Freehan of Chicago (Gleason, 1987).

After much discussion, the bishops issued the following decree (#199):

1. Near every church, where one does not already exist, a parochial school is to be erected within two years from the promulgation of this Council, and to be supported 'in perpetuum', unless the Bishop decides it is to be delayed on account of grave difficulties.

2 A priest, who during this time obstructs by his grave neglect the

building or maintaining of a school or does not obey after repeated admonitions of the Bishop, must be removed from that Church.

3   The mission or parish that so neglects its duty to help the priest in the building or maintaining of the school, that on account of this supine negligence it is not possible to build the school, is to be reprimanded by the Bishop, and by this more efficacious and prudent manner persuaded to give the necessary support.

4   All Catholic parents are bound to send their children to parochial schools, unless either at home or in other Catholic schools they provide sufficiently and fully for their Christian education, or on account of a good reason approved by the Bishop, and with the appropriate precautions and remedies, they are allowed to send them to other schools. Which Catholic school, however, is to be left to the decision of the Ordinary.

(Guilday, 1933)

Support for Catholic schools was not as strong as these decrees might imply.

> Great leeway was left for episcopal discretion in determining whether a school was Catholic (which might permit compromises with the state), in disciplining pastors and congregations, and in allowing exceptions to parents who wished to send their children to non-Catholic schools.
>
> (Gleason, 1987: 133)

Support for parochial schools has never been unanimous in the Catholic community, and the decrees of the Third Plenary Council did not make it so. For example, Archbishop Ireland (1897) of St Paul addressed the annual convention of the National Educational Association in 1890.

> I am a friend and an advocate of the state school. In the circumstances of the present time I uphold the parish school. I sincerely wish that the need for it did not exist. I would have all schools for the children of the people to be state schools.
>
> (1897: 199)

The following year he turned over the parochial schools in Faribault and Stillwater, Minnesota to the state to be administered as public schools. The school board hired the faculty, including the religious sisters, to teach the ordinary school curriculum during school hours. They taught religion after school. His plan was opposed both by

German Catholics who saw it as a violation of the decrees of the Third Plenary Council of Baltimore and by non-Catholics who saw it as an attempt to get the state to finance Catholic education.

Initially, the strongest opposition to Ireland's plan in Faribault and Stillwater were the German Catholic newspapers, *Amerika* of Saint Louis and *Columbia* of Milwaukee, and the German Jesuit missionaries. The German Jesuits used their influence in Rome to begin a Vatican investigation of the archbishop. It was only the strong support of Cardinal Gibbons of New York that led to a decision by the Holy See to accept the plan (Ellis, 1952). However, within two years, the school board had decided not to renew the contracts

The strong support of the German bishops for Catholic schools was a reflection of their interests both in Catholicism and in German culture. German was the language of the German Catholic schools. These schools served the children and grandchildren of German immigrants. They wanted their children and grandchildren to learn the German language and German culture but the English language and American culture were the norms in public schools.

While Catholics in the more urban centres set up parochial schools in opposition to the public schools, in the more rural sections of the country Catholics and Protestants had to co-operate in order to build schools (Walch, 1996).

CO-OPERATIVE EFFORTS IN SAVANNAH AND POUGHKEEPSIE

The best-known examples of this co-operative effort were in Savannah, Georgia and Poughkeepsie, New York. In 1862, Bishop Verot of Savannah made an appeal to the school commissioners for financial assistance for the Catholic schools. It was denied due to the financial constraints of the American Civil War (Gannon, 1964). After the war, Verot sent a letter to the mayor and the aldermen of Savannah requesting that the Catholic schools of the city be united with the public school system.

The Board of Education, initially opposed this plan, arguing that 'The classification of pupils according to religious faith once inaugurated, must, in principle, be extended to all denominations – and Hebrew, Roman Catholic, Baptist, Methodist, Episcopalian, Unitarian, Lutheran, Swedenborgian, and whatsoever denomination else may exist' (Savannah, 1868: 4–5).

Two years later, in 1870, an agreement was finally reached. The

Catholic schools of Savannah were received under the control of the Board of Education. The agreement stipulated that the teachers in these schools were to be members of the Catholic Church and were subject to examination and were appointed by the Board. Religion classes were held each day from 8.30 to 9.00 before the beginning of the official school day (Powers, 1956). The Savannah Plan was terminated by action of the Board of Education on 18 December 1916 (ASBE, 1916) after a complaint from a local citizen that the agreement violated the Georgia State constitution by using public funds for sectarian schooling. This agreement, set in place before the Third Plenary Council of Baltimore, remained essentially unchanged by the Council decrees for 32 years.

A similar plan was promoted in Poughkeepsie in upstate New York. In 1873, Archbishop McCloskey of New York and the School Board of Poughkeepsie entered into an agreement whereby the parochial schools of Saint Peter's Church were leased for one dollar per year by the Board for specific hours during the school day. The Board assumed the costs of maintenance, salaries, and textbooks. The church reserved the right to use the buildings outside of school hours (Cramer, 1890). The official school hours were from 9 to 12 and from 1.30 to 3. Religious exercises were conducted before and after school hours, with religious instruction during the lunch break (McSweeney, 1887).

A serious conflict arose concerning the habit worn by the Sisters of Charity. A local resident protested to the Board that sisters in habit were teaching in a public school, operating in buildings owned by a church. The pastor proposed that the sisters be allowed to wear secular dress during school hours. The sisters refused. On 23 December 1887 the Board voted to terminate the plan. The major issue was that the wearing of a religious habit 'constitutes a sectarian influence, which ought not to be persisted in' (Assembly Documents, 1899: 111). A second issue was the permanent leasing of private facilities for public use.

Although Savannah and Poughkeepsie are the best-known compromise plans, they were not the only ones. The Sisters of Charity, the religious community founded by Saint Elizabeth Seton and part of the Vincentian family, were involved in many of the controversies, including the one in Poughkeepsie. In 1885, Saint Raphael's Church in Suspension Bridge (Niagara Falls, New York) had placed its school under the Board of Education of the Union Free School District No. 7. Three Sisters of Charity continued to teach in the school. New

York State Superintendent Draper (Assembly Documents, 1888) ruled that the wearing of a religious habit was a violation of the state constitution. In 1895, West Troy, New York hired religious sisters to teach in the public schools. Before this plan was found unconstitutional (Assembly Documents, 1897) the West Troy school district was absorbed into the Watervliet District, which renewed the arrangement with the sisters. When Skinner again ruled that the habit constituted a sectarian influence, there was so much dissension on the Board that they refused to hire anyone – superintendent, principals, teachers, janitors – for the 1897–8 school year. Eventually, the New York Supreme Court (Hutchinson v. Skinner) decided that the wearing of a religious habit did constitute a sectarian influence.

Despite this ruling, in 1901 the public school district in Lima, New York hired two Sisters of Charity to teach in a school that had formerly been a parochial school. Skinner (Assembly Documents, 1903) again ruled that it was not permissible for them to teach in their habits. The following September, the school district hired one of these two sisters and another sister. They continued to teach in habit. During the last month of the school year, the sisters were notified that they could no longer teach in habit. They persisted and continued to teach in their habits until the end of the school term. When their pay cheques were withheld, they sued. In O'Connor v. Hendrick, the court decided that Board owed the sisters only the amount that they had earned prior to being notified that they could no longer teach in habit.

The court (Hysong *et al.* v. Gallitzin) in Pennsylvania reached an entirely different verdict. In Gallitzin, when the parochial school was closed, it was turned over the Board of Education. Four Sisters of Charity were hired by the Board to teach in the former parochial school. When a new school was built, the Board hired six sisters to teach. The court ruled that it was permissible for the Board to hire the sisters, because their exclusion from hiring would be a violation of their First Amendment rights. As long as these sisters provided no sectarian teachings and conducted no sectarian religious exercises, they were allowed to wear their habits in the public school classroom.

There are many other examples of co-operation, in this period around the Third Plenary Council. There were plans at Mount de Sales in Macon, Georgia (Zettler, 1890), at Saint Mary's Academy in Augusta, Georgia (correspondent, 1890), at Saint Patrick's in New Haven, Connecticut (Buetow, 1970), at Saint Peter's in Hartford,

Connecticut (Buetow, 1970), and in Alpine, Michigan (Richter v. Cordes: 285).

Protestant churches also sought compromises with the public school authorities. Beck (1965) reported that several Lutheran congregations in Pennsylvania turned their schools over to the public school authorities during the middle of the nineteenth century. These schools were to be conducted 'under the joint direction of the congregation and the local school-board, the members of which sometimes, in thickly settled Lutheran communities, were members of the Lutheran congregations within the district' (1965: 81). He cited as examples the Heidelberg School in Berks County, Pennsylvania as well as schools in Coopersburg, Shiremanstown, Greensburg, and Trappe. Lutheran pastors were frequent visitors in these schools.

Despite numerous setbacks, efforts to find an accommodation continued well into the middle of the present century. In 1933, five Catholic schools in Vincennes, Indiana, closed and public schools opened in three of the buildings. The school board hired the previous faculties, including the sisters who continued to teach in habit. Holy pictures and statues remained in the classrooms, and every morning, before school, the parish priest would conduct religious instruction in the church next to the school. In Johnson v. Boyd (1940) the Indiana Supreme Court ruled that this arrangement was constitutional. In a study conducted in 1937, Cronin and Donohue called these jointly administered schools 'Catholic Public Schools'. They investigated 140 of them, and speculated that there were about 340 elementary and secondary schools in which 'church and public school authorities participate jointly in the administration of the schools' (Cronin and Donohue, 1937: 1).

An analysis of these attempts to find an acceptable accommodation between the religious and secular purposes of education would not be complete without a mention of Revd James J. Tighe (1890) and what he called 'The Pittsburg [*sic*] Failure'. In 1887, he was elected Principal of the public school that was next to his church. He closed his parish school, took off his Roman collar, was called 'Mr Principal' and administered the school as a public school. He would gather the Catholic students for religious instruction in the parish church for a half-hour before school began. After two and a half weeks, only 56 students were attending religious instruction. More than 300 pupils had transferred with him to the public school. He wrote: 'I presided over a school that according to the American idea could not offend Protestant, Jew, Turk, infidel or agnostic, but which I now see must have offended the great God grievously' (p. 7). He resigned his position, re-opened the parish school and brought the Catholic children back with him to the parochial school. He remained convinced that 'a combination of the Catholic Church with the Public School System is an utter impossibility'.

TWENTIETH-CENTURY GROWTH OF THE CATHOLIC SCHOOL SYSTEM

The period after the Third Council of Baltimore was one of unprecedented growth for the Catholic school system. When the bishops issued their decrees in 1884 about one-third of Catholic parishes had schools. There were 6613 churches and 2532 schools (McAvoy, 1966). Sixteen years later, in 1900, there were almost 4000 Catholic schools. In the next two decades an additional 4103 schools would be opened. By 1966, the year in which the Catholic schools reached a peak of 13,292 schools (Jacobs, 1998), the percentage of churches with schools had doubled to two-thirds. These schools had enrolled over five a and half million students, almost 47 per cent of the Catholic school-age population in 1965 (Walch, 1996). It is worth noting that, even at its height, there were still one-third of Catholic parishes without schools, and over half the Catholic school-age population (53 per cent) did not attend Catholic schools.

Ellis Island opened in 1891 and remained the major centre for immigration into the United States until 1954. Combined with the bishops' concern for the education of youth, Catholic immigrants fuelled the rapid growth of the Catholic school system. A second factor was the changes occurring in American society.

During the latter part of the nineteenth century and the early part of the twentieth century, schools began to reflect a national concern for business. In the latter half of the 1880s, the United States

> moved from a society and people who lived in agrarian and rural villages and small communities into an urban, industrial society whose number-one identity and purpose is the production of material objects and instruments during the day and their destruction [consumption] at night.
>
> (Etzioni, 1984: 222)

The emergence of a consumer and capitalistic society had an effect on education.

With the development of the common schools, educators in the 1890s deliberately sought to break the ties that bound children to their natural communities. 'America's public school system was conceived as an agent of the state, not of the family' (Kane, 1995: 2). America was a land of immigrants, and there were fears that ethnic and religious schools would deepen the divisions of language, religion, and customs in society.

> The task of the state (as some educators saw it then) was to break the power of the family over its children; to liberate the children from the narrow horizons, the dogmas, the language, the narrow subcultures, the self-serving power of their parents.
>
> (Coleman, 1990: xiv)

Up until this time, much of the industry was out of, or close to, the home. A girl still learned domestic skills from her mother and from others in the neighbourhood. A boy learned his craft from his father or a neighbour. With the advent of the industrial revolution, fathers went somewhere else to work, and so education of the boys was given over to the state.

With passage of child-labour laws, and the subsequent need to do something with children, compulsory attendance laws were passed in all of the states. The law in Oregon went further than that in most states, and required all children to be educated in the state-supported schools. The law did not prohibit churches and other groups from operating schools, but it did limit this right by requiring that all children attend public schools, while allowing them to attend other schools for after-school programmes. The Supreme Court in 1925 ruled (Pierce v. Society of Sisters) that the state may not compel students to attend the public school.

The period after the First World War was marked in the United States by a rapid increase in the percentage of children attending school and in the length of time that they remained in school. The mandatory attendance laws required not only boys, but girls as well, to attend school. Besides the increase in the number of girls attending school, the law also required black Americans to attend school. Initially, some states provided education for black Americans in separate-but-equal schools. However, in 1954, the Supreme Court (Brown v. Board of Education) determined that separate schools were not equal, and mandated that all state-supported schools in the United States were to be integrated.

Religious schools were influential in this decision. At one time, most religious schools were segregated. In the years, however, before the Supreme Court decision, many religious leaders determined on principle that their schools should be integrated. For example, Archbishop O'Boyle of Washington, DC, in 1951 ordered the integration of all Catholic schools in his archdiocese. Several weeks before the issuing their landmark decision in Brown v. Board of Education, Chief Justice Earl Warren and two associate judges visited Cardinal O'Boyle and inquired about the peaceful integration of the Catholic schools as a model for their own decision.

THE VINCENTIANS' SCHOOLS OF EDUCATION

At the Third Plenary Council the bishops recognized that if Catholic parents were to be persuaded to choose Catholic schools for their children, then these schools had to be at least the equal of the public schools. In their pastoral letter they wrote: '[W]e must also perfect our schools. We repudiate the idea that the Catholic school need be in any respect inferior to any other school whatsoever' (Nolan, 1984: 125).

In order to improve the Catholic schools, the Council mandated in decree 203 that each diocese establish a Diocesan Commission on Schools to test all teachers, both religious and lay, who wished to teach in Catholic schools. The purpose was to ensure that 'only good and capable teachers are provided for these schools' (Scanlon, 1967: 305). In addition, the council mandated (decree 204) that every diocese create School Commissions for different areas and nationalities, composed of one or more priests, to inspect schools in cities and rural districts.

In response to the growing need for teachers in the Catholic schools, and especially the need to provide teachers, both religious and lay, with an education that was the equal of the public school teachers' education, bishops approached various colleges to sponsor schools of education. This contributed to changes in the Vincentian universities. The universities were originally established for males. The Catholic school teachers were both religious sisters and lay teachers, predominantly female. Saint John's established its School of Pedagogy (now the School of Education and Human Services) in 1908. DePaul established the School of Education in 1918, although it had been conducting extension courses for Catholic women for several years prior to this. Commencing in 1914, women could earn the Bachelor of Education degree during these summer sessions

(Birney, 1961). The first two women to receive degrees from Niagara graduated in 1935 with Master of Arts degrees.

CATHOLIC EDUCATION TODAY

Although the number of Catholic schools has declined since the 1960s, the need for Catholic schools remains. Research has found that children learn best in those schools where the children have a strong sense of community (Bryk and Driscoll, 1988). Although Catholic schools have adopted the same basic subject discipline approach that most public schools have, there is a greater sense of community in Catholic schools. This sense of community is based on three core features: (1) a shared value system, which provides a set of expectations that motivate and guide behaviour; (2) a common agenda of activities that provides a base of common experiences for students and faculty together; and (3) the shared interactions among faculty and students, who are brought into contact with one another in situations outside the classroom (Bryk *et al.* 1993). Many students learn best in the community of the Catholic school. Bryk *et al.* (1993) opined that there were four characteristics found in Catholic high schools that accounted for the effectiveness of these schools – a delimited technical core, communal organization, decentralized governance, and an inspiration ideology.

Catholic schools have a strong core curriculum with few elective courses. These schools have a narrow vision of what elements should be part of an education. They set the same basic academic goals for all students, with few differences and very limited tracking. This delimited core is at the heart, according to Bryk *et al.*, of the success of these schools.

The second characteristic is the communal organization of these schools. There are numerous occasions during which children and adults interact with one another in the school – the shared academic experiences, the religious programmes and retreats, and extra-curricular activities, all of which also contribute to the traditions of the school whereby those in the present are joined with those who have gone before and those who will follow after them. The collegiality of the faculty is also a part of this communal organization. The faculty interact with one another as friends in mutual trust and concern, and bring this concern to their interactions with their students. Finally, there is a shared commitment to a set of values, which forms a community in which each person is respected and receives care.

The decentralized governance of Catholic schools is seen in the leadership role given to the Principal. Even in those schools that are part of a larger system, Principals in Catholic schools are relatively autonomous. Generally, they are chosen to be Principal from among the faculty of the school, and find their loyalty directed to the school and not to the larger system.

Finally, an inspirational ideology permeates these schools. There is a commitment to what is true and what is ethical. This affects not only the curriculum of the school, but also the dialogue that occurs within the classroom, and the interactions of the school community with the world. A religious atmosphere flows throughout the school and integrates all elements of the school into a cohesive whole.

Many children learn best in Catholic schools. This is especially true of students in impoverished urban schools. These students are often the new immigrants coming from Latin America, from Asia, and from Eastern Europe. Black Americans are seen by some as involuntary immigrants (Fordam and Ogbu, 1986), whose culture clashes with American culture. These new immigrants often live in stratified neighbourhoods and stratification of neighbourhoods assured that public schools were stratified (Friedman, 1955). Differences in the racial balances among neighbourhoods created differences in educational opportunities. Research (Neal, 1997) has found that many minorities in urban Catholic schools outperform their peers in the stratified urban public schools.

Perhaps the most serious threat to the existence of Catholic schools today, especially in the urban centres, is finance. The financial support of Catholic schools has been a prominent concern since the trustees of Saint Peter's church sought funding in 1806 for its parish school. Catholic parents are taxed to support the public school and then are asked to pay tuition for their children to attend Catholic schools. The Congregation for Catholic Education (1998) called this 'an almost unbelievable financial burden on families choosing not to send their children to state schools, and constitutes a serious threat to the survival of the schools themselves' (Article 7).

Although Saint John's and DePaul remain committed to the Catholic schools of their cities, they are also concerned about the needs of all children. Saint John's and DePaul characterize themselves as Catholic schools that are metropolitan and urban. This is a commitment to help the cities to educate all the children of the city as a way to solve the despair of so many urban inhabitants. Through their schools of education, both Saint John's and DePaul seek to provide quality teachers for the Catholic and public schools of the city. In addition, these universities seek qualified graduates of urban schools and, through extensive financial aid programmes, make the opportunity available for them to graduate from college. In this the universities are continuing the tradition of Saint Vincent de Paul who was 'keenly aware of the vital place of education in a holistic approach to the service of the poor' (Sullivan, 1997: 13).

CONCLUSION

The history of education in the United States is the history of an immigrant people. Dissenters and loyalists founded schools in the East, missionaries from Catholic Europe established schools in the West. Church and state struggled over the plight of immigrant children. At first, Catholics and Protestants clashed. Later, the Catholic bishops founded the Catholic school system because of the lack of religious instruction in the public schools. Today the Catholic schools are schools of opportunities, especially for urban minorities. In 1994, Saint John's University began its 125th academic year with celebration at Saint Patrick's Cathedral in New York. In the entrance procession, students carried the flags of 120 nations and each flag was carried by a current student born in that country. Four years later, during the centennial celebration of its founding, the students from 'DePaul University performed a new university anthem, DePaul University, Our Home of Hope and Grace'. The second verse is: 'Gathered are we, an urban family, Sharing our lives, and our hopes and dreams. Gath'ring strength from our diversity, DePaul University, where learning lights our way'. The history of Catholic education, especially in the Vincentian traditions, continues to be the story of immigrants.

REFERENCES

Primary Sources

(1806) Laws of the State of New York, Albany, NY: Websters and Skinner.
(1813) Revised Laws of New York State.
(1824) New York State Session Laws.
(1840) The memorial of the members of the congregation of Saint Peter's Church (Barclay Street) in the City of New York, Dunwoodie: Archives of the Archdiocese of New York.

(1842) Annual report of the Superintendent of Common Schools. Assembly documents of the State of New York. Sixty-fifth Session, 1(12), Albany: Thurlow Weed.

(1842) Laws of the State of New York (Sixty-fifth Session), Albany: Thurlow Weed.

(1868) Report of the Board of Public Education for the City of Savannah and the County of Chatham to the mayor and aldermen of the City of Savannah upon the petition of the Roman Catholics of Savannah for a division of the public school fund, Savannah, GA: Morning News Steam Power Press.

(1888) Thirty-fourth annual report of the State Superintendent of Public Instruction. Documents of the Assembly of the State of New York, One hundred and eleventh session, 1(7), 854–9, Troy: The Troy Press Company.

(1897) Forty-third annual report of the State Superintendent of Public Instruction. Documents of the Assembly of the State of New York, One hundred and twentieth session, 16(71), Part I, 174–92, Albany: Wynkoop, Hallenbeck, Crawford Company.

(1899) Forty-fifth annual report of the State Superintendent of Public Instruction. Documents of the Assembly of the State of New York, One hundred and twenty-second session, 10(56), 110–19, Albany: Wynkoop, Hallenbeck, Crawford Company.

(1903) Forty-ninth annual report of the State Superintendent of Public Instruction. Documents of the Assembly of the State of New York, One hundred and twenty-sixth session, 11(58), 164–7, Albany: Wynkoop, Hallenbeck, Crawford Company.

(1916) Annals of the Savannah of the Board of Education (ASBE).

(1917) Minutes of the Common Council of the City of New York 1784–831, New York: City of New York.

Court Decisions

Brown v. Board of Education, 347 U.S. 483 (1954).

Hutchinson v. Skinner, 49 N.Y.S. 360, 21 Misc. Rep. 729 (1897).

Hysong *et al.* v. School District of Gallitzin, 164 Pa. 629, 30 Atl. 482, 26 L.R.A. 203 (1894).

Nance v. Johnson, 84 Tex. 401, 19 S. W. 559 (1892).

O'Connor v. Hendrick, 184 N. Y. 421, 77 N. E. 612; 7 L. R. A. (N.S.) 402 (1906).

Pierce v. Society of Sisters, 268 U.S. 510 (1917).

Richter v. Cordes, 100 Mich. 278, 58 N. W. 1110 (1894).

State ex rel Johnson v. Boyd (Ind.), 28 N.E. (2d) 256; 217 Ind. 348 (1940).

Secondary Sources

Ahlstrom, S. *A Religious History of the American People* (New Haven: Yale University Press, 1972).

Beck, W. H. *Lutheran Elementary Schools in the United States: A History of the Development of Parochial Schools and Synodical Educational Policies and Programmes* (Saint Louis: Concordia, (1965).

Birney, J. D. 'The development of departments of education in Catholic universities and colleges in Chicago, 1910–1960', unpublished doctoral dissertation, Loyola University, Chicago, (1961).

Bourne, W.O. *History of the Public School Society* (New York: William Wood & Co, 1870).

Bryk, A.S. and Driscoll, M.E. *An Empirical Investigation of the School as Community* (Chicago, IL: University of Chicago, 1988).

Bryk, A.S., Lee, V. E. and Holland, P.B. *Catholic Schools and the Common Good* (Cambridge, MA: Harvard University Press, 1993).

Buetow, H.A. *Of Singular Benefit* (New York: Macmillan, 1970).

Burns, J.A. *The Catholic School System in the United States: Its Principals, Origin, and Establishment* (New York: Benziger, 1908).

Burns, J.A. *The Principles, Origin and Establishment of the Catholic School System in the United States* (New York: Benziger, 1912).

Carper, J.C. 'History, religion, and school: a context for conversation', in J.T. Sears and J.C. Carper. (eds) *Curriculum, Religion, and Public Education* (New York: Teachers College Press, 1998), pp. 11–24.

Carper, J.C. and Layman, J. 'Independent Christian day schools: past, present, and future', *Journal of Research on Christian Education*, 4(1) (1995): 7–19.

Cassidy, F.P. 'Catholic education in the Third Plenary Council of Baltimore', *Catholic Historical Review*, 34(3–4) (1948): 257–305, 414–36.

Coleman, J.S. 'Choice, community and future schools', in W.H. Clune and J.F. Witte (eds), *Choice and Control in American Education: Volume 1. The Theory of Choice and Control in Education* (Bristol, PA: Palmer Press, 1990), pp. ix–xxii.

Congregation for Catholic Education 'The Catholic school of the threshold of the third millenium', *Catholic Education: A Journal of Inquiry and Practice*, 2(1), (1998): 4–14.

Correspondent 'An unsuccessful attempt at Suspension Bridge', *The Independent*, 42(2179) (4 September 1890): 6.

Cramer, G.E. 'The Poughkeepsie plan', *The Independent* 42(2179) (4 September 1890): 5.

Cronin, J.T. and Donohue, F.J. 'Catholic public schools in the United States', *Institute of Catholic Education Research, Bulletin*, No. 1, mimeographed (New York: Fordham University, 1937).

Cubberley, E.P. *Public Education in the United States* (Boston: Houghton Mifflin Company, 1919).

Dolan, J.P. *The American Catholic Experience: A History from Colonial Times until the Present* (Garden City, NY: Doubleday, 1985).

Ellis, J.T. *The Life of James Cardinal Gibbons, Archbishop of Baltimore, 1834–1921*, (2 volumes) (Milwaukee: Bruce Publishing Company, 1952).

Etzioni, A. 'Can schools teach children moral values?' in P.A. Sola (ed.) *Ethics, Education and Administrative Decisions: A Book of Readings* (New York: Peter Lang), pp. 215–25.

Farley, J.M. *History of Saint Patrick's Cathedral* (New York: Society for the Propagation of the Faith, 1908).

Fordham, S. and Ogbu, J.U. 'Black students' school success: coping with the burden of "acting white"', *Urban Review*, (1986) 18(3): 176-206.

Friedman, M. 'The role of government in education', in R.A. Solo (ed.) *Economics and the Public Interest* (New Brunswick, NJ: Rutgers University Press, 1955), pp. 123–44.

Gannon, M.V. *Rebel Bishop: The Life and Era of Augustin Verot* (Milwaukee, WI: Bruce, 1964).

Gleason, P. *Keeping the Faith: American Catholicism Past and Present* (Notre Dame, IN: University of Notre Dame Press, 1987).

Guilday, P. (ed.) *A History of the Councils of Baltimore, 1791–1884* (New York: Macmillan Company, 1933).

Ireland, J. 'State schools and parish schools', in *The Church and Modern Society: Lectures and Addresses* (New York: D.H. McBride & Co., 1897).

Jacobs, R.M. 'U.S. Catholic schools and the religious who served in them: contributions in the first six decades of the 20th century', *Catholic Education: A Journal of Inquiry and Practice*, 2(1), (1998): 15-34.

Kane, P.R. 'Privatization in American education', *Private School Monitor*, 17(1), (1995): 1–12.

Kashatus III, W. C. 'The making of William Penn's "Holy Experiment" in education', *Journal of Research on Christian Education*, 4(2), (1995): 157–81.

Kehoe, L. (ed.) *Complete Works of Most Rev. John Hughes, D.D*, two volumes, 2nd edn (New York: American News Company, 1865).

Lannie, V.P. *Public Money and Parochial Education: Bishop Hughes, Governor Seward, and the New York School Controversy* (Cleveland, OH: The Press of Case Western Reserve University, 1968).

Laycock, D. 'Summary and synthesis: the crisis in religious liberty', *George Washington Law Review*, 60(March), (1992): 841–56.

McAvoy, T.T. 'Public schools versus Catholic schools and James McMaster', *Review of Politics*, 28(1) (1966): 19–46.

McKey, J.P. *History of Niagara University, Seminary of Our Lady of Angels, 1856–1931* (Niagara, NY: Niagara University, 1931).

McSweeney, P.F. 'Christian public schools', *The Catholic World*, 44(264), (1887): 788–97.

Monroe, P. *Founding of the American Public School System: A History of Education in the United States* (New York: Macmillan Company, 1940).

Neal, D. 'The effects of Catholic secondary schooling on educational attainment', *Journal of Labor Economics*, (1997) 15: 98–123.

Nolan, H.J. (ed.) *Pastoral Letters of the United States Catholic Bishops, Volume I: 1792–1940* (Washington, DC: United States Catholic Conference, 1984).

Peterson, P.E. 'Monopoly and competition in American education', in W H. Clune and J.F. Witte (eds) *Choice and Control in American Education: Volume 1. The Theory of Choice and Control in Education* (Bristol, PA: Palmer Press, 1990), pp. 47–78.

Poole, S. 'Ad cleri disciplinam: the Vincentian seminary apostolate in the United States', in J. Rybolt, S. Poole, D. Slawson and E. Udovic (eds) *The American Vincentians: A Popular History of the Congregation of the Mission in the United States, 1815–1987* (Brooklyn, NY: New City Press, 1988a): 97–162.

Poole, S. 'The educational apostolate: colleges universities and secondary schools' in J. Rybolt, S. Poole, D. Slawson and E. Udovic (eds) *The American Vincentians: A popular history of the Congregation of the Mission in the United States, 1815–1987* (Brooklyn, NY: New City Press, 1988b): 2091–346.

Powers, M.F. '*A History of Catholic Education in Georgia, 1845–1952*, unpublished paper (Washington DC: Catholic University of America, 1956).

Pratte, R. *The Public School Movement* (New York: David McKay Company, Inc., 1973).

Ravitch, D. *The Great School Wars: New York City, 1805–1973* (New York: Basic Books, 1974).

Ryan, L.R. *Old Saint Peter's* (New York: US Catholic Historical Society, 1935).

Scanlan, W.G. 'The development of the American Catholic Diocesan Board of Education, 1884–1966', unpublished doctoral dissertation, New York University, (1967).

Sullivan, L. *The Core Values of Vincentian Education* (Chicago: DePaul University, 1997).

Tighe, J.J. 'The Pittsburg failure'. *The Independent* 42(2179) (4 September 1890: 7–8).

Walch, T. 'From doubts to affirmation: reflections on the recent history of Catholic parochial education', *Catholic Education: A Journal of Inquiry and Research* 1(2), (1996): 120–9.

Zettler, B.M. 'A Catholic public school in Macon', *The Independent* 42(2179) (4 September 1890): 8.

10

WRESTLING WITH MANAGERIALISM

John Sullivan

IN GENESIS 32 we read about Jacob wrestling (presumably) with God (or God's angel) in the night before meeting and being reconciled with his brother Esau, from whom he has, for so long, been estranged. The struggle for Jacob is both unavoidable and important; it is life-changing in a mysterious way. In similar fashion, I suggest, the wrestling match between Catholic educators and all that is implied in the spectre of 'managerialism' is one that is unavoidable, important and crucial for the healthy development of Catholic schools. It is a struggle from which one can re-learn what is essential and distinctive within Catholic education and at the same time be reminded of the gap that always exists between claim and reality. In the course of this wrestling it becomes clearer which principles and practices affecting education deserve to be embraced, as part of an openness to and a willingness to learn from the world, and also those which, after due testing, must be resisted as hostile to the Gospel.

This chapter offers a critique of the managerialist imperative in education and shows how some features of managerialism are both highlighted and compounded in Catholic schools. In what follows I describe a problem which I believe is widespread in education at the end of the twentieth century and then suggest that it has particular relevance to Catholic education. First, I describe managerialism. Second, I relate this to recent government policies for education, in particular, competition and inspection. Third, I indicate some concerns about accountability and certainty in education. Fourth, I bring out how the managerialist context can distort the emphasis on mission in a Catholic school. Fifth, I summarize the work of a recent critic of managerialism in education (Neil Postman) and point to the relevance of his plea for some overarching narrative which can direct and inspire school work. Sixth, I suggest that the documents of

Vatican II and subsequent theological developments provide a context and prompt for a reappraisal of the Catholic 'story' of education, although this opportunity has received only a patchy response so far. Finally, I pick out some of the ways in which managerialism is at odds with a Christian perspective and I point to some of the principles which should permeate any serious attempt to address managerialism with discernment and constructively.

MANAGERIALISM

In my work as an educational management consultant I have come to recognize the defects of 'managerialism' and the dangers posed for schools by too ready an adoption of the managerial imperative. What are these defects? Much of the managerial literature aimed at improving educational practice seems to display a universalism which is blind to cultural differences, curriculum specialisms, the climate of particular communities and the role of traditions as foundations for identity and our outlook on the world.[1] As Starratt puts it, 'Achievement in school means meeting uniform standards set for everyone more often than a personal response.'[2] Such standardization diminishes education, rather than enhances it.[3] Atomistic objectives and competencies are described without reference to the perspectives and passions of the people involved.[4] A false sense of certainty and the dangerous illusion of control are hinted at as the desired outcomes if the relevant competencies are developed. In reality, there are so many variables involved in education that, no matter how confident a teacher is in employing a range of techniques, they can never claim predictive powers with regard to their effects with any particular group of pupils. This would not allow for a free response on their part. The ambiguity, complexity, particularity, creativity, unpredictability, open-endedness and essentially personal dimensions of educational practice can disappear when too strong an emphasis is laid on 'managing' education.[5] In the industrial model of school, alongside line management and total quality control,

> budgets are kept and scrutinized by accountants, press officers try to ensure a positive public image, and performance indicators are put in place to monitor output variables. Above all, there is concern that the product, that is the student, should be delivered effectively and efficiently in accordance with the requirements of the various customers, for example, employers, government, further and higher education.[6]

This is not to reject the important part that sound management can play in education.[7] Pupils and teachers can benefit enormously from effective management and they suffer greatly in its absence. Many of the skills outlined in educational management literature, if sensitively employed with intelligent attention to context and to purpose, do enhance the quality of learning and assist in harnessing the talents of each for the good of all.

But too great a readiness to map out performance indicators, programmes of study, attainment targets, development plans, and the scaffolding of competencies required at various stages through-out the teaching profession[8] can lead to specifications which are too elaborate, leave too little to chance, reduce the possibility of appropriate reciprocity and interaction between teachers and learners and slip too easily into conceiving of education as a technique requiring merely one-way transmission. The outcomes of educational exchanges are essentially unpredictable and unamenable to control, even at the same time as teachers intend them to be purposeful, orderly and carefully structured.[9]

COMPETITION AND INSPECTION

Attempts to predict and specify educational practice too closely are encouraged, in some cases enforced, via recent government policies. These policies have provided fresh impetus in the task of articulating the distinctive nature of Catholic education. For the purposes of this chapter, two aspects to this fresh impetus will be picked out, one negative, in the form of a sharp challenge, the other positive, in the form of an opportunity. When taken together these two aspects have caused the Catholic community to re-emphasize that the difference between state-sponsored and church-sponsored education goes well beyond a particular diet of religious instruction and more attention to collective worship.

First, there is the spur provided by features of government policy which those concerned for the health of Catholic education perceive as being detrimental to its flourishing. The encouragement of increased competition between schools, which was intended to act as a lever for raising standards and widening choice, has been seen by some Catholics (as well as by many others) as having effects which are detrimental to sound education, damaging to pastoral care and undermining community spirit.[10] Moral dilemmas arise for schools about the tactics they might employ for survival in a competitive atmosphere. For example, will they be tempted to give less attention to (or even to be less ready to admit) those pupils who appear to contribute least to the schools' reputation in examination league tables?[11] Will they be so ready to collaborate with other schools when they are encouraged to view educational provision as a competitive market?

> Competition brings the temptation to play the system to the advantage of one institution . . . It tends to undermine the integrity of the school as a moral society . . . [so that it] cease[s] to take the broader view and to feel concern for the whole service . . . Competition poisons the wells of community.[12]

Second, there is the opportunity provided by new arrangements for school inspection.[13] Catholic diocesan authorities and many Heads of Catholic schools have tended to welcome the requirement on teachers in all schools to promote spiritual and moral development and to be inspected on this, even if their understanding of spirituality, morality and development differs in important respects from that of the government and despite the generally anti-OFSTED feeling among many teachers.[14]

They have also welcomed the opportunity for Catholic schools to have a separate and parallel inspection which focuses directly on the provision of religious education, collective worship and the religious ethos of the school – all in the context of the specifically denominational aims and values.[15] This arrangement is an encouragement for those who espouse the importance and role of such schools in our society. The fact that all maintained church schools are subject, on a regular basis, to this form of inspection, the outcome of which is published immediately afterwards, injects an element of urgency into the deliberations of teachers about the denominational nature of their school and their work within it. Preparation for inspection, dialogue with inspectors during the process and communication with parents and governors about the outcomes, combine to stimulate considerable discussion about the distinctive nature of church schools and the implementation of their mission.

There is the danger, however, that, by focusing too closely on how we might recognize the quality of Catholic education in the context of an inspection, an interpretation of Catholic education might be distorted. Giving a proper emphasis to evaluation is well overdue, but an evaluation-led approach to clarifying the special character of Catholic education is not enough by itself. An inadequate philosophical underpinning of the enterprise of Catholic education opens the way to sloppy thinking, to ambiguous expression, to unclear boundaries, to uncertainties at the level of policy, to the danger of internal incoherence, to fudging 'hard' cases, to capitulation either to secular take-overs or to theological imperialism. Clarity about identity, purpose and mission is needed in order to deal with a host of difficult questions, for example,

- What percentage of pupils can come from non-Catholic families without detriment to the Catholic character of the school?
- Are non-Catholic colleagues to be considered second-class citizens in terms of the ideal to be aimed for in staff appointments and promotions? (Should all senior positions be held by Catholics?)
- What are the criteria for establishing who is a Catholic? (And who applies these criteria?)

There are many other controversial issues to be addressed, including, for example, appropriate lifestyle for teachers, if they are to be considered as models for pupils, school behaviour policies which are congruent with aims and mission, grounds for advocating pupil exclusions, criteria for making decisions over school budgets and priorities, and so on.

ACCOUNTABILITY AND CERTAINTY

More frequent inspection is just an example of one of the key features of the managerial movement within education – an emphasis on accountability, which requires continuous monitoring and regular evaluation. These practices are likely to become much attenuated if they are part of a managerialism which is insufficiently informed by a carefully thought through educational philosophy and ethic (which includes, for example, a view of the human person, society, well-being, education and relationships). Lacking such a foundation, the practice of monitoring can very easily slip into increased surveillance for increased compliance and evaluation can be reduced to counting what is easily measurable. The attempt to increase control through the practices (and associated external agencies) of monitoring and evaluation is likely to induce fear and resistance on the part of both teachers and students.

Furthermore, it is clear that educators who accept too readily the managerial approach seek to reach certainty about those short- and medium-term outcomes which are amenable to objective measurement. As shown above, this is to seek certainty at the wrong 'end' of education. It would be better to look for certainty at the beginning of our endeavours, to aim for greater clarity about our purposes in education and those beliefs and values which frame the whole process for us.

Two caveats are necessary here. First, workable 'visions' for education only emerge in the light of a considerable degree of trial and error. Practices become clearer as a result of both successful and unsuccessful practice. The emphasis on clarity about purpose rather than outcomes is more a matter of the degree of priority to be accorded to principles and aims. These are by their nature rather general and elusive. It can be too readily assumed that they are both understood and accepted, leading too swiftly to a concentration on apparently more concrete and measurable behavioural outcomes as indicators of progress. Judgements about pupil achievement, teacher performance, the quality of a course, the effectiveness of a policy or the value added by a school cannot be reached without a proper weighing of the aims and purposes of the people involved, and with regard to these aims and purposes, their grounding, worth and coherence.

Second, teachers should seek an objective view of the effectiveness of their efforts, the curriculum and the school as a whole. However, monitoring and evaluation, like other 'tools' of management, should serve, rather than obscure, a larger vision and purpose which is at the heart of the educational endeavour.

CATHOLIC SCHOOLS AND THE DOWNSIDE OF MISSION

Catholic schools probably suffer as much as other schools from the defects of managerialism. Furthermore, the potential for managerialism to damage education is strengthened in a context, like that of a church school, which gives high priority to a mission statement and which heavily underlines the legitimacy of authority (divine, scriptural, ecclesial).[16] In such a context, it is often too readily presumed, and with insufficient warrant, that certain ideals are shared and a particular code of behaviour accepted.[17] After a Headteacher has been appointed by school governors there can be a temptation to confuse the general mandate to lead with his or her personal vision of Catholic education for this particular school.[18] Sometimes the comment that 'this is a Catholic school' precludes debate and gives the impression that the essence of Catholicism is uncontested by Catholics themselves and that the application of Catholic beliefs to the practice of education is straightforward.

In his analysis of 'mission' in organizations generally, Pattison considers its connotations of higher purposes, of obedience to superiors, of urgency, and of implementation being both inexorable and costly. While the notion has galvanizing power, it is also open to defective interpretations.

> Mission may appear to justify narrowness, imperialism, conquest, and changing others and the world rather than living alongside them. The implicit radical, invasive, sectarian, dualistic overtones of this concept may energise outreach at the expense of seeing people outside the organisation as 'objects' to be saved.[19]

If employed in this way, the concept is liable to support a drive for distinctiveness which, in failing to attend to the particular circumstances and needs of individuals, is insufficiently inclusive. Catholic schools, which by their nature are more liable than many to the use of the language of 'mission', need to guard against these dangers.

For a variety of reasons, which are explored later, many teachers who work in Catholic schools do not have a clear view of Catholicism. As a result, they lack any distinctive vision of Catholic education. This makes some aspects of school evaluation especially perplexing or even burdensome for them, at the same time as it makes more complex the task of Catholic school management and leadership. All teachers are subject to scrutiny and pressure through appraisal, inspection and league tables based on pupil performance.[20] In Catholic schools they are also inspected by diocesan-approved officers who report on the quality of the school as a Catholic community. This inspection assesses the degree to which the school mission is being implemented, as shown by religious teaching, worship, permeation of Catholicism through the curriculum and school life and community relations. Furthermore, there are additional expectations as regards their own example as teachers. In these circumstances it is not surprising that some teachers in Catholic schools perceive the recent emphasis on monitoring, evaluation and school review as a form of increased surveillance for increased compliance.

NEIL POSTMAN AND NARRATIVE

Yet, when they are set in a larger context of long-term goals, pervading values and well-founded principles, some of the strategies employed in school management can be freed from the manipulative functions to which they are prone. Neil Postman recently advocated a return to the 'metaphysical' rather than the 'engineering' aspects of education, that is, answers to the question 'why?' have priority over 'how?'[21] Postman argues that education flourishes best when it is sustained by an overarching narrative, a story that 'tells of origins and envisions a future, a story that constructs ideals, prescribes rules of conduct, provides a source of authority, and, above all, gives a sense of continuity and purpose'.[22] This kind of narrative must have 'sufficient credibility, complexity and symbolic power' to enable those who rely on it to organize their lives around it.[23] Such a story will 'give point to our labours, exalt our history, elucidate the present, and give direction to our future'.[24]

Postman reiterates my concern that education under the sway of managerialism is in danger of seeking to *control* the process of learning, but with no worthy end in view. If schools are to be important sites for education, what goes on there must engage our attention, arouse our interest, capture our energies and direct our efforts. For this to occur, education must serve non-trivial ends and offer a god or gods who call us to give ourselves fully to a larger, worthy purpose. In this process our lives will not be confined or diminished but liberated and enhanced. Those who start the educational journey with ends in mind, can also demonstrate flexibility about routes and allow for detours, backtracking, starting again and changing direction.

Postman's primary aim is not to justify or to demonstrate the coherence of a particular narrative but to emphasize that any enduring educational endeavour needs to draw upon a comprehensive and powerfully illuminating and motivating 'story'.[25] This 'story' will be 'foundational', that is, it will provide key concepts, goals, metaphors and values for the conduct of education, but it is not to be held uncritically, nor is it unrevisable; indeed, the best of stories will have the capacity to cope with criticism, revision and constant adaptation to changing circumstances. Neither the basis nor the plausibility of Postman's thesis rests upon religious assumptions. He proposes several stories or myths as frameworks for education (for example, democracy, America, multi-culturalism and spaceship earth).[26] Many of them are held much more lightly than are the key narratives of any particular religion. By comparison with these, Postman's myths make fewer demands and they are more vulnerable to modification and even jettisoning, if they no longer serve their purpose. His proposals are intended to prompt us to relate education to our greatest purposes and priorities in life.

Such a desire is, of course, not new. Indeed, it is a traditional view of both education in particular and of society in general that there is need of 'some higher spiritual principle of co-ordination to over-come the conflicts between power and morality, between reason and appetite, between technology and humanity and between self-interest and the common good'.[27] But it is a view which has been considered outmoded for some time in mainstream educational thinking. This is due to its being seen as connected too closely with discredited religious world-views, which no longer command alle-giance, and also because education is seen as having internal aims, rather than as serving extrinsic purposes.[28] With the failure of the Enlightenment project to deliver all that was expected of it in terms of rationality, autonomy and well-being, and with a re-appraisal of the limits of individualism, the need for community, the foundations of reason and shortcomings of materialism, this traditional view of the centrality of narrative is once again considered worthy of serious attention.[29] While I acknowledge that the diverse forms of post-modern critique which follow the supposed failure of the Enlightenment project call into question the possibility of such narratives, for the purposes of this argument I assume that such critiques can be met.[30]

The term 'narrative' here is being used in a special sense. The focus is less on the chronological ordering of events which make up a 'story' and more on the ordering of lives which can follow from adopting the 'story' as a guide for life, one which structures our priorities, elicits our energies, sustains our efforts in the face of difficulties and one which encourages us to co-operate with others who share a 'story' that embodies ideals. In this sense the story is normative. It tells us how things *should* be, rather than how they *have* been. Even when the story appears to be based on the past, for example, a divine revelation or a salvation event, its significance for those who adhere to it is its promise for the future.[31] This kind of story is meant to provide us with a vision towards which we can strive.

One of the characteristics of leadership, as distinguished from management, is the presence of such vision and the capacity to inspire others to engage with it. If the possessors of a vision seek to prescribe too closely the details of the route to be taken, rather than to inspire others to make the journey towards the ends held up before them, they slip into managerialism. In seeking such a level of control, they betray a lack of trust in others and in the intrinsic attractiveness of the goal.

VATICAN II

In describing the managerial imperative I have noted both negative and positive features, the first to be avoided, namely the danger of seeking excessive control, which squeezes the life from teaching and learning, and the second to be provided more abundantly, namely visionary leadership set in the context of some overarching 'story' or rationale for education.

The details, emphasis and framing of this 'story' have undergone significant revision as a result of the Second Vatican Council (1962–65) and theological developments since then. The council gave respectability and prominence to notions of collegiality, pluralism and diversity, the social apostolate and a more inclusive attitude within the church. Its deliberations prompted a rethinking of key concepts which have a bearing on education: truth, knowledge, salvation, humanity, conversion and revelation. Important council documents were issued which re-expressed the mind of the church with regard to its own nature and constitution, to revelation, ecumenism, the role of the laity, missions, non-Christians and religious freedom. Post-Vatican II theology often displays a noticeably different style and tone, by comparison with earlier this century: it seems less confident and certain; it relies less on logic; it is more sensitive to outside perspectives; it takes into account diversity and plurality; it is less imperialist; it adopts a historical rather than a classical mentality; it gives greater weight to co-operation and dialogue with those who are outside the Catholic community and it brings out more clearly the social implications of gospel teaching.

This has led to changing expectations of the laity in the life of the church and also, to some degree, a recognition that the experience, perspectives and contributions of women have been neglected by theologians and church authorities. Religious education in Catholic schools in the years after the council reflected some of these changes: its central focus was not so obviously doctrinal; its tone was less dogmatic and authoritarian; it adopted more frequently a multi-dimensional approach to the study of religion; it sought more explicitly to take into account the experience and viewpoints of pupils; it was more open to criticism and questioning; it was more open to and positive about non-Catholics.

These theological developments, when taken together, add up to a major reinterpretation of the nature of Catholicism. This inevitably has important implications for Catholic education. I am not suggesting that the majority of Catholic teachers have assimilated this rethinking in any depth. On the contrary, for reasons that are beyond my brief here to demonstrate, I believe that many Catholic teachers exhibit serious gaps in their theological understanding. Many Catholic teachers who present themselves for interview for senior posts in Catholic schools are clearly personally committed to Catholicism in their private lives and can give evidence that they are both academically and professionally well qualified and highly competent. Yet they appear to lack confidence when asked to articulate how their work can contribute to the distinctive Catholic ethos of the school and they seem ill-equipped to relate their faith perspective to their prospective teaching and leadership responsibilities in anything other than superficial terms.

These gaps in their understanding are due to several factors: changes in the pattern of family and parish life, confusions in Catholic education in the period after the council (arising from an inadequate understanding of these theological developments), and the pressures of accommodating themselves to secular requirements for professional accreditation. Catholics have enjoyed the same massively increased participation in further and higher education as the rest of society. Many Catholic teachers have studied in secular colleges and universities, without a surrounding Catholic 'plausibility structure'.[32] Even among those whose studies were carried out at Catholic institutions of higher education, many have come into contact only rarely with explicit expressions and explanations of a Catholic world-view. This would have been, in some cases, partly through their deliberate choice to avoid any engagement with Catholicism. It would also, in part, be due to the large numbers of non-Catholic students working alongside them whose main needs were for academic and professional qualifications, rather than for personal formation. For all students, in any case, the rules of validation of degrees and accreditation and certification of professional training deflected much of the energies of higher education staff towards meeting secular requirements, thereby leaving much less time and energy for study of the religious dimensions or implications of their subject matter.

MANAGERIALISM AS CHALLENGE

Managerialism challenges Catholic educators in three ways. First, it tempts them to import into schools priorities (for example, concern for their market position and success in narrowly prescribed league tables) and modes of working (for example, enforced compliance and alignment within the school as an organization and 'zero tolerance' of failure) which sit uneasily with, even when they do not directly contradict, key features of Catholic education. Second, by pressurizing school leaders to establish ever-increasing levels of control over key aspects of teaching and learning, it underlines the dangers of a one-sided emphasis on distinctiveness within the context of Catholic education. Without an adequate emphasis on inclusiveness, new control mechanisms in the service of an authoritative, universal and unavoidable mission can become overbearing and pay too little attention to local realities and needs. Third, the lack within managerialism, of an adequate 'story' with which to frame and give purpose to schooling, should prompt Catholic educators to re-present their own account of the nature and purpose of education as an important resource for rectifying the shortcomings of managerialism. Andrew Morris's comment is pertinent here: 'In England and Wales the current public debate about [school] effectiveness is often separated from philosophical issues concerning the nature and purpose of education, and it is conducted under an assumption that all schools seek the same primary objectives.'[33]

Managerialism might, with some justification, be considered as a kind of heresy. Like a heresy it is one-sided, partial, lacking connectedness with the whole, and therefore lacks correction from the whole. Pattison brings out how some of its fundamental assumptions are problematic from a Christian perspective:

- the world and other people exist for the benefit of organizational survival, exploitation and expansion;
- human beings can control the world and create a better future if they use the right techniques;
- individuals must be subordinate to greater goals decided by their superiors;

- relationships are fundamentally hierarchical and require clear lines of upward accountability and downward responsibility;
- the nature and condition of work should be such as to extract the maximum from the employee;
- everything worth doing can in some way be measured;
- the future can be planned and colonized.

Such views are 'wildly over-optimistic, narrow, Pelagian, and utopian'; they trivialize human nature and endeavour.[34]

In an imaginative mythological exploration of some of the assumptions lurking within managerialism, Chater identifies 'systemania' and 'permacrisis': the first offers a cult of constant change; the second seems to delight in a state of permanent crisis.[35] Service to these 'gods of mismanagement' causes individuals to be subordinated to the institutions in which they work and diminishes, rather than promotes life in them. Chater helpfully identifies one of the side-effects of 'permacrisis':

> when a real personal crisis occurs . . . the resources for dealing with it are severely depleted. Compassion and empathy are related creativity: they flow when the organisation is sufficiently at ease to allow them space and they are reduced or stopped when the organisation is driven by a struggle to survive.[36]

In order to counteract some of the destructive forces unleashed by these 'gods', he argues for the development of a 'spirituality of management', where there is 'a dialogue between authentic spiritual traditions and the skills of management'. This will foster the flourishing of vision, creativity, intimacy, reverence, openness and inclusiveness.

I have not suggested that we can do without management and some elements of managerialism. In accepting the need for monitoring and evaluation of policies and achievements and in its sensitivity to 'customer' perceptions and needs, the managerial movement has prompted all schools to become both more realistic and more service-oriented. Relying too much on good will in the management of school affairs and leaving everything to the Holy Spirit are not signs of faith but of irresponsibility. Just because the practice of education can be interpreted as part of a life journey, our openness to the transcendent does not mean that we should not attend to the here and now.

Salvation as a central concern of our faith must not be confused with success, nor should it be confused with safety. Salvation cannot be grasped; it cannot be achieved through our own efforts; it is the work of grace, costly grace; it is not under our control. Too marked an emphasis on control in education crushes professionalism, kills creativity, prevents experiment, inhibits questioning, undermines openness, freezes reinterpretation, obstructs mutuality and reciprocity and damages community building.

A healthy approach to managerialism will allow for two-way accountability. It will treat leadership and management as a leaven within a community, allowing fermenting from within. Power should always be used for service, in remembrance that the Kingdom transcends our institutions, schools, even our churches; loyalty to these must be subject to and circumscribed by truth. Leaders who want to be listened to must themselves learn to listen and attempt to cultivate not docile obedience but strong allegiance from pupils and staff. To do this requires the promotion of discernment, trust and encouragement throughout the school community. Both in curriculum planning and in the context of professional development the personal and the spiritual should not be neglected. Some of the implications of such a stance are as follows:

- work needs to be reintegrated into the totality of our lives;
- we need to be very careful about the notion of 'zero tolerance';
- a wider and deeper sense of 'vocational' must be fostered;
- the contemplative as well as the active dimension of life needs attention;
- measurement – of all kinds – is less important than relationship; and
- authority structures and hierarchy should always be treated as less important than our common discipleship.

In helping Catholic schools to respond constructively to the managerialist imperative certain themes frequently recur. Three examples are given below.

One recurring theme is the nature, scope and importance of *spiritual leadership* in the life and work of a school, whether this is thought of as facilitating the staff as a Christian community, maintaining a Christian spirit in the midst of pressure, supervising the RE programme, leading liturgy and corporate worship, promoting the spiritual development of all or acting as a constant advocate for the mission. How do I live out the spiritual side of leadership? What do I do to nurture my own and others' 'spiritual side'? What have you found most replenishing for yourself? Which motivations, feelings and priorities have sometimes got in the way or clouded your vision? How are your beliefs about spirituality related to your view of teaching and school leadership – with regard to the *person*, the *task*, the *performance* and the *context*? How could you spot the difference between new levels of performance and new levels of life in staff and other members of the school community?

Another is the centrality of the *mission* of the school. Reference might be made to its wording. Do we understand what it says? Do we mean what it says? Does it excite, inspire and concentrate the minds of all associated with the school, offering a sense of common purpose and direction? Does it provide a basis for communication with internal and external audiences about institutional activities? Does it provide a torch and a touchstone – can it be used repeatedly to inspire, encourage and evaluate? Has the communication – including listening – included all relevant people – pupils, staff, parents, governors? How is it being applied to specific areas of school work and life? Are its values reflected in the development and action plans which structure school priorities and projects, in the way people behave, in how resources are allocated and in how people are treated? What kinds of aftercare or nurture are considered for the mission: in monitoring its implementation, evaluating its use, reflecting on its appropriateness, with regard to prayer, celebration and revision – who is involved, when and how?

Third, in reviewing progress and considering *performance indicators*, how do we know if we are doing well? Apart from examining the customary information about examination results, test scores, and figures for attendance and punctuality, staying on and drop-out rates, exclusions, the number of targets met and so on, is consideration also given to those original performance indicators given to the church, the fruits of the Spirit: love, joy, peace, patience, kindness, goodness, faithfulness, gentleness and self-control (Gal. 5:22)? When are these qualities most needed and most tested in school life, teaching and management? Are we living the sacraments in school life, for example, in our practice of reconciliation, healing, encouragement and strengthening, thanksgiving and community building, in witnessing and calling others to do the same? How would you evaluate the work of a school chaplain? What criteria and sources of evidence would be relevant? What considerations or factors should be borne in mind?

CONCLUSION

Wrestling with managerialism takes place in various contexts and over many different issues. It occurs in the classroom and in the staff room, in meetings with parents, governors and a wide range of external 'authorities' such as inspectors and diocesan and local education officers. The struggle is revealed in arguments about priorities and progress, about policies and plans, and it is as evident in the way students and staff are invited to join schools as it is in the ways that their achievements and contributions are evaluated and publicized afterwards. I have tried to indicate how, as teachers in this wrestling match, we might endeavour to uphold certain principles and qualities.

First, priority is given to substantive ends and purposes over techniques and skills in continuing professional development activities. Second, we should always be people-centred rather than oriented solely on 'success', by whichever criteria happen to predominate at this moment, for it is the person, and not particular competencies which should be the subject of the curriculum, including the in-service curriculum. Third, we should be conscious that sharing vulnerability is an essential route towards professional growth, more fruitful in the long run than planned control or ever greater efficiency and productivity. This is not to deny that there is a major (and inescapable) moral challenge for schools and colleges in how they address poor performance and under-achievement by either students or staff.

Managerialism, as a challenge, cannot be ignored or avoided; this would be irresponsible escapism. Not to take up the challenge of the managerial imperative leads inevitably to becoming a victim of it, a puppet, dancing to its unseen hand. On the other hand, neither can managerialism be swallowed whole, accepted uncritically, because some of its elements and assumptions are alien both to education and to the professionalism which should serve education. A principled discernment is what is required.

There are, then, several ways in which Jacob's wrestling with his unseen adversary finds an echo today in educators' wrestling with managerialism. First, the engagement is necessary and must be faced. Second, we may not appear to 'win' the encounter. Third, we will be changed in the process of struggle. And fourth, while we do not know the effect on his assailant of Jacob's wrestling, we do have reason to believe that our struggle with the managerial imperative, seeking a balanced discernment and response, will assist in the process of damage limitation, and more positively, in harnessing the energies of the world for good and in opening them up for conversion into the more abundant life in Christ. At this testing moment in *our* salvation history, with opportunities for reflection and prayer as key ingredients of our professional development activities, we may emerge as still incomplete, but new persons.

NOTES

1   For examples of such management literature, see Brent Davies and John West-Burnham (eds), *Reengineering and Total Quality in Schools* (London: Pitman, 1997) [for the deficiencies of the metaphor of engineering as applied to education see Postman, note 21, below]; Brent Davies and Linda Ellison, *School Leadership for the Twenty-First Century* (London: Routledge, 1997); Dilum Jirasinghe and Geoffrey Lyons, *The Competent Head* (London: Falmer, 1996); S. Murgatroyd and C. Morgan, *Total Quality Management and the School* (Buckingham: Open University Press, 1993). For criticisms of managerialism in education and for analyses of various associated deficiencies relating to markets, competencies, and other defects such as confusing management with leadership, as well as for questions about the applicability of private sector, commercial and industrial models of management to public sector services, see: Stephen Ball, S. Gewirtz and R. Bowe, *Markets, Choice and Equity in Education* (Buckingham: Open University Press, 1995); David Bridges and Terence McLaughlin (eds), *Education and the Market Place* (London: Falmer Press, 1994); S. Ranson and J. Stewart, *Management for the Public Domain* (Basingstoke: St Martin's Press/Macmillan, 1994); Gerald Grace, *School Leadership* (London: Falmer Press, 1995); and Ruth Jonathan, 'Illusory freedoms: liberalism, education and the market', *Journal of Philosophy of Education*, 31(1) 1997.

2   Robert Starratt, *Leaders with vision* (Thousand Oaks, CA: Corwin Press, 1995), p. 98.

3   Richard Pring brings out the shadow side, the consequences (in most cases unintended) of recent government education policy: 'The advisory bodies have been abolished; the Schools Council closed down; Her Majesty's Inspectorate as an independent critical voice emasculated; the countervailing influence of local education authorities enfeebled; the language of education impoverished; the curriculum imposed by politicians; the inevitably perennial deliberation over what is worth learning foreclosed.' 'Values and education policy', in Mark Halstead and Monica Taylor (eds) *Values in Education and Education in Values* (London: Falmer Press, 1996), p. 117. Cf. also his 'Markets, education and Catholic schools', in Terence McLaughlin, Joseph O'Keefe and Bernadette O'Keeffe (eds) *The Contemporary Catholic School* (London: Falmer Press, 1996) (hereafter, *CCS*).

4   Ronald Barnett provides a sustained critique of recent reliance on competencies in higher education in *The Limits of Competence* (Buckingham: Open

University Press, 1994). His criticisms are relevant to the wider field of educational management. Richard Roberts provides a brief yet powerful critique of the damaging effects of some of the measures which accompany managerialism in higher education in 'Our graduate factories', *The Tablet*, 11 October 1997: 1295–7. A notable exception in educational management literature to the omission of treatment of the personhood and emotions of leaders and teachers is David Loader, *The Inner Principal* (London: Falmer Press, 1997). Loader shows that a new sensitivity to self, a new awareness of others and a better understanding of the educational task are intimately connected with one another.

5   For a different set of criticisms of what she calls 'Jurassic Management', see Helen Gunter, *Rethinking Education* (London: Cassell, 1997).

6   Jasper Ungoed-Thomas, 'Vision, values and virtues', in Halstead and Taylor, *Values in Education*, p. 144.

7   'Of itself, management is neither moral or immoral; its primary concern is logic, efficiency, order, predictability, and productivity'. Starratt, *Leaders with Vision*, p. 109.

8   As laid down in 1996 by the Teacher Training Agency for newly qualified teachers, for subject leaders, for those preparing for Headship and for experienced Headteachers.

9   Margret Buchman and Robert Floden (eds) *Detachment and Concern: Conversations in the Philosophy of Teaching and Teacher Education* (London: Cassell, 1993), pp. 211–16, bring out several dimensions of uncertainty in teaching, for example, those relating to assessments of student learning, to the effects of their teaching, as well as uncertainties about content and the scope of teachers' authority. 'Too much uncertainty may be disabling, but too much certainty can lead to boredom and stagnation or to the mistaken sense that teaching is mechanical', ibid., p. 216. Donal Murray brings out a different aspect of uncertainty for teachers: 'the great paradox of education is that it is an enterprise in which adults attempt to prepare young people to live in a world which the adults cannot even imagine' (*A Special Concern – The Philosophy of Education: A Christian Perspective* (Dublin, Veritas, 1991), p. 3.).

10 See, for example, the comment by O'Keefe and O'Keefe in *CCS*, p. 306: 'The competitive climate in which Catholic schools function places self-interest, competition, success and the power of personal choice high on the agenda.' Complaints levelled at government policy, apart from the deficiencies of a market-led approach to provision and the dangers of competition, include the narrow focus on education for economic needs, the weakening of local education authorities and the increase in state control. On the concern that Catholic schools are deflected from the transmission of Catholic culture by their accommodation of pressures for results set by the state, see Christopher Dawson, *The Crisis of Western Education* (London: Sheed and Ward, 1961), p. 111.

11 According to Nicholas Pyke, 'schools no longer have time to concentrate on the vulnerable' ('Young minds in trouble', *The Tablet*, 15 February 1997: 211). On this point, see also Gerald Grace, 'The future of Catholic schools', in *From Ideal to Action* (Dublin: Veritas), p. 195.

12 John Prangley, 'Examination factories', *The Tablet*, 15 February 1997, p.208.

Prangley warns that the 'subtler, deeper purposes and goals of schools are not easy to determine in an objective way and so now tend to be neglected in the classroom and in governors' meetings'. He refers (p. 207) to the 'relative neglect of the children with special needs, at both ends of the ability scale, as their performances cannot be so significantly changed' [as those on the borderline of a pass].

13   The introduction in 1993 of a new national system of inspection has forced all schools to review their progress towards providing high quality teaching, high standards of pupil achievement, effective opportunities for spiritual, moral, social and cultural development and value for money in the use of resources.

14   The following comment brings out a key difference: 'Although both the National Curriculum Council and OFSTED make it clear that spiritual and moral development do not necessarily depend on religious belief, in the Catholic synthesis of the human and the divine they must,' *Spiritual and Moral Development Across the Curriculum* (London: Catholic Education Service, 1995), p. 3.

15   This form of inspection, called a Section 23 (formerly Section 13) inspection, is also available for Anglican and Jewish schools. Of course such communities, along with the Catholic community, have always had the right to inspect their own schools. Now state funding, albeit at a very low level, is available for these religious inspections, with the minimum of strings attached. Control over the content and conduct of these inspections remains with the respective religious communities.

16   Stephen Pattison, in *The Faith of the Managers* (London, Cassell, 1997), p. 2. highlights the religious tone and imagery used in much management language. He refers to management as 'a set of ideas, rituals, practices and words . . . that provide a total world view and way of life that binds existence and organizations together and shapes people, purposes and actions in a fundamental way', cf. ibid., p. 39.

17   Pattison refers to the tendency, in organizations under the sway of managerialism, to require an 'unthinking acceptance of "official" reality as determined from above,' ibid., p. 54.

18   Furthermore, as Pattison says, 'just because something is called a vision does not mean that it is automatically good, true, unchallengeable, right and useful for the organization,' ibid., p. 70.

19   Ibid., p. 71.

20   In England and Wales compulsory teacher appraisal was introduced in July 1991, the new, regular and comprehensive system of inspection started in September 1993 and, after a turbulent introductory period, the publication of national league tables for pupil performance in schools became a reality by 1995. Pattison compares the function of appraisal (or individual performance review) with that of confession in mediaeval Catholicism. 'It is a means of engendering conformity and control in the individual,' He goes on to claim that 'appraisal is, in some ways, the most personally immediate sign and sacrament of the modern managed organization'. Ibid., pp. 196–7.

21   Neil Postman, *The End of Education* (New York, Vintage Books), 1996, p. 3.

22   Ibid., pp. 5–6.

23   Ibid., p. 6.

24 Ibid., p. 7.

25 'The idea of public education depends absolutely on the existence of shared narratives *and* the exclusion of narratives that lead to alienation and divisiveness,' Postman, *End of Education*, p. 17.

26 Postman also reviews, as narratives which have served in the past as a foundation for education, nationalism, reason, communism, science, technology, economic utility and consumership. He considers several possible candidates for the future, for example, the fallen angel, humans as word-weavers and world-makers. For an alternative rendering of key narratives or perspectives which have informed western education, see E.D. Macpherson, 'Chaos in the curriculum', *Journal of Curriculum Studies*, 27:3, May–June (1995), pp. 263–79, where he summarizes (at pp. 273–4.) Platonic, republican, scientific, do-it-yourself, neo-Marxist, service of God as well as precise curriculum engineering views.

27 Christopher Dawson, (originally writing in 1961), quoted by V.A. McClelland in *Christian Education in a Pluralist Society* (London, Routledge, 1988), p. 28.

28 Although R.S. Peters (whose landmark study, *Ethics and Education* (London: Allen and Unwin), was published in 1966) was not guilty of separating educational aims from consideration of the good life, much work in philosophy of education which followed in his footsteps in the 1960s and 1970s did appear to disconnect educational analysis from larger social and spiritual purposes. In an increasingly plural and secular society it is not surprising that discussion of education policy becomes detached from particular narratives which might hold the allegiance of only a minority of citizens and appeals more and more to general procedural (rather than to substantive) principles.

29 Alasdair MacIntyre has been a leading figure in restoring narrative to academic respectability. See especially his *After Virtue* (1981) and *Whose Justice? Which Rationality?* (1988), both London: Duckworth.

30 For penetrating analyses and judicious assessments of the significance of postmodernism for either religious or educational theory and practice, see Michael Paul Gallagher, *Clashing Symbols* (London: Darton, Longman & Todd, 1997), Chapter 8 and also his chapter, 'The new agenda of unbelief and faith,' in Dermot Lane (ed.) *Religion and Culture in Dialogue* (Dublin: The Columba Press, 1993).

31 In the case of the Christian 'narrative' its normative status depends upon claims about *historical* truths and it also partially depends on the proclamation of truths about how things *are*.

32 For an analysis and employment of the notion of 'plausibility structures' which legitimate and provide support for a worldview or way of thinking, see the works of Peter Berger, for example, *The Sacred Canopy* (New York, Doubleday, 1969).

33 A. Morris, 'Catholic and other secondary school: an analysis', *Educational Research*, 40:2, (1998), p. 188.

34 Pattison, *Faith of the Managers*, pp. 161–2.

35 Mark Chater, 'The gods of mismanagement: a mythological exploration of our management predicament', *School Leadership and Management*, 18:2 (1998), pp. 231–8.

36 Ibid., p. 235.

11

CONTEMPORARY YOUNG ADULT CATHOLICS IN ENGLAND: FAITH AND EDUCATION

John Fulton

THIS CHAPTER focuses on the world-views and religious practice of young adult Roman Catholics. The questions we are asking for present purposes are as follows: what changes have occurred in contemporary society which affect the cultural and spiritual values of young adults today? What kind of faith do Roman Catholic young adults experience in the complex and contemporary world in which they live? To what extent has Catholic schooling had an influence on their lives? This chapter looks first at the relevance of the social environment and how it might affect religious identity today. The second and principal part of the chapter looks at a sample of young adult Roman Catholics in England and examines the nature and content of their faith commitment as these appear in their own life stories. In the final part, we note briefly the varying experiences of religious and secular education these young Catholics have had, and suggest the way in which we should consider the impact of present-day Catholic school education on faith. The young Roman Catholic adults who participated in the research were interviewed as part of an international study of young Catholic adults. The other countries participating in the research are Ireland, Italy, Malta, Poland and USA.[1] The findings presented here are partial and indicative, as the life history data set has not yet been thoroughly analysed.

CHURCH DECLINE, SOCIAL CLASS AND CULTURE

The Catholic Church in England and Wales had official Sunday attendance figures of just under 2 million in the 1960s, two decades before it reached its peak in registered membership of $4\frac{1}{4}$ million in 1980 (see *Catholic Directory for England and Wales*, 1961 and 1971; also, in more detail, Hornsby-Smith, 1989: 1–21). Church attendance declined in 1997 to less than 1.2 million, and looks set to decrease further over the next decade (Brierley, 1994). Bearing in mind that these figures were probably never that reliable, but also that Catholics today are less rigid in their interpretation of Sunday obligation, we must still accept the numerical decline in religious practice and accompanying decrease in church association the figures represent. The number of clergy has diminished by a third over the same period, and is likely to continue to do so as ageing priests fail to be replaced. The root causes of numerical decline for both laity and priests are in dispute. Some point to the part-modernization of the church from the Second Vatican Council (1962–5) onwards as the cause (Flanagan, 1996). Others say the church would have shrunk anyway, because of the changing circumstances of modern life (Hervieu-Léger 1993). Some even argue that the church has not been modernized enough (Hornsby-Smith *et al.*, 1995). The research is thus also appropriate in trying to find out just what kind of Roman Catholics adults are emerging in the church today, and how they relate to the influences and culture of the contemporary world.

The process of growing up for today's young adult generation has been very different from that of their parents. For those entering the labour market in the 1970s, job stability was still to be found on the tail of the industrial post-war boom. There was a relatively easy transition from school to work, as labour was plentiful even if one left school at fifteen or sixteen. Young adults were also able to marry relatively early as they often earned sufficient money to set up their own home or rent the numerous council house dwellings then available. If one was sick or unemployed, benefits or dole were also still widely available. Consequently, the pattern of marrying and having children early established in the post-war period was still quite common.

If we consider 'young adulthood' in a more cultural way than simply a specific age range (the one we have chosen is 18–30), we can define it in terms of its social role: that period of the life course in which basic socialization, including personality formation, has been concluded (post-childhood, post-adolescence, post-school), where some state of semi-independence from the authority of mentors has been achieved but without yet achieving economic and social stability, and a degree of experimentation is sometimes undertaken in an effort to find one's social place and sexual identity. Such a situation was accomplished in the 1960s when one married or set up home on one's own. Most parents of our present young adult generation thus had a relatively short young adulthood, up to about 24 years old, then settling down into full adulthood, with marriage and child-rearing. Today, the passage from young to full adulthood takes place over a much greater span, anything up to 35 years of age, and there is both less marriage and less stability over the period. Both uncommitted and committed sexual partnerships are more frequent. The impact of job insecurity on marriage plans and the arguably consequent and wide acceptability of living together place young people in situations where decisions on sexuality, identity and morality are more complex: the decision on deferral of sexual relationships for a lengthy period clashes with increasing possibilities of sexual pleasure and personal intimacy in a world of vastly increased personal moral autonomy. The parents of the generation we are considering only experienced such a situation for a much shorter period of time, and, if they were Catholics, sometimes not at all.

The increase of job insecurity took place in the late 1970s and developed rapidly during the early years of Thatcherism. The collapse of the youth job market, much related to the collapse of heavy industry (Jones and Wallace, 1992; Roberts, 1995), and the massive diversification of employment forms, particularly the growth of the service sector (Furlong and Cartmel, 1997; Bynner *et al.*, 1997) have affected the whole 16 to 35 age range. Many young people stay on in education until 18 and as much as a half continue in full or part time education for a decade or more afterwards. Part-time employment has grown, even for university students. In addition, there has been the massive growth of female employment. And though most employed women are in part-time or low paid employment, they consider they have a right to work and are as good at the job as men. Also, as the research of Bynner *et al.* (1997) shows, inequality between sections of the young adult population has grown significantly, and along traditional class lines. The school leavers of the 1970s could still expect to find full-time work in unskilled or low skilled occupations. Today a prolonged period of part-time training and part-time work is the best they can hope for, and those with few or no qualifications can expect lengthy periods of unemployment, a situation which may continue for most of their lives. Consequently, the experiences of contemporary young adults are incredibly diverse in terms of work, home arrangements and cultures. Bynner divides young people up into those 'getting on', those 'getting by' and those 'getting nowhere', a 30/30/40 per cent split according to Will Hutton (1995). Those getting by and getting on are evenly split. Those getting nowhere are at 40 per cent; additionally, they are highly susceptible to depression and to social marginalization (Bynner *et al.*, 1997: 77–96).

Such experiences have probably had a dramatic effect on the faith and church attendance of Roman Catholics. Fewer young adults can be found in church at Sunday Mass than 20 or 30 years ago. The age at which Catholics marry today is probably in line with the national pattern, where the median age of marriage has moved for men from 23 in 1971 to 28 in 1993, and for women from 21 to 26. This explains why it is that family Masses on Sunday are still attended by significant numbers of children, but with parents who are mainly in the thirty plus age bracket. Living together, especially if one's partner may be of another faith or of none, is likely to be an additional factor in the absence of unmarried young adults from the eucharistic celebration.

YOUNG ADULT CATHOLICS IN ENGLAND

With this in mind, we now approach the empirical investigation itself on which the chapter is principally based and focus on the faith and morality of young adult Catholics. The young Catholics in the sample number 51. The life histories which have been collected from them have been divided into 1) those of *former* or *distant* Catholics; 2) those of *intermediate* Catholics (still in touch which the church but with activity limited to either frequent or infrequent church attendance); and 3) those of *core* Catholics (active in the institutional church beyond regular attendance). There are at least fifteen in each group. They have also been split into 1) single males; 2) single females; and 3) married or partnered people. Again, there are at least fifteen of these in each group. Young adults were traced through both higher educational and parish networks. The life history schedule itself focuses on collecting information on the key stages of life (family, education, and work) and on relationships, religious orientations and practice, and personal and social morality.

Some three-quarters of our life-history sample have either been through university or were completing it in 1997. The sample thus represents mainly those among the Catholic population who have been academically successful, most of them having achieved that success via Catholic schools. The majority of them have been either to the old universities or to what are now the Catholic university colleges, with only three having experienced the old polytechnic/

new university sector. Eight people from lower-class backgrounds have succeeded in joining the middle classes, making the most of their undoubted skills and abilities. All of these are well aware of the labour market advantage they have acquired through their education. Within the sample as a whole, the men are somewhat more likely to have moved into business careers and the women into working with people. This gender division roughly follows the national employment trend for young adults (Bynner, 1997). Additionally, there are more teachers in the sample than would nationally be the case.

We already know that by the 1960s, ethnicization – the social separation of Catholics from the cultural life of the country – was breaking down completely and this decline of the Catholic ghetto was especially apparent among the young (Kokosalakis, 1971). By the early 1970s the percentage of Roman Catholics marrying other than Catholics was reaching 75 in a number of parishes. As we arrive into the 1990s, we can say, even on the basis of the present findings of the research, that the predominant 'sin cycle' of Roman Catholic religiosity over the previous hundred years (sin, confession, communion, sin . . .) has all but disappeared especially among young adults, who have never known the old regime. Correspondingly, the power of the clergy over souls has massively declined. A new structure, albeit with contradictions and weaknesses, has emerged. It would not be too strong to say that the majority of young Catholic adults today are qualitatively different from their pre-1950s predecessors in their religious and moral experience. The following findings might help the reader decide whether or not these changes are to be considered a decline of religious consciousness (secularization) or an appropriate change (modern religion). The findings can be reviewed under the following headings: 1) changes in belief in the transcendent and in the structure of religious experiences; 2) the replacement of the sin cycle by communal religiosity and intimacy; and 3) some initial reflections on the role or impact of Catholic education. We will take these in order.

CHANGES IN BELIEF IN THE TRANSCENDENT AND IN THE STRUCTURE OF RELIGIOUS EXPERIENCES

Belief in God and the transcendent is still substantial even among young former Catholics. Only two from this group of life histories turn out to be atheist (George, Beth), three have a vague notion of a

supernatural rather than a personal God (Colin, Maureen, Douglas),
and one further person (Sam) finds an aesthetic path to the impersonal transcendent. In terms of the remaining 45, who believe in at
least a personal God, what is not certain is the degree to which there
has been a change in the way God is experienced. It has proved one
of the most difficult areas to research without putting words into the
mouths of respondents. Belief in God does appear to have become
more sensed and emotional in form rather than image-specific and
cognitive. Gill, who has been deeply affected by the Lourdes experience, is one of a minority who imagine God as Father:

Gill: For some it's Jesus and his life, for some it's the heavenly father – now
       that's me, but most of all Mary – very much the father figure, but Mary
       as a friend. (Intermediate, single)

Most respondents are at a loss to describe God and appear bereft of
any ready analogies:

Crystal: I have found [thinking about God] quite difficult actually. I think
          probably the person I could most relate to of the Trinity is Jesus . . . .
          (Core, single)

Surprisingly and yet again, Jesus Christ as the core of religious
experience is only strongly affirmed by three people, Frances and
Linda, both core Catholics, and Harry, now a Protestant evangelical,
who left Catholicism because Mary and the saints seemed more
important to it. For most, Jesus is rather the person in the accounts of
God's work, but is not personally encountered in religious experience. A further four indicate both the Spirit and either 'God' or
'Jesus' as subject of their religious relationships. Others relate more
generic religious experiences: 'Sometimes I go to Mass . . . and I have
some kind of special thing' (Alan, Core, single).

   If the faith of the pre-1960s period was underpinned by the fear of
sin and hell, there is no such fearful urgency about belief today.
Believing itself is indeed an issue. It might well be that uncertainty
about it affects at least a significant number of young Roman Catholics, particularly as they are not readily responsive to the authority of
the church on personal matters. However, lest anyone might infer
that the young people interviewed find their own judgements continually undermined, we can point out that the majority of the 34
young adults presently in the core and intermediate category demonstrate in the main a clear conviction about the presence of God or of
a transcending and intelligent power. Those who are still doubtful

approach the issue with meditative quiet rather than panic, and are not guilty or distressed about their questioning.

As we examine further the faith experience itself, it will be useful to take account of the situation which triggers it. For example, Douglas (intermediate single) who was formerly a Catholic out of habit rather than conviction experienced an accident in which two family members died:

> Douglas: It was a car accident. Two cousins, two very young girls in the back [both died] . . . It made me less religious and question things. One way you would look at it and say: things happen for a reason; or another way: if there was a God why would this happen? . . . I think the questioning definitely goes on . . . I'm on the fence. Also I'm more Catholic, I've moved more to that side than to the atheist side, definitely. (Intermediate, single)

Among definite believers, some hold their faith with very firm conviction. God is there for them in a deeper and more personal way than for the majority. This conviction has usually been triggered by a chain of experiences or one experience only. Cathy has known a violent father in the home, and beatings for herself and her mother were frequent. God was a solace in such times and grew in her consciousness over the period. After one particularly bad morning at home, she went into the school chapel as she often did, to be alone:

> Cathy: The chapel is just outside the playground where it is completely noisy, yet it was completely quiet; and I just suddenly felt so calm, and you know suddenly relaxed and just felt that I was one with everything. Everything just seemed – I just seemed to be in with everything, in with nature . . . I suddenly stopped crying. I felt calm and relaxed. I knew everything was going to be OK. It was only once but you know I always related back to that. It was very close and just – you know, a religious experience, God being there with me, very close . . . (Core, single)

Other young people had one crucial experience at a retreat or on the Lourdes pilgrimage like Alan (core, single), or through involvement with charismatics, like Eddie:

> Eddie: It wasn't like a conversion experience as such . . . As a young person I always believed in God and wanted to be a nice person . . . One of my parents started going back to church . . . [Dad] just wanted to be part of our community . . . [But then] my parents became Christian, or they had this experience . . . [I was] about 14 . . . [They joined] a charismatic group . . . and we [the three children] used to

go along with our parents . . . and play football outside the church while the prayer meeting was going on. Gradually we would come into the church . . . [We found out] there's something different . . . They were lively, they kind of believed, they – it wasn't stale, boring, it was like . . . with meaning . . . So we kind of became interested in that, and got more involved. (Core, single)

Frances (previously disliked going to church):   When I was thirteen . . . I did Confirmation and we went away on three days retreat and it was an amazing experience. It sort of opened my eyes to it, my whole perception about church and about God. And I became more involved after that rather than less . . . [Before that] I was very much of the opinion that God was a judge . . . [The change] meant a number of things. I went away with people I had not seen eye to eye with . . . And I was at peace with them . . . and there was a positive feeling . . . And the liturgy was different . . . The idea that God was your friend was something I had not come across before. [Before the change] it was only about giving up, now it was receiving an awful lot as well, so that I should be going because I want to and not because I have to . . .

J.F.   Mass had been boring for you?

Frances: Yes, but I would never have been able to admit that because to have done so would have been a terrible thing. (Core, single)

Such religious experiences have been shared by a number in the sample (e.g. Linda, core, single). Other religious experiences have been more passing, but have still left a taste and a desire:

Evelyn: When I was younger, about seven or eight, I was really happy at Mass. I suddenly knew there was a God and that everything would be OK, that everything was all right. And I wanted to become a nun. I desperately wanted to keep hold of this feeling. But when I came out of Mass it all sort of floated away gradually. I have always remembered that experience because it had an effect on me at the time. I hankered after that again but I don't know where that came from. (Intermediate, single)

Nine respondents have done at least half of their degree in theology, simply as lay people, something which had not even been possible in the first half of the century. These are far more knowledgeable about their faith than a comparable sample of middle-class churchgoers from the 1950s, and yet they are the first to say that theology has not fulfilled them religiously and, if anything, has provided a further test of their faith. For example Paula (core, single) found theology at her university of choice dry and threatening to her faith, and moved on to another university where intellectual theology in the lecture theatre was partnered by religious friendship and community within the staff-student campus life. Neil (intermediate, single) had benefited more from the philosophy than the theology in his degree.

As already seen, the Virgin Mary has not completely disappeared from the religious experience of young adults. To some extent, devotion to her represents the continuation of traditional Catholicism for a portion of our young adults. But the spirituality within which she is present today is a melding of the old and the new. Mary has either a more or an equally living sense of presence as God has in the experience of eight of the seventeen core Catholics so far interviewed. It is the single most common personal religious relationship and was initiated during different Lourdes youth and disabled pilgrimages spread over a ten-year period (Taizé pilgrimages are only mentioned twice). Those who experienced Lourdes have come from at least two different directions, university chaplaincies and their own parishes. In one case, it was the secondary school which was involved in a regular diocesan visit to Lourdes. Pilgrimages to Lourdes have long been a characteristic of English Catholicism, but the content of them has changed over the years. One could say that some components of them have been modernized. Traditionally, diocesan pilgrimages often included the disabled, assisted by men of all ages, and focused on devotions, preaching and contemplation at the grotto where Mary is alleged to have appeared. Disabled and some able-bodied pilgrims would bathe in the waters from the spring, and participate in the daily procession and the Mass. In so far as England is concerned, the new elements have been the setting up of youth pilgrimages, with young able-bodied men and women assisting disabled youth and children, and the increased importance of communal worship and activities, and especially the Mass or Eucharist, celebrated in the large modern basilica constructed in the 1950s. The pilgrimage is by train or coach, lasting about six days including two days' travel. The young helpers have a one-to-one relationship with their disabled charges, and look after their every need.

The first pilgrimage was the most important for each of the eight Marian-oriented respondents. There are two principal high points in the accounts. One is spending time at the Grotto, in quiet prayer or simple silence, and frequently weeping for joy in experiencing the caring presence of Mary. In Gill's case, the first pilgrimage came at a time she was beginning to drift away from the church as her brothers were doing. The experience in fact triggered the development of her religious commitment:

Gill: I go to church every Sunday . . . My older brothers don't . . . They have just given up . . .It's just something that's gradually faded out . . . I've just come back from my seventh time at Lourdes . . . I think it's changed me a lot. I think I was at the stage when I was beginning to go through the stage my brothers have gone through . . . The minute I got there I absolutely loved the place. I'd never go without taking the [handicapped] children. Went down to the Grotto at night and it was amazing. I cried my eyes out . . . It never stops having an effect on me. It's been like a drug . . . It just came to me at the right time . . . (Intermediate, single)

Phrases used to describe the pilgrimage are summarized in one pilgrim's own reflections: 'The best thing I have ever done . . . a week of your life that builds you up for a year . . . you get your priorities and perspectives, though not necessarily morally . . . you get close to the people you were with . . . you make friends for life' (Alan, core, single). In two life histories, the experience has been clearly one of renewal of an already present committed faith; in the other six, life perceptions have been changed from a customary to a committed Catholic Christianity. The experience has also heightened their sense of responsibility for others. One person also talks of empowerment: being made capable of taking initiatives in favour of other people, something she felt incapable of doing before. It would appear that, if there is something that modernity fails to remove from religion, it is the effect of certain holy places, whose sacrality can increase with improved and cheaper communications rather than the reverse. This does not mean the Lourdes pilgrimage is a great event for all. Two other interviewees had a distinct impression that the Lourdes experience was rather 'tacky' as one of them put it, and they remained ambivalent about their visit.

THE RELIGIOUS EXPERIENCE OF COMMUNITY

We should note that all but one of the occasions for religious commitment and personal change we have encountered so far have been parish, university chaplaincy or school initiated, and that proximate triggers have been pilgrimage, a visit to the school chapel, a retreat. Another element has been the experience of the religious gathering, which in turn has produced a heightened sense of religious community. Such awareness is also one of the principal high points of the Lourdes experience, especially the principal gathering of the pilgrimage in the basilica, during the Mass shared with 5,000 or more other young helpers and their young disabled charges. A number of the respondents articulate their experience of community, sense of oneness and the presence of the supernatural either at this event or in the subsequent relationships formed. So strong is the bond overall developed that it can remain after coming back from Lourdes, and involves friendship with the disabled children as well as with fellow helpers:

Alan: When you come back you are close to those people you were with. People at my college can't understand that ... They have had the same experience as you. It's amazing how close you stay to them because there is something in common you have never said but – it's there ... (Core, single)

This religious experience of community, however, is not confined to those who have been to Lourdes, but is also shared by a significant number of other young adult Catholics, who experience the same in certain parishes or chaplaincies they have come to love:

Debra: [Mass] is quite a social – you know, you meet at Mass and you get together. I find that during the holidays [at home] when there's no [participatory] Mass I don't very often go. Because, I feel, the reason you go to Mass is to be part of a community and I feel in that community at the [Mass I go to in the university chaplaincy]. I mean, OK when I move away I'll find another parish and build up that community there. (Core, single)

For some, religious community is an experience to be sought and treasured beyond the occasion of worship. Paula (core, single but soon to marry) belongs to a lay religious community which spends four hours together on Sunday afternoons and evenings, with an additional two-hour session one day a week for group meetings and prayers. As one might expect, the presence of God in the community is as important to her as other cases of divine presence experienced in her religious life and commitments.

One should mention that five of the sample spontaneously said that reading or hearing the Scriptures, and/or listening to the sermon, was the main element in their community worship. Reflecting on how she appreciated and benefited from studying Scripture at a Church of England secondary school, one of them says:

Karen: If you ask me even now, you know, why do I go to church, why do I like going to church, what part do I enjoy best, I actually enjoy

Scripture, I enjoy the Bible readings. I can really try and imagine myself there and what seems the most simple thing, I don't have to go and analyse what's this about and what's that about and what makes me a Catholic rather than something else. That to me doesn't interest me, I just want to go in there, don't worry, there's one God and I reading the Scripture and, you know, it's just – think about how it was in those days . . . it's wonderful for me. That's how I, you know, that's why I go to church every Sunday, really. (Intermediate, partnered)

If one looks at the members of our sample, the top-down conversion of the Tridentine Mass into a fellowship ritual of Word and Sacrament has had some success. Of course, this generation has known hardly any other form of worship, being born in the late 1960s or in the 1970s. But it still remains true that a significant number of interviewees spontaneously and without prompting have introduced their own experience of the faith community. In these cases at least, there is a clear experience of religious solidarity. This sense of fellowship (the word itself was not used by informants) was also positively desired, and some were prepared to go from church to church to find it.

Despite this positive element, there is also evidence that the bond experienced is often relatively weak in a number of ways. In only a few cases does the experience develop into friendship awareness beyond the sacred space of the church. Most are often not concerned with inserting themselves into the local community, partly because they are passing through. Second, the experiences of community only occur when the liturgy is enthusiastic, meaningful and well prepared, all of which requires at least a clearly committed and sensitive priest. This has usually not been the case in the majority of parishes known to our sample, and Sunday Mass has often been 'boring'. Teresa (core, single) and Rachel (intermediate, married) have had more felt religious and communal worship in fundamentalist evangelical churches than at Mass.

The only ones who have to move frequently because of their job and who miss participation in the more general life of the local *parish* community were one of the two couples interviewed. Rachel and Oliver both experience the loss of local community as a spiritual drawback:

Rachel: The one thing we did feel in C'town, when we first went . . . we became part of the community there and became involved and I think that is something that possibly we miss here because we

> haven't really [got involved] . . . [Parish involvement] is the begin-
> ning of the community for you and I think that again is the
> important side. We are very insular at the moment because we don't
> know which way we are going, we don't want to commit ourselves
> . . . (Intermediate, married)

In the discussions on the significance of communion reception, it is
also clear that the rite is sometimes experienced as a weak and
routine exercise. There is little sense of the presence of Christ in all
but a few cases, despite some prompting on my part, though there is
something special or sacred about it. Also, the 'Liturgy of the Word'
– the Bible readings, prayers and priestly homily, which usually take
up half of the Sunday celebration – does not make an impact in many
cases, despite the favourable remarks of our five biblical enthu-
siasts.

Towards the end of 40 of the interviews, a battery of straight
questions was asked that refers mostly to everyday life commitments
and to social and personal values. One of these is, 'What is the single
most important thing in your life?' The majority have responded with
'my family and close friends' or 'my partner, family and close friends'
or other similar phrases. In a number of the remaining life histories
there are references to both the importance of close friends and the
desire for a life-long intimate partner. Almost all the transcripts thus
indicate that the predominant life concern of young Catholic adults
is both present and future family, or both present and future loved
ones including those friends who are envisaged as 'friends for life'.
Intimacy is thus a core value shaping their construction of life style
and priorities. It is the generalized goal of personal fulfilment which
their generation has, one they share with the vast majority of those
who are not Roman Catholic (Giddens, 1991; Beck, 1992; Collins,
1998), but one which has a this-worldly stress while not excluding an
other-worldly purpose. Only with these relationships in place do life
and career seem to be viewed as fulfilling.

In this context, the presence of intimate or close relationships at
the spiritual level, both human and transcendent, take on a particular relevance for human fulfilment in contemporary society. If such
religious relationships are so important, why, then, are they not more
present in the sample of life histories we have assembled? Is it simply
the lack of opportunities (retreats, pilgrimages, well prepared liturgies, religious personalities)? Or is it refusal on the part of individuals
to take advantage of opportunities offered? Religious life once
offered such opportunities, but with the enhancement of the value of

sexual intimacy, even by the contemporary church itself, that route is clearly less desirable to all our sample. We must ask ourselves to what extent the existence of such human and spiritual needs for intimacy and the shortage of their religious counterparts are recognized in the pastoral planning of church mission.

THE ROLE OF CATHOLIC EDUCATION

We are still at the early stages of the analysis of those sections of the life histories which focus on the effects of Catholic education. However, it is possible to bring into focus the variety of school careers, and the religious convictions of respondents. Our qualitative sample of life histories shows what people with a long experience of Catholic schools (and colleges) might have already concluded: (1) children actually react differently to the same school; (2) the Christian Catholic ethos in Catholic schools varies widely, not only in terms of affecting the religious commitment of pupils, but also in the type of religious influence it has exerted; and finally (3) some committed Catholics come from outside the Catholic education system, and their Catholicism has been developed in either the family or the parish or both. We will illustrate some aspects of these points in turn.

Different reaction to the same school

Kevin, Ian and John all attended the same Catholic secondary school and were in the same age group. Kevin was also educated in a Catholic primary school. In addition, his father, who works in insurance, is a practising Catholic, while his mother has no religious affiliation. Kevin calls himself a Catholic, but since he was sixteen has not been to church and has no interest in it. He does not pray, and his long-term girl friend has no religious affiliation. Also, he found religious education at school a waste of time. Ian, who went to a state primary, but has both parents Catholic and running a small business, is a dedicated and practising Catholic, prays, and goes out with the daughter of a core Catholic family. In addition, he found the same religious classes as Kevin interesting and appreciated his Catholic education as a whole. John has a similar background to Kevin but has disconnected from Catholicism altogether, though his mother still practises. John, however, also notes that in the secondary school (the same one as Kevin and Ian), there were clearly separate friendship groups, those who were involved with the school's religious activities and those who had entirely secular interests. Both groups still worked hard at their subjects, but viewed each other from a distance.

Catholic ethos in Catholic schools

Eddie went to Catholic schools, but his father, who was a Catholic, played little part in his religious education, though his mother, an Anglican, took him to school as a child. His memories are that he was brought up to say his prayers mainly by his grandmother, a deeply committed Catholic. He loved his Catholic primary school, much less his Catholic secondary, though he (like most others) cannot remember anything about religious education or prayers at primary school. He remembers 'boring mass and boring sermons' at his parish church. As we have noted, Eddie becomes a committed religious person through his parents' 'conversion' via charismatic renewal. Frances (core), too, had a similar family and parish experience. Helen, with practising Catholic parents, remembers the religious aspect of her secondary schooling negatively, especially doing religious education for GCSE:

> Helen: You did have religious education twice a week. You studied other religions [as well] and St Mark's Gospel . . . [The Gospel was taught the] same as I'd done it before . . . I still had to study it for GCSE – had to do it. Got an 'A', but it was drummed into you. (Intermediate, single)

Debra's life at Catholic school was quite miserable on all fronts, mainly because she was dyslexic, but her disability was not picked up until the sixth form. It was her family's religious life and her own parish life which promoted her Christian commitment. Eileen (distant, partnered) enjoyed her local Catholic primary school and even her local secondary, but found the religious education very poor. She cannot remember anything about the effect of the Catholic ethos on her. Later, she was accepted into the sixth form of a well-known Catholic private school to do 'A' levels including Religious Studies. But she got no religious support at all, despite the fact that priests were running the school. She thinks that religious support was better further down the school, but the only thing the priests were concerned about at sixth form level was high academic grades. They refused to take her on for a particular 'A' level subject because they did not think she would score an A. This has left a bad impression on her. In addition, her parents always saw her attendance at Mass as an obligation, and she was forced to go to church up until she left home for university. She now no longer goes to church. George (former, single) has had a Catholic school education, always been interested in religion and always debated it. But over his years at Oxbridge he has come to believe in God no longer and has left the church.

Development of Catholicism

Harry, while having a practising Catholic mother, has never attended a Catholic school, but went to prestigious fee-paying ones, a secular primary and an Anglican secondary. He attended catechism classes for his first communion and his confirmation, has been taught to pray at home, and is one of the three Oxbridge life histories. At university he has stayed faithful to his religious practices, and considers himself a staunch believer. He is active in his home parish. Linda (core) has come from a secularist home background and had no experience of a Catholic school. She got involved with the Christian Union via a local Church of England school, and became an evangelical Christian. When she experienced overt fundamentalism from within the movement, she resolved to take her love for Jesus elsewhere. The first church she walked into was Roman Catholic and she concluded it was right for her.

The only general statistical survey ever done in this country on the effect of Catholic education or the lack of it on Catholics was by Hornsby-Smith and Lee (1979: 76–105). Without raking up old controversies, the conclusions of two pieces of research from the past are worth remembering. Spencer's study (1968) which was based on a small number of parishes showed that respondents who had no Catholic schooling had marginally better Catholic profiles than those who had. Greeley *et al.*'s (1976) US national sample showed Catholic schools producing more Catholic activists than the state system. They concluded that Catholic schooling in the USA has reinforced the faith otherwise acquired in home and parish and that this has resulted in the increased parish activism. While Spencer's research was too localized to have wider statistical inference, Greeley's reliable research refers to an entirely different system of Catholic schools, the fee-paying US system whose primary branch has now been decimated since their study took place. However, Greeley's moderate claim is likely to be the best one could establish for the English system by statistical studies and is in fact supported by

Hornsby-Smith and Lee's findings. By this we mean that home, parish and school have mutually reinforcing effects, particularly where good home is partnered by good parish and good school. Even so, good home and good parish come first, with school complementing or reinforcing their work. However, a very good school might be able to make up for a poor parish experience.

CONCLUSION

An attempt has been made to sketch out salient characteristics of the contemporary religious faith of young Catholic adults in England on the basis of a small but rich data set. A limitation of the sample is that it is heavily weighted towards the well educated (those 'getting on') with only five belonging to anything lower. Substantial additional research would have to be done if a class-balanced picture were to be achieved.

While this report has concentrated on religious faith, other papers from the research project have reported on the decline of priestly and parental authority, the corresponding growth in young adult personal moral autonomy, the continuance of a strong sense of the sacredness of human life, and clear concerns for the poor and marginalized of society, the environment and the plight of the Third World (Fulton and Dowling, 1997; Fulton, 1999). The general conclusion to the present analysis of the religious faith of young adult Catholics in England is that it is relatively strong and designed to cope with living immersed as citizens in a pluralistic world of all faiths and none. The passing of ethnic Catholicism and its features of the sin cycle and an authoritarian priesthood was inevitable, and could only have survived by erecting sect-like boundaries around an ever-decreasing population of socially marginal Catholics (Fulton, 1997). Modern young adult spirituality is strong in its critique of the contemporary world and looks as if it is able to grow, provided it is nourished by the religious community in which it lives, with its triple rooting in the family, the parish and the school. But part of that nourishment also has to be in terms of intimate relationships, both with God and with another human person, and probably other (non-sexual) close friendships also. This demand, shared in its secular component by contemporary non-religious young people, is perhaps the central reason why celibacy has declined in its attraction to modern young people, and accounts more than materialism for the fall in vocations and religious life. Going back to traditional Catholicism is not an option without fragmenting the English and Welsh churches. If anything, it may be that the institutional church has to evaluate further the transformation of contemporary society and rebuild itself into a form and shape which recognizes many of the moral gains the contemporary culture has made, while exposing with care and accuracy its accompanying losses.

The research shows the interweaving of family and parish in the structuring of religious commitments, with Catholic schooling having an additional but significant effect. The outcome of this support can be seen in the fact that religious experience is still alive, but refers more to peace, divine presence and community rather than to traditional symbolic referents (sacraments, the sacred, the saints), or to any sense of relief at being in a state of grace. Religious leaders should perhaps be worried about some of the weaker aspects of sacramental experience, while welcoming the growth of the sense of Christian community. Our young people are also more outgoing towards the needs of the world than previous Catholic generations. They are generally positive, open to life, and feel supported by, rather than dependent on, their religious faith. If there is a key concern to their existence, it is their search for intimacy and the hope that they will initiate and sustain loving relationships with significant others for the whole of their lives. And yes, they are this-worldly rather than other-worldly oriented, and share in a number of the values of the 'New Generation' of 18–35 year olds (Wilkinson and Mulgan, 1996), particularly those of the 'post-materialists' rather than the 'pleasure seekers' or the individualists. Do they perhaps express a form of contemporary religion, a Christianity for a contemporary world?

NOTE

1   The other persons working on the project are Anthony Abela (University of Malta), Irena Borowik (Jagiellonian University, Krakow), Teresa Dowling (University College, Cork), Penny Marler (Samford University, Birmingham, Alabama) and Luigi Tomasi (University of Trento).

REFERENCES

Beck, U. *Risk Society: Towards a New Modernity* (London: Sage, 1992).
Brierley, P. *UK Christian Handbook 1994* (London: Evangelical Alliance, 1994).

Bynner, J., Ferri, E. and Shepherd, P. (eds) *Twenty-Something in the 1990s* (Aldershot: Ashgate Press, 1997).

Catholic Directory for England and Wales (London: Burns and Oates, 1961).

Catholic Directory for England and Wales (London: Burns and Oates, 1971).

Collins, S. 'Immanent faith: young people in late modernity', in L.J. Francis (ed.) *Sociology and the Curriculum: A Theological Perspective* (London: Cassell, 1998).

Flanagan, K. *The Enchantment of Sociology: A Study of Theology and Culture* (London: Macmillan, 1996).

Fulton, J. 'Modernity and religious change in Western Roman Catholicism: two contrasting paradigms', *Social Compass* 44 (1997):115–31.

Fulton, J. 'Young adult Catholics', in M. P. Hornsby-Smith (ed.) *Catholics in England 1950–2000* (London: Cassell, 1999).

Fulton, J. and Dowling, T. 'Society and belief today: Roman Catholic young adults in Britain and Ireland', in Ulrich Nembach (ed.) *The Impact of Change on Contemporary Religion* (No. 17 of *Forschungen zur Praktischen Theologie*) (Frankfurt: Peter Lang, 1997).

Furlong, A. and Cartmel F. *Young People and Social Change: Individualisation and Risk in Late Modernity* (Milton Keynes: Open University Press, 1997).

Giddens, A. *Modernity and Self-Identity* (Cambridge: Polity, 1991).

Greeley, A.M., McCready, W.C. and McCourt, K. *Catholic Schools in a Declining Church* (Kansas City: Sheed and Ward, 1976).

Hervieu-Léger, D. *La Religion Pour Mémoire* (Paris: Les Éditions du Cerf, 1993).

Hornsby-Smith, M.P. *Roman Catholics in England: Studies in Social Structure Since the Second World War* (Cambridge: Cambridge University Press, 1987).

Hornsby-Smith, M.P. *The Changing Parish: A Study of Parishes, Priests and Parishioners after Vatican II* (London: Routledge, 1989).

Hornsby-Smith, M.P. *Roman Catholic Beliefs in England: Customary Catholicism and Transformations of Religious Authority* (Cambridge: Cambridge University Press, 1991).

Hornsby-Smith, M.P., Fulton, J. and Norris, M. *The Politics of Spirituality: A Study of a Renewal Process in an English Diocese* (Oxford: Clarendon Press, 1995).

Hornsby-Smith, M.P. and Lee, R.M. *Roman Catholic Opinion: A Study of Roman Catholics in England and Wales in the 1970s* (Guildford: University of Surrey, 1979).

Hutton, W. *The State We're In* (London: Cape, 1995).

Jones, G. and Wallace, C. *Youth, Family and Citizenship* (Buckingham and Philadelphia: Open University Press, 1992).

Kokosalakis, N. 'Aspects of conflict between the structure of authority and the beliefs of the laity in the Roman Catholic church', in M. Hill (ed.) *A*

Sociological Yearbook of Religion in Britain, vol. 4. (London: SCM Press, 1971), pp. 21–35.

Roberts, K. *Youth and Employment in Modern Britain* (Oxford: Oxford University Press, 1995).

Spencer, A.E.C.W. 'An evaluation of Roman Catholic educational policy in England and Wales 1900–1968', in P. Jebb (ed.) *Religious Education: Drift or Decision?* (London: Darton, Longman and Todd, 1968).

Wilkinson, H. and Mulgan, G. *Freedom's Children: Work, Relationships and Politics for 18-34 Year Olds Today* (London: Demos, 1996).

12

MISSION INTO THE MILLENNIUM

Mary Eaton

HISTORY AND BACKGROUND

BROOK-GREEN HOUSE, Hammersmith, near London

> The Committee most earnestly invite the co-operation and assistance of all who are interested in the moral and religious condition of poor children. In the most populous towns of Great Britain the poorest class of the population is Catholic. The offspring of this class must not be neglected. Religion and social policy equally forbid it. The Committee, then, implore the aid of the rich and benevolent, and will thank fully receive any contribution confided to them for the diffusion of sound education among the Catholic poor.
>
> Charles Langdale, Chairman
Scott Nasmyth Stokes, Secretary

The education of Catholic children has been a recognized priority of the Catholic Church in Britain pre-dating the re-establishment of the Hierarchy in 1850. The foundation of the Catholic Poor Schools Committee in 1847 is evidence of the importance given to this project, and the development of that committee during the subsequent century and a half, into the Catholic Education Council and then the Catholic Education Service marks the continued importance given to education. Church involvement in higher education arises from the priority given to the education of the Catholic poor. Until recently Catholic higher education was concerned solely with the training of teachers for Catholic schools. In this, Catholic higher education in Britain differs from that in continental Europe, the USA and Australia. There different traditions have led to the establishment of Catholic universities.[1] Here in Britain there has been a long slow

Table 12.1 The dates for the establishment of Catholic Teacher Training Colleges in England

Date	Name	Student gender
1850	St Mary's, Hammersmith	(for men)
1856	Mount Pleasant, Liverpool	(for women)
	St Leonard's-on-Sea	(for women)
1863	St Leonard's-on-Sea closes	
1874	Wandsworth	(for women)
1903	Adelphi House, Salford	(for women)
1904	La Sainte Union, Southampton	(for women)
1905	Wandsworth moves to North Kensington	
1905	Endsleigh, Hull	(for women)
1906	Fenham, Newcastle upon Tyne	(for women)
1914	St Paul's, Selly Park, Birmingham	(for women)
1926	St Mary's moves from Hammersmith to Strawberry Hill	
1927	Holy Child, Cavendish Square, London	(for women)
1946	North Kensington moves to Roehampton (Digby Stuart)	
	Selly Park moves to Rugby	
1946	Coloma, Croydon	(for women)
	Maria Assumpta, Kensington	(for women)
1948	De La Salle, Manchester	(for men)
1958	Coloma moves to West Wickham	
1965	Christ's, Liverpool	(for men and women)
1966	Trinity and All Saints, Leeds	(for men and women)
1967	Mary Ward, Windsor	(for women)
1968	Mary Ward moves to Nottingham	
1968	Newman, Birmingham	(for men and women)

Source: Annual Reports of Catholic Poor Schools Committee and Catholic Education Council.

process to achieve university status for post-school Catholic education which encompasses more than teacher training.

Until very recently, the history of Catholic higher education in England was a history of gradual growth and little substantive change. From 1850 to 1950 there was a steady increase in the number of Catholic training colleges for teachers, and only one closure (see Table 12.1). Fifty years ago there were twelve colleges, each training a small number of students by contemporary standards, in single sex institutions (ten for women; two for men). The number of colleges

Table 12.2 The distribution of students between teacher training and
non-teacher training courses in Catholic colleges in 1982

Name of institution	Teacher training		Non-teacher training	
	Men	Women	Men	Women
Fenham, Newcastle upon Tyne	28	56	–	–
La Sainte Union, Southampton	51	244	25	105
St Mary's, Strawberry Hill	123	279	296	412
Trinity and All Saints, Leeds	95	225	220	387
Newman, Birmingham	65	185	–	–
Christ's and Notre Dame, Liverpool	98	271	129	200
De La Salle, Manchester	150	161	166	170
Digby Stuart, Roehampton	22	169	100	273

Source: Annual Report of Catholic Education Council (1982)

remained constant until the late 1960s when there was a rapid
increase in provision to sixteen. It was during this period in British
education that the graduate training of teachers became widespread.
At first the three-year certificate was followed by an optional fourth
year to complete a BEd degree (1968). Later graduate entry to
teaching became universal, either through a four-year degree which
incorporated the teacher training component within an undergraduate programme, or by a first degree followed by a one year
postgraduate certificate in education. It was during this period that
most of the Catholic colleges diversified their provision. Following
the recommendation of the 1972 James Report that teachers no
longer be trained in monotechnics, many of the colleges began to
offer other degree programmes. By the 1980s the non-teacher training students out-numbered the teacher training students in half the
Catholic colleges (see Table 12.2.)

   However, this time of change also saw a series of closures and re-
groupings among the Catholic colleges leading to the present
situation (see Table 12.3). At the time of writing there are five
Catholic colleges: St Mary's at Strawberry Hill, near London; Trinity
and All Saints at Leeds; Newman at Birmingham, Liverpool Hope;
and Digby Stuart which is part of the Roehampton Institute in South
West London. Digby Stuart is the Catholic college of the ecumenical
structure which is the Roehampton Institute. Liverpool Hope is an

Table 12.3 The closure and regrouping of Catholic teacher training colleges

Year	Name of institution	Status
1969	Holy Child, Cavendish Square	Closed
1977	Coloma, West Wickham	Closed
	Endsleigh, Hull	Closed
	Maria Assumpta, Kensington	Closed
	Mary Ward, Nottingham	Closed
	St Paul's, Rugby	Closed
	Sedgley Park	Closed
1975	Digby Stuart joined Roehampton Institute	
1980	Christ's and Notre Dame joined the Liverpool Institute	
1985	Fenham, Newcastle upon Tyne	Closed
1990	De La Salle, Manchester	Closed
1996	La Sainte Union, Southampton	Closed

Source: Annual Reports of the Catholic Education Council

ecumenical organization incorporating both Catholic and Anglican faith traditions.

For the original Catholic colleges their identity and mission were clear. They were Catholic in their student intake, in the work of the institutions and in the presence of a religious order. Aspiring students needed a letter of recommendation from the parish priest as evidence of their standing as practising Catholics. The student body consisted entirely of Catholics. Each college was concerned with the training of teachers, with producing Catholic teachers for Catholic schools and thus playing a central role in the evangelizing work of the church. Religious orders constituted the providing bodies. In most cases the religious order provided the grounds and the buildings of a college; in all cases the roles of Principal, Vice-Principal and many senior staff were held by members of the providing order. These nuns or priests lived in community with others of their order on the campus. This provided not only evidence of a visible faith commitment but also the basis of the college community which so many staff and students valued.[2] It also gave scope for distinctiveness within the Catholic tradition as the charism of each order made its own mark on the work of each college.

Of the five Catholic colleges in England today only one has a religious at the head; this is also the only one with a woman at the head.[3] The others have lay men as Principals, or the equivalent.[4] Lay men and women occupy other senior staff roles. The number of religious as teaching staff is greatly reduced and no longer is there a religious community of priests or sisters living on the campus of each college. Among the lay staff Catholics constitute a minority. The student body is no longer exclusively Catholic, nor are Catholics in the majority. The exception, in some of the colleges are the students on the teacher training programmes. In most of the colleges these courses are only one part of a much wider portfolio. In what sense then are these colleges 'Catholic'? Is their Catholicism important to the colleges, to the church and to the wider world? These questions lay at the centre of the interviews conducted with the Principals and other staff of the five Catholic colleges.

The data for this chapter are derived from a series of interviews and from 25 years of working in Catholic colleges. For the purposes of the research I visited each of the five colleges and interviewed each institutional head as well as members of staff who were seen as key players in, or relevant commentators on, the mission of the college. I also drew on the personal experience of working in the sector during a time of change, of a decrease in the number of Catholic institutions and of an increase in the types of programmes on offer to students.

The interviews were unstructured and lasted for approximately one hour. Interviewees were invited to discuss the form and content of Catholic higher education, particularly as it was delivered in their own colleges. Issues of identity and mission were explored in order to gain an understanding of Catholic higher education in England at the end of the twentieth century.

The mission statement of each college articulates the Catholic dimension of the life and work of the college and makes an explicit commitment to ecumenical dialogue with people of other faiths. Communal worship is recognized as part of the life of each college. Each mission statement makes a commitment to the provision of educational opportunities for those who have had little chance to develop their full potential. All but one of the mission statements make an explicit commitment to the provision of teachers for church schools. The similarity between the mission statements of each college can be seen as the implicit acknowledgement of a common heritage. The differences between the colleges lie in the way that heritage has been developed and in the ways in which it is now delivered in each institution.

In listening to these interviews, and reading the transcripts, I was aware that three themes dominated the discussions which arose in answer to questions on the identity, mission and practice of the colleges:

- Community;
- Tradition;
- Curriculum.

COMMUNITY

In each interview the making of community was recognized as a defining characteristic of a Catholic college and a necessary part of the work of that college. All the colleges were proud of the sense of community which characterized life there, for students and staff. This was an aspect of personal experience chronicled and quantified in the inspection of external agencies such as the QAA and OFS-TED.[5] Such inspecting bodies had commented favourably on the ethos of all the colleges and on the strength of the student support services which were found there. This making of community was seen by those interviewed as the necessary pre-condition for any enterprise that continued the mission of the original founders.

> Ethos is a very over-worked term, but research has demonstrated that successful schools are the ones with a positive ethos. That positive ethos is about how people relate to each other. It's an elusive thing. You can't prescribe it and you can't make people do it but you can create the conditions in which it can happen. It's about team-work, it's about sharing, it's about understanding, it's about inclusion rather than exclusion.

This theme was taken up and developed by those from other colleges. Each of the colleges had one geographical site and this was recognized as important in the creating of community. Contrasting his institution with a large civic university one Principal said:

> They have scores of buildings strung out across the city – on an average day the average student won't meet the Vice Chancellor, wouldn't know what the Vice Chancellor is like, wouldn't meet chaplains, deans and so on. Whereas here there is only one way to walk through the campus – on the pathways; there's only one place to eat – the refectory – and every student has the opportunity to stop me, for instance. They can't help but see the chaplains who are in the most visible base at the centre of the campus and so it genuinely is a collegiate atmosphere and the staff are committed to

being supportive of that atmosphere and ethos. So I think it is very different, and deliberately so.

The deliberate creation of that which had previously occurred as a by-product of a resident religious community was the policy of Catholic colleges at the end of the twentieth century. The single campus was prized, the opportunities of meeting and working together were emphasized. In one college all staff are entitled to a free lunch which encourages a gathering together daily in the refectory. In another the Principal uses a series of evening meals as a way of building community with new students:

> I speak to every resident first year student, one to one, through chaplaincy suppers. I would think we had failed if a student didn't recognize me in the street. I couldn't guarantee that I could put a name to all of them, but I would expect to know my own students. That is qualitatively different to a large civic university. I think that's part of what the community of the church is witnessing too. It's difficult to maintain with QAAs and OFSTEDs. How you prioritize the community aspect alongside your academic and professional role is a tricky one. But community has to be at the heart of a Catholic college.

So, in the name of community-building, Catholic Principals were open to being accosted by students as they crossed the campus, greeted by students in the high street, mixing with students in the bar, and even in one exceptional case, parachuting with students out of an aeroplane!

Central to such community-building is the role of the liturgy. Each college had a chaplaincy and at least one resident Catholic chaplain. In each of the colleges the chapel occupies a central place on the campus and is the focus of communal worship. Daily Mass is a common feature, ecumenical worship is available in some of the colleges. While these services might not be attended by large numbers of staff or students, they provide the small nucleus of a faith community, with individuals drawing strength from each other's presence. The persistence of such groups gave others the opportunity to join in at those times when they too felt the need to be part of the visibly worshipping church. Sunday Mass is a particularly significant event in those colleges with a residential community of students and staff, and with college members who live nearby and worship at the college chapel. In such cases the college community is expanded and enriched by the presence of the family and friends of college members. Where chaplains and chaplaincy teams are able to

facilitate the variety of talents to be found among such congregations, the result is a liturgy which stimulates and validates the faith
community which it celebrates. For some students it is an opportunity to experience for the first time a sense of contributing to and
being part of a worshipping community which sustains, and is sustained by, its members.

Chaplaincy programmes of lectures and training, retreats and
prayer were also ways in which the faith tradition was developed and
community was built. Opening such events to the local community
allows for an interaction with others and the development of an
ethos of service as part of the practice of faith. In a number of the
colleges the chaplaincy provides the focus for work on local, national
and international projects. Helping the housebound in the area,
providing assistance for handicapped children on pilgrimage to
Lourdes, raising funds for charity and raising consciousness on
global issues of justice were all aspects of the work being co-ordinated
by the chaplaincy teams within the Catholic colleges.

In one college the academic year began with a day of recollection
for staff led by an internationally recognized authority on prayer.
The day was well attended by men and women of many faith traditions and all areas of the college. Although led by a Catholic priest
the day was experienced as inclusive and relevant to all faiths.

By such means the Catholic colleges in the late twentieth century
draw on the traditions of their founders and take them forward. The
religious community of the past, on campus, would meet and eat and
worship together as part of their rule – their religious way of life. This
provided a focus for the community life of the college – a community
life which now needs to be deliberately nourished in different ways.
In one of the colleges this is being attempted by the establishment of
an 'intentional' residential community which consists of three religious sisters and six students. The community was established in
September 1998 and will be reviewed and renewed each year. The
order will provide three sisters and six students will be chosen from
those who apply. Applications are invited from women and men. The
current student group of six women includes three who have experience of community life: one a religious sister from Ghana and two
with experience of lay community in the UK. The community meet
for evening prayer each day and eat together once a week. Daily Mass
is celebrated for those who wish to attend, and most do. The
presence of the community on campus has provided a focus for
others and there is an almost constant stream of visitors calling in for

coffee and conversation. So far the hopes of the Principal at the planning stage have been fulfilled.

> One of the criteria drawn up for selection of students was an openness to keep widening the ripples of this community through house Masses and so forth. They will all play together and eat together sometimes and each do their own thing at other times. I think it's an initiative that could make a lot of difference to the sense of community on campus.

This is one way of exploring alternative forms of religious community, in order to give a religious dimension to the college community.

TRADITION

The sense of community that was being carefully and deliberately constructed at each of the Catholic colleges was not only a way of relating current college members to each other; it was also a way of meeting with, and taking forward the work of those who had been part of earlier college communities. Each Principal is aware of the heritage of Catholic education in England and specifically in his or her own institution. And each is aware of the way that heritage is being developed to meet contemporary needs:

> The founders of the college opened up access to higher education for a previously excluded group – women. That spirit needs to live on, but ironically some of the excluded groups now are young white men. They're not excluded by law but they are excluded because they are apathetic and can't see that there is a role for them and I think we can offer something which really does touch them and teach them and gives them an opportunity to develop and flourish as rounded human beings and citizens. And I think that's very important so I feel that we can live out the faith in the broadest sense of the founders and we re-invent it in the mission for current and future eras.

Such development was seen as vital for the institutions and for the church.

> Our heritage does matter to me – to preserve, develop and expand. I like the idea that the students have a sense of tradition; I like them to know a bit of the history of the place. I'm not sure you can hand on a vision in a way that permits it to stay static. Religious orders are contracting, wanting to move out of formal education. Now we have to prepare the next generation to have the confidence to take over

and not to fossilize Catholic education in a model that used to be celibate and religious. Part of the responsibility must be giving the next generation of interpreters of the vision the right to develop that vision. Unless there is harmony between visionaries of the past and of the future, then I think the institutions could fall in the middle.

One way of extending and developing the original vision and mission is to take the commitment to teacher education beyond the stage of initial training.

A central part of our service is to support the work of the church in education. That used to be about the initial training of teachers, now it's much more about continuing professional development. One of the most difficult issues that Catholic education faces at the moment is getting people to take on headships of schools. Part of it is because of that sense of undertaking a moral or spiritual leadership role in school.

Developing Masters programmes in school leadership, and delivering these programmes in centres away from the college but near to the working teacher is another way in which the tradition of teacher education and provision for schools is continued.

Many of the religious orders which had been active in the founding of the Catholic colleges and had staffed so many of the Catholic schools are now withdrawing from education and declining in numbers. If lay people are to fill the roles which are left, in education and elsewhere, the necessary training and formation must be provided. The Catholic colleges are well placed to offer this and this was recognized by those working within them:

One of the challenges for all of us is to continue to find ways in which the roles that have been taken in the past by full-time 'church professionals' are taken by committed lay people.

Drawing on the tradition of religious education for schools, some of the colleges were exploring ways of providing religious education for those involved in pastoral ministries: in parishes, prisons, hospitals and other areas previously served by the clergy and religious.

CURRICULUM

Each of the colleges was established to provide Catholic teachers for Catholic schools. Education and Religious Education are still at the centre of the curriculum of each college, and recognized as vital to the validity of the college.

> It would be a threat to our future if we didn't have a strong presence
> in Theology and if we didn't have a strong base in Education.

These sentiments were echoed by the leaders of each of the Catholic
colleges. However, a Catholic identity was seen to go beyond these
original and clearly demarcated areas of mission. The mission was
now being delivered through other subject areas and through new
ways of offering these areas.

> We encourage all staff responsible for course proposals to give
> consideration to the Catholic or religious dimensions of the cur-
> riculum.

In the different colleges this was being played out in different ways.
In one college modules in Theology with a specifically Catholic
dimension (e.g. Vatican II Documents; Spirituality) were available to
students not taking Theology as a main subject. In another college
new course programmes were being developed to draw on Catholic
traditions and social teachings. Thus an academic Development
Studies programme would articulate with the practical work of a
major Catholic charity. A new Media programme would offer modules of relevance to a broadcasting church. The Business Studies
programme had been developed with an emphasis on Business
Ethics and was located in the Department of Theology and Religious
Studies. In Sociology funded research was being undertaken in areas
that had a clear relevance to the original mission of the college: the
religious experience of young people; the Christian Socialist Movement, and also in areas which drew on the charisma of the founding
order by working with women in prison and women in secure
psychiatric units. A post-graduate Centre for Religious History had
been established to draw on the research strengths of resident
scholars and provide a focus for others working in this mission-
related area. Such a centre would also be able to provide a physical
location for archive material in need of a home as religious institutions shrink, change and relocate.

While the church was being served at a national level by the
provision of an archive by one college, another college was focused
on the needs of the church at a local level – specifically a deprived
area of the inner city.

> We recruit around the main campus. We have a dozen places
> around, sometimes Catholic primary schools, sometimes voluntary
> sector groups where we put on an out-reach degree. So we take

higher education to people where they feel comfortable and then eventually progress to the mother house – the main campus.

At this college the outreach strategy goes beyond providing programmes in pre-existing venues; it extends to the creation of new areas for college activity: areas which continue earlier church activity:

> We are building a new campus in a very disadvantaged area of the city, using a church and a school which we bought from the archdiocese and which had run into all sorts of difficulties. We are there helping the community by converting redundant church school property into a major resource for the immediate community.

For this college, and for at least one of the other colleges, outreach provision was seen as a way of meeting the mission by taking the educational enterprise to people who would otherwise be unable to gain access to higher education, or particularly Catholic higher education. The mission relatedness was seen to be as much in the way the provision was made as with the provision itself; it is this which constitutes 'witness'.

> For me the really prime thing is about witness rather than about doing things that are necessarily clearly labelled 'churchy'. I think it's actually much more about saying 'Who are you here for?' Clearly in here we've got far more opportunity – working in particular areas of this city with people who are trying to achieve regeneration and trying to work with social groups four and five. The projects we have started here really build on a long tradition of doing that, but they are ways of doing that for our own time.

Even within the main campus there are ways of addressing the curriculum that have been developed to be mission-related: a pedagogy that embraces the values of living in community. At one of the colleges a series of modules has been designed to be part of the learning and teaching experience of all students and staff.

> They are a way of building community because everybody will have a shared experience – something in common which cuts through the tendencies of modular schemes to fragment. It has built in it the notion of students being in a group with a tutor, to reinvigorate the old academic and personal tutor idea, but all geared toward student responsibility and autonomy.

This series of modules is very much focused on the needs of the student groups attending the college.

> We have lots of students who don't really understand what higher
> education demands of them, and we have a desire for each student
> to be seen as a whole person. We've put that together with the
> notion of certain things we'd like all students to do. We've put in a
> dimension about ethics so that all students will actually have the
> opportunity to engage with questions like 'What are my values and
> what are other people's values?' as part of that curriculum

This programme contrasts with programmes in other institutions
which might seek to build in core skills as a common unit, but would
not necessarily be concerned with the values of those involved in the
process. For the Catholic college learning is part of a richer tradition.

> We want this to be a community experience. It's about building
> community, it's about building relationships, it's about ensuring
> that our access mission is carried out through the way in which
> students are brought into higher education.

Central to the transmission of the curriculum are the staff who work
in the Catholic colleges. No longer predominantly members of a
religious order, or necessarily Catholic, these are the men and
women who take forward this work of the church on a daily basis.
Each Principal discussed the staff as the whole staff, not just the
teaching staff and each saw all the staff as part of the college
community.

> We have 600 staff. We have 800 on the payroll but 600 FTE and of
> these about 200 are lecturers. I would say that the longevity of
> service and the loyalty of, say, the catering staff are remarkable and
> are linked to them feeling comfortable with the church, as they
> would see it, as an employer in a city where jobs have been scarce
> ... they feel valued by our predecessors, colleagues and gover-
> nors.

The academic staff formed part of the total staff – valued for what
they could contribute. Another Principal commented:

> I think the threats we face lie within us rather than outside. I think
> the biggest threats we face are loss of confidence and loss of will.
> There has to be, across the college, a group of staff in different
> areas who believe that we bring something, who believe there is a
> purpose to being here, who are in this area through a positive
> choice to work in it. If you have a strong sense of mission you can
> survive the most incredible outside pressure. I think the greatest
> hope is in the people. There are signs of hope, certainly in a
> number of the younger people on the staff.

This sentiment was echoed by others.

> The average new lecturer has a lot of choices now and we tend to attract people who like the mission. They could be academics anywhere and they like what the college stands for. I'm sure that's true of the other church colleges.

Consistency and diversity characterized discussion of the staff and their work, consistency of values, diversity of practice.

> There is a set of values that underpin what we do and they're not that different from the values of the 1920s and 1930s, although the place would be quite different at that time. If you bring together students of different generations, their experience of the college is completely different. To me, being here, being a student here is actually a much richer experience than I had as a student in a big city university. I don't look back on that with anything like the same sense of valuing that our own students do.

Catholic colleges are part of a larger enterprise, part of the church active in education, as it has been for centuries and in a specific way in Britain for the past century and a half. Today Catholic colleges are fewer in number but those that remain have grown in size and enterprise. Active in a secular society, these institutions have to be able to justify their existence to government inspection and funding agencies and to the relevant church authorities. Their Catholicism no longer rests on the baptismal identity of recruits, the religious identity of a providing order or a curriculum sharply focused on the needs of Catholic schools. But changes in the colleges are a part of changes in the wider society and changes within the church. Many of the changes in the colleges are a result of meeting the changing needs of society and church. In doing so the colleges hold fast to their Catholic identities and develop them in response to different needs. Just as different charisms characterized the religious orders who founded the early colleges, so different charisms are at work in the different Catholic colleges of today as each seeks to meet, in different ways, the needs of the church at local, national and inter-national levels. Yet within these different responses there is a common theme, one which is recognizably 'Catholic' in the way in which needs are addressed and the church is both served and serving. Through the building of community in an increasingly anonymous society, through drawing on tradition in an increasing ahistorical society, through the development of a curriculum which recognizes both community and tradition, the Catholic colleges continue to be part of the enterprise of Catholic education. One of those interviewed was drawing on a wide personal experience of educational institutions, large and small, religious and secular in formulating this conclusion – and these words speak for the others:

> When you look at Catholic education, whether it's primary, second-ary, sixth form colleges or higher education, there is something very different about the preoccupations of the people who are committed to that. There is a very strong emphasis on the person as a whole person, it is this notion of the person 'in the round' and everything having an interconnection and things not being some-how separate dimensions of existence but everything being of a piece and all the people who work with and for you, and that you work with, also being of a piece. I think there is a theological understanding that's behind that which is the interconnectedness of all of creation.

It is this which defines the diversity and distinctiveness of the Cath-olic colleges as they move forward in time, thought and task.

NOTES

1   Cf. Philip Gleason, *Contending with Modernity: Catholic Higher Education in the Twentieth Century* (Oxford: Oxford University Press, 1995) and Theodore Hesburgh, *The Challenges and Promise of a Catholic University* (Notre Dame: University of Notre Dame, 1994).

2   See Michele Dowling, 'Propagation of the faith: St Mary's College and the training of Catholic teachers, 1944–72', chapter 7 in this volume, and Mary Eaton, 'What became of the children of Mary? Post-war women in the Catholic church', in M.P. Hornsby-Smith (ed.) *Catholics in England 1950–2000* (Lon-don: Cassell, 1999).

3   When the religious orders supplied the senior staff women Principals were in the majority.

4   The chief executive of Liverpool Hope is the Rector, however, in order not to attribute quotations to individuals I use the title 'Principal' for each head of a Catholic college.

5   The Quality Assessment Agency is the government-funded body that monitors the standards in higher education in the UK. The Office for Standards in Education is the body that monitors standards of teaching in schools and the standards of courses for training teachers.

INDEX

DATE DUE